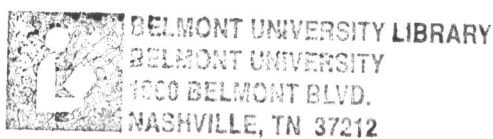

Politically Speaking

POLITICALLY SPEAKING

A Worldwide Examination of Language Used in the Public Sphere

EDITED BY
Ofer Feldman and Christ'l De Landtsheer

Westport, Connecticut
London

Library of Congress Cataloging-in-Publication Data

Politically speaking : a worldwide examination of language used in the
   public sphere / edited by Ofer Feldman and Christ'l De Landtsheer
       p.   cm.
   Includes bibliographical references and index.
   ISBN 0-275-96122-2 (alk. paper)
   1. Discourse analysis—Political aspects.   2. Rhetoric—Political
aspects.   I. Feldman, Ofer, 1954– .   II. Landtsheer, Christ'l De.
P302.77.P65   1998
410'.41—dc21   97-49249

British Library Cataloguing in Publication Data is available.

Copyright © 1998 by Ofer Feldman and Christ'l De Landtsheer

All rights reserved. No portion of this book may be
reproduced, by any process or technique, without the
express written consent of the publisher.

Library of Congress Catalog Card Number: 97-49249
ISBN: 0-275-96122-2

First published in 1998

Praeger Publishers, 88 Post Road West, Westport, CT 06881
An imprint of Greenwood Publishing Group, Inc.

Printed in the United States of America

The paper used in this book complies with the
Permanent Paper Standard issued by the National
Information Standards Organization (Z39.48–1984).

10 9 8 7 6 5 4 3 2 1

Every reasonable effort has been made to trace the owners of copyright materials in
this book, but in some instances this has proven impossible. The author and publisher
will be glad to receive information leading to more complete acknowledgments in
subsequent printings of the book and in the meantime extend their apologies for any
omissions.

Contents

Illustrations	vii
Preface	ix
1. Introduction to the Study of Political Discourse *Christ'l De Landtsheer*	1

I. The Nature and Scope of Political Discourse

2. The Pervasiveness of Islam in Contemporary Arab Political Discourse: The Cases of Sadat and Arafat *Raphael Israeli*	19
3. The Changing Political Language of Germany *Christa Lang-Pfaff*	31
4. The Political Language of Japan: Decoding What Politicians Mean from What They Say *Ofer Feldman*	43
5. The Rhetoric of Jewish Cohesion and Territorial Attachment in Rabbinic *Midrashim* *Carol B. Conaway*	56
6. Pragmatic Ambiguity and Partisanship in Russia's Emerging Democracy *Richard D. Anderson, Jr.*	64

II. The Discourse of the Political Elite

7. The Crisis Tool in American Political Discourse 79
   Amos Kiewe

8. Discourse as a Stage for Political Actors: An Analysis of Presidential Addresses in Argentina, Brazil, and Venezuela 91
   Maritza Montero and Isabel Rodriguez-Mora

9. The Method of Argumentation of Jean-Marie Le Pen, Leader of the French Extreme Right Wing, in an Important Political Television Program 106
   Simone Bonnafous

10. The Media, the Markets, and the Crash: A Consideration of Financial Press Narratives 117
    Matthew G. Sorley

11. The Political Rhetoric of a Unified Europe 129
    Christ'l De Landtsheer

III. Methods in the Study of Political Discourse

12. Political Interviews: Television Interviews in Great Britain 149
    Peter Bull

13. Functions of Recent U.S. Presidential Slogans 161
    Herbert Barry III

14. Political Language in an Environmental Controversy: Integrative Complexity and Motive Imagery in Advocacy Propaganda and the Press 170
    Peter Suedfeld, Loraine Lavallee, and Jennifer Brough

15. Post-Realism, Just War, and the Gulf War Debate 184
    Francis A. Beer and Robert Hariman

Epilogue: Where Do We Stand? 195
Ofer Feldman

Index 205
About the Editors and Contributors 209

Illustrations

TABLES

6.1	Modality in Authoritarian and Electoral Speech	69
8.1	Interlocutors	101
8.2	Allies, Opponents, and Enemies	102
13.1	Slogans by President Carter	163
13.2	Slogans by President Reagan	164
13.3	Slogans by President Bush	165
13.4	Slogans by President Clinton	166
14.1	Average Integrative Complexity Levels for Source Groups	175
14.2	Motive Imagery Scores	176
14.3	Values Endorsed by Source Groups	178
14.4	Newspaper Coverage of Participants' Positions	179

FIGURE

11.1	Metaphorial Power in European Parliamentary Rhetoric by Political Groups, 1981–1993 (Dutch Proceedings)	140

Preface

Politically Speaking: A Worldwide Examination of Language Used in the Public Sphere is a study of political language. In this book, as the title suggests, we offer an overview of the characteristics, nature, and content of language in politics. We also look at the various roles of language in the political domain. Our goal is to bring together essays with essential information on specific issues of relevance to political language in both Western and non-Western societies. To reach that goal, we give a special emphasis to relatively recent new topics that have stimulated additional interest in the study of political discourse in general and the roles that the language of politicians, government officials, and news media play in contemporary politics in particular.

The chapters in this volume provide reviews of recent important research, include extensive lists of up-to-date references, and draw on the authors' own research that presents original or updated findings. All of the chapters point to a wide diversity in directions of research, methods of examination (theoretical, analytical, descriptive, qualitative, quantitative, and empirical), and approaches to analyzing the functions language plays in the polity. From this diversity emerge subtle links between culture, political culture, and the language which politicians, other power elites, and the public use in their symbolic interaction.

Thus, this anthology details and analyzes the recurrent theme of political language from different perspectives—political science, psychology, philosophy, sociology, economics, religion, public administration, mass communication, and linguistics. Critical eyes focus on the discourse of press reports, political orations, election propaganda, ideological treatises, and political party programs. The result is an overview of the "art" of political language; an analysis of the rhetoric of American presidents, Arab leaders, and French presidential candidates; reports on the changes in the rhetoric of leaders in Russia; and discussions of the political language in such non-Western countries as Japan, Argentina, Brazil and Venezuela.

This volume stakes out what we believe to be some important potential areas in political language research. It is divided into three main parts: "The Nature and Scope of Political Discourse," "The Discourse of the Political Elite," and "Methods in the Study of Political Discourse."

We sincerely hope this book will encourage and further stimulate worldwide research on political language.

We would like to express our thanks to Praeger Publishers for granting permission to reproduce excerpts from Amos Kiewe's *The Modern Presidency and Crisis Rhetoric* (Westport, CT: Praeger Publishers, an imprint of Greenwood Publishing Group, Inc., 1994).

On a personal note, Ofer Feldman expresses his deep gratitude to his wife, Rie, and their children, Utai and Iri, for their support throughout this project. Christ'l De Landtsheer dedicates this book to her parents, who first taught her to like politics.

CHAPTER 1

Introduction to the Study of Political Discourse

CHRIST'L DE LANDTSHEER

Where does an introduction to political language studies begin? Although the need has certainly been felt for an approach combining political and linguistic (linguistics being the theory of [the functions of] linguistic signs, a component of semiotics, the theory of [the functions of] signs in general [Ramat, 1976: 44]) or semantic (semantics being the science of [word-] meaning [Ullmann, 1962: 1]) information, explicit attempts to formulate this kind of approach, until now, have been hard to find. From the 1980s onward there has been an increasing interest in the language of politics (political rhetoric, political speech, political style, political discourse), but research on the subject has been fragmentary and unfortunately not very methodological.

Politically Speaking: A Worldwide Examination of Language Used in the Public Sphere aims at formulating and exemplifying a general approach to political language (political semantics). The chapters in this volume indicate current trends in research on language and politics. This introduction provides a detailed description of these trends and notes both the origins of research and the prospects for further research. These questions seldom have been the subject of inquiry. The main reasons for this can be found in the interdisciplinary character of the field and its epistemological implications, and the immense amount of material to explore. An incomplete picture, only in black, grey, and white, is the best result one can expect from such an exploration because much work still needs to be done in this area. Similarly, a preoccupation with one aspect, the verbal notion of language, can be justified. In order to inventory ways of examining the subject area, this introduction highlights historic developments and regional traditions, disciplinary foci, and methodological options. Meanwhile, it specifies its own political-semantic point of view. Both in this introduction and throughout this volume, the focus lies on research that pays equal attention to linguistic and political aspects, with the purpose of collecting information (political and social-scientific) on the language of political processes. This focus has been inspired by Lasswells' writings, including his statement in Lasswell, Leites et al. (1949: 38) that certain changes in style may indicate the gradual decline of democratic feeling or reveal the groundswell of a gathering crisis.

DEFINING POLITICAL DISCOURSE

An initial discussion about the definition of attempts and concepts in the political discourse area of study is helpful in explaining the definitive step indicated in the book title, *Politically Speaking: A Worldwide Examination of Language Used in the Public Sphere.*

Political Language, Discourse, Speech, Rhetoric, and Propaganda

Political language, political speech, political rhetoric, and political discourse are apparently interchangeable terms that political officials, such as scientists, politicians, and journalists, use to denominate the relation between language (linguists distinguish between language as a vehicle of communication and speech as the use of that vehicle by a given individual on a given occasion [Ullmann, 1962: 19–23]) and politics. The distinction between these terms, in my point of view, does not seem to be of primary importance for the scholar in political language (political-semantic) studies, even though the terms represent different traditions of study.

Most of the contributors to this volume use the term *political discourse*, which seems to be the term now most commonly used, to refer to political language. However, discourse (corpora of meaningfully related signs [Hak & Helsloot, 1991: xiv]) is the fetish of postmodernism (Rosenau, 1992). The postmodern approach is represented in this volume by Beer and Hariman in Chapter 15, and somewhat more moderately by Sorley in Chapter 10. Other scholars in this volume use the term but, unlike the above-mentioned authors, do not practice postmodernism (or are not even inspired by linguistic structuralism).

Political language is a term introduced by pioneers of both propaganda research and the social sciences. To many scholars it sounds old-fashioned; nevertheless, it represents the prestigious political-psychology tradition (founded by brilliant political scientists and psychologists). When the aim is to influence power, and there is some impact upon power, we speak of the political function of language (Lasswell, Leites et al., 1949: 8), and when we speak of the science of politics, we mean the science of power.

Hence, the language of politics is the language of power. Contributors to this volume who still prefer the old-fashioned term form part of the political science tradition (Lang-Pfaff in Chapter 3) or the political psychology (and propaganda) tradition (Suedfeld, Lavallee, and Brough, in Chapter 14). But political psychology contributors also use the term *political discourse* (Montero and Mora in Chapter 8) or *political rhetoric* (De Landtsheer in Chapter 11).

The terms *political speech* and *political rhetoric* (rhetoric being public persuasion on significant public issues [Windt & Ingold, 1987: xvi]) are currently used by communication scientists and belong to the tradition of rhetoric studies (founded in antiquity). Several studies in this volume originate in this tradition. Conoway (Chapter 5) presents a less typical example of this approach than does Kiewe (Chapter 7).

Both public opinion and social science associate political language with propaganda, the organized action to influence and lead public opinion (Van der Meiden, 1988: 58). I would discourage this association. Both concepts deal with mass communication (public communication), but the focus of political language is on communication and its forms (the purposeful exchange of symbols), whereas propaganda focuses on action. Besides, political language encourages a scientific attitude that is both neutral and critical; propaganda seduces us to neglect the less manifest and less purposeful ways in which people's opinions and behavior are influenced in society. Further, propaganda is an outdated term to denominate political language, because it insufficiently takes social-scientific developments into account. The negative connotations to this term are well deserved. Finally, I would suggest to limit its use to crisis, war, and totalitarian communication, which is, in fact, what pioneers of propaganda research (Lasswell, Lerner, & De Sola Pool, 1952) did.

It can be concluded from the above that a general approach to political language benefits from a non-dogmatic position, in which most terms that denominate the subject area (political language) are equally accepted. The subject area itself, however, should be described and even defined.

Politics

From my review of literature I conclude that the limiting definition of political language (which depends upon the preferred concept of political language) is affected by one's definition of language and politics.

The concepts of politics and the political are items in political theory and political philosophy under much discussion, from which stems one of the more traditional viewpoints: politics refers to activities and institutions related to state organization (Gruenert, 1974: 2). Moderate viewpoints such as ours emphasize political functioning (Lasswell, Leites et al., 1949: 8) or the negotiating of power or social conflict (Nimmo, 1978: 6). The broad concepts often identify politics as an aspect of language. These are mostly inspired by sociology (Mannheim, 1960: 278–79) and cultural anthropology (Malinowski, 1944: 74–75). Politics is driven by instinctive mechanisms (Mannheim, 1960: 279), motives (Mills, 1940), and needs (Malinowski, 1944: 74, 75), and can thus be summarized as a satisfaction of needs. Situations are affected by particular motives, which also determine the vocabulary (Mills, 1940). Classic Marxist conceptions of linguistic philosophy reflect Mannheim's (1960: 239) concept of global ideology (utterances reflect social structure). Modern structuralists' concepts are influenced by Mannheim's (1960: 238) concept of specific ideologies (ideology equals lies). Moreover, the definition of politics considers it to be a political action, according to Shapiro, because when one makes choices one starts by choosing words (1982: 3). Those who control discourse control society. Politics is discourse, and discourse is politics (Shapiro, 1982: 1–2).

Language

Popular concepts of language (those found in dictionaries and in official circles) tend to limit language to verbal or written utterances, contrary to scientific concepts, which generally include nonverbal utterances.

Politics, like communication, is a process, writes Nimmo (1978: 7), and, also like communication, politics involves speech. This is not speech in the narrow sense of the spoken word but speech in the more inclusive sense, meaning all methods by which people exchange symbols—written and spoken words, pictures, movements, gestures, mannerisms, and dress. Scientific concepts of language often identify language with communication or regard language as a purposeful means of communication (Schaff, 1960: 292). Both linguists and communication scientists consider language a system of signs (Schaff, 1960: 292) or a medium to exchange symbols (Nimmo, 1978: 70; Meadow, 1980: 22).

When broad concepts of language and politics coincide, language is mainly considered a power strategy. This attitude again results from cultural, anthropological, and sociological insights. Social phenomena are always uttered (Malinowski, 1944: 23); these utterances do not necessarily include speech, whether spoken or written. The principles on which society is based are not always uttered in public speech (Mannheim, 1960).

Political Language

I must conclude from our review that the concept of political language that is commonly used among scholars is restricted in the ideas of both language and politics. Edelman's former definition is representative of this restriction: Politics is largely a matter of words. Negotiations are held, speeches are made, debates take place, bargains are struck. Beyond these oral discussions are other forms of political speech, wherein written communications, such as laws, proclamations, treaties, and other political documents, are created. This commonly used concept suggests that political language is public communication on the subject of politics. One can find it in the language of newspapers, television, and radio (including parliamentary debates, mass meetings, party meetings), propaganda (including publications for elections and other political pamphlets), and administrative, judicial, and diplomatic language (including law texts, treaties and international political negotiations) (Edelman, 1974a, 1974b; Fagen, 1966; Nimmo and Swanson, 1990).

Some scholars developed even more restricted concepts, as they equated political discourse to polemic or argumentative language (Klaus, 1971) or to political vocabulary (Prost, 1969: 117), either separately or as levels of analysis within the concept of language use in politics (Dieckmann, 1975: 47). Others refer to semantic criteria (content) or sometimes to pragmatic ones (functions and effects) in order to identify political language.

Popular (political language) concepts used by the public, politicians themselves, and literary writers tend to be restricted to the speech patterns used by politicians. Negative connotations such as demagoguery and lies are always involved. Orwell's definition (1950: 336) adequately illustrates these popular concepts: The political dialects to be found in pamphlets, leading articles, manifestos, White papers and the speeches of undersecretaries do, of course, vary from party to party, but they are all alike in that one almost never finds in them a fresh, vivid, homemade turn of speech.

The chapters in this book—indeed—focus mainly on the language used by political leaders (Israeli, Montero and Rodriguez-Mora, Anderson, and Kiewe) and other people involved in politics (politicians and journalists, Feldman), eventually mediated through television (Bull and Bonnafous), uttered during parliamentary debates (De Landtsheer), or conceived for propaganda (Barry). Both the title and the choice of chapters for *Politically Speaking: A Worldwide Examination of Language Used in the Public Sphere*, however, express a somewhat broader political language concept than the one that is commonly used among scholars. The lyrics of songs have been important in revolutions, but the significance of the music itself is not without political importance either. Reich (1983) made the remark that the Nazis copied the revolutionary music of their socialist enemies and put Nazi lyrics to it. Besides the analysis of classical political literature, such as the works of Stendhall, Rousseau, and Orwell, the political function of recent romantic (e.g., South American, South African) literature and poetry has also been demonstrated. Public language that does not directly address political issues can also be considered political language. This is what could be learned from the chapters dealing with religious texts (Conaway), scientific discourse (Beer and Hariman and Lang-Pfaff), financial newspapers (Sorley), and discourse on environmental subjects (Suedfeld, Lavallee, and Brough).

The perception that symbols (signs which solidify abstract concepts for the audience [Schaff, 1960: 172]) vary according to ideology and the political system, and that terms from another sphere of life are often incorporated in the political vocabulary (Dieckmann, 1975: 8–9) supports our main (moderate) point of view. Language that obviously deals with political issues cannot be seen in isolation from everyday language because, depending upon its use, all language can become political language. The fact that language is used in the public sphere implies that it may be relevant for the citizens in a political way. This may be one focal point, in order to narrow down the subject. I prefer the term *public sphere* over *public* because it includes informal polite conversation which is indeed relevant in the process of forming a political opinion.

Language use in the public sphere as a definition of political language acknowledges current scientific developments in (international) communication theory, focusing on the growing power of the mass media, new communication technologies, the trends of globalization and commercialization. This moderate view obviously has been inspired by the critical approach of communication theory, which acknowledges the political function of almost all public utterances; however, the editors do not share its emphasis (from cultural studies) on popular culture (Hariman, 1995: 190), which includes television and news (Neuman, Just, & Crigler, 1992). Even though in this volume the broad view of modern structuralists, traditional Marxists, and anthropologists (according to that theory, almost every form or style of communication or language can be political) is not discussed, this introduction reflects approaches based on these views. The broad view is tempting and thought-provoking, as can be gleaned from Beer and Hariman in Chapter 15, but the moderate view, at least for the scope of this volume, is more useful (neutral, straightforward, and generally applicable).

EXAMINING POLITICAL LANGUAGE

Rhetoric, the faculty of observing in any given case the available means of persuasion (Roberts, translation of Aristotle, 1954: 24), is the oldest approach to political language. Its influence on contemporary political language studies is a more direct one than Orwell's, whose thesis (1949, 1950) that political language can covertly influence political thought, indirectly influenced many literary and scientific writings, such as research in political communication, political psychology, and postmodernism.

Rhetoric

This overview of trends in research should start with the oldest (i.e., the rhetorical) approach. Both Israeli (in Chapter 2) and Kiewe (in Chapter 7) illustrate what an interesting rhetorical analysis may look like, in the same way as they illustrate the exceptional rhetorical capabilities of Anwar el-Sadat and Yasir Arafat (Chapter 15) and of recent American presidents. Israeli convinces the reader that both Sadat and Arafat possessed or possess these capabilities. In addition, Israeli's comprehensive political and psychological picture throws a new light on the personalities of these Arab leaders. Kiewe presents studies in presidential rhetoric, a field of study (Windt & Ingold, 1987) that is practiced at American university departments of speech and communication and has a significant influence on communication science. Nevertheless, rhetoric has an even wider influence, as law, for instance, has also been studied from a rhetorical point of view (Witteveen, 1988). Both Israeli's and Kiewe's accounts of the rhetoric of political leaders surpass the often unsatisfactory superficiality (for scholars) of the rhetorical genre, which can be characterized as varying from the descriptive to the journalistic, focused on recent events, and primarily critical in nature.

Political Communication

Political communication studies are based on origins other than the rhetorical approach. Feldman's Chapter 4 strikes me as a typical (political) communication scientist's approach. Feldman's symbolic-interactionist approach indeed focuses on what Meadow considers to be the essence of political communication, a process involving interchange among political actors that takes place within a political context and involves the exchange of symbols to some political end (Meadow, 1980: 22). Graber (1976) and Edelman (1974b) are among the first scholars in political communication who presented such a symbolic approach. Feldman's picture of the informal contacts between Japanese politicians particularly reminds me of Edelman's (1974a) critical-ironic symbolism of the political language of the helping professions. Nimmo and Swanson's (1990) reader introduces political language as one of the new directions in political communication research. Indeed, the discipline neglected the subject of language for decades.

Political Psychology and Propaganda

Lasswell and his disciples (the brilliant pioneers, who, in their research on propaganda, invented scientific content analysis) were aware, since the thirties, that language is a powerful source of information for all social scientists (Laswell et al., 1949, 1952). Their work, the result of a survey that began during World War II in the Experimental Division for the Study of Wartime Communication, was aimed both toward developing new research tools and toward offering effective aid on war problems (Lasswell et al., 1952: 26). While dealing with political propaganda and political newspaper articles (and other forms of political communication), their work summarizes the so-called quantitative-semantic and political-semantic approaches. At least five chapters (6, 8, 11, 13, and 14) of *Politically Speaking* are written in the vein of this important tradition. Quantitative semantics was used to denominate quantitative empirical research; political semantics was used in connection with the study of style (Lasswell, et al., 1949: 8–9). In a modern version, I would define political semantics as the political study of meaning or the study of meaning in politics, thereby referring to both quantitative and qualitative research.

Chapter 14, co-authored by Suedfeld (psychologist); Chapter 6 by Anderson (political scientist); and my (communication scientist) Chapter 11, however, in Lasswell's view, are quantitative-semantic analyses because they statistically test political-semantic hypotheses. They remind one of De Sola Pool's article on variety and repetition in political language, which statistically tests a former qualitative statement by Lasswell on the style of crises. Pool concludes that, during wars and in totalitarian regimes, there is a standardization of political language (De Sola Pool, 1956: 217–31; Lasswell et al., 1949: 28). Anderson demonstrates that Russia's democratically elected politicians use forms of linguistic modality that differ from those used by their communist predecessors. Suedfeld shows how environmental conflict in Canada results in lower integrative complexity and higher need for power imagery levels in information campaigns and newspaper coverage. From my metaphorical analysis of European parliamentary rhetoric can be learned that European identity has started to overrule national identities. This volume contains two propaganda analyses, or political semantic analyses in the strict sense of Lasswell: political semantics examines key terms, slogans and doctrines from the point of view of how they are understood (Lasswell et al., 1949: 8–9). Chapter 13, Barry's analysis of slogans by Carter, Reagan, Bush, and Clinton, and Chapter 8, Montero and Rodriguez-Mora's examination of presidential addresses (1990–1996) by the leaders of Argentina, Brazil, and Venezuela, show how to perform a systematic qualitative analysis on political texts.

Political Vocabulary

The pioneers were not the first ones who scientifically dealt with political symbols. Since roughly the beginning of the twentieth century, several works have been published in which the vocabulary of politics has been described (glossary) and even analyzed (Dieckmann, 1975). The first political dictionaries were inspired by the language of the French revolution (Frey, 1925; Ranft, 1908). They were followed by research on the history of the use of certain terms, their changing meanings, and the contexts in which they have been used. The scope of subjects seems unlimited. So are the viewpoints and disciplines about which later studies were undertaken. As noted in the following paragraphs, France (Frey, 1925) and Germany

(Radike, 1849; Ranft, 1908) developed particular traditions of political language study.

Historical Semantics

A historical-semantic approach is given in Chapter 5 by Conaway. The concepts of peoplehood and national territory, Conaway argues, used within a particular type of rhetoric within the Jewish tradition (*midrash*), created positive and enduring concepts of Jewish national identity that may have influenced political behavior. Historical semantics (sémantique historique) was developed in France in the early 1960s for the purpose of enriching history with linguistic data (Robin, 1971).

Political Lexicology

The contribution to this volume by Bonnafous (Chapter 9) represents political lexicology (lexicologie politique), another French tradition of political language studies, which is practiced at the Ecole Normale Superieure de St. Cloud. It is closely related to historical semantics (Dubois, 1964; Prost, 1969), but is focused on actuality, by means of descriptions (mostly quantitative) of newspapers and oratory (e.g., frequencies of assertions and rhythm in Charles de Gaulle's and Francois Mitterand's speeches) (Bonnafous & Willems, 1981). Most of the work of political lexicology shows an analogy with the applications of quantitative content analysis techniques that were developed in the United States by the earliest social scientists.

German Political Language Studies

German political language research has its own tradition. It is characterized by a preference for qualitative analysis and theoretical-philosophical studies (the usefulness of language in society) (Klaus, 1971; Ludz, 1980). German equivalents (*Ideengeschichte, Wortforschung, Begriffs-geschichte*) of historical semantics and political lexicology (the study of, respectively, the historical and the actual political use of words) are closely related to political philosophy (the study of the history of ideas). Political language of Germany, the political-philosophical account by Lang-Pfaff (Chapter 3), represents the unique German tradition. Since World War II, political language (*Politische Sprache*) formed in Germany, both in the former East Germany (e.g., Klaus, 1971) and in West Germany (e.g., Dieckmann, 1975), has been a separate field of study. On several occasions, linguists and political scientists joined efforts (e.g., Burkhardt & Fritzsche, 1992). Scholars connected the political message to the political system in matters of content, vocabulary, stylistic aspects, and rhythm of speech. They concentrated on Nazism (Schnauber, 1972; Seidel & Seidel-Slotty, 1961) and on the division of Germany, including the language of the cold war opponent (Pelster, 1966; Schmidt, 1977). East Germans performed political-ideological research; the West Germans mostly described the vocabulary of historical periods (Gruenert, 1974; Jaeger, 1971), with a preference for parliamentary rhetoric (Pelster, 1966).

In Chapter 3, Lang-Pfaff portrays how both German politicians and scholars, on several occasions during the last century, were faced with fundamental changes in the political system and corresponding changes in political discourse. Lang-Pfaff states that scholars, far too often, allow themselves to be directed by political motives or run backward or ahead of events. The division of Germany engaged both politicians and scientists in a cold war; unification created the need for a new political vocabulary, almost like the end of the criminal Nazi regime had done before (Eroms, 1988). German scientists now live in a political-linguistic laboratory.

Official Language

Research into the use of language in the judicial, diplomatic, and governmental systems has been executed since roughly the beginning of this century, and, because of its political importance, it plays a special role. Research on terminological uniformity and on official language has been stimulated by the European Commission and by national governments. Scholars study the semantics of certain judicial and jurisprudential terms and texts because their interpretations result in consequences for politics and law practice (law linguistics). Further, the uniformity of official language has been of especially great concern to totalitarian regimes and to new countries wanting to liberate themselves from colonial influences.

Sociolinguistics

The influence of language on perception, its power to alter a world view, and the function of language as an agent of cultural or racial domination are widely discussed controversial factors in social linguistics. The claim that language can convey cultural and political domination has been elaborated in several anthropological works relating to culture (e.g., Bloch, 1975; O'Barr & O'Barr, 1976), most often for a colonial or an exotic setting (ethnolinguistics). Within sociology, qualitative and quantitative research has been undertaken into relationships between linguistic characteristics and group characteristics, such as class, gender, race, or ethnicity. Sociolinguistics provides correlational research between linguistic variables, mostly in everyday language, and social structure.

Discourse Analysis

At the base of discourse analysis lies linguistics, which is currently practiced in the Netherlands and Great Britain. Part of it focuses, mostly qualitatively, on political discourse (i.e., media texts and news reports). Bull's review (Chapter 12) of current research on political television interviews in Great Britain reveals much about the demagoguery of leading British politicians during the last two decades. Also, Bull shows what a discourse analysis looks like. The leading journal on the subject, *Discourse and Society* (1997), and its Dutch editor, Teun A. van Dijk, consider such an approach a detailed, systematic, and theoretically based analysis of text and talk.

The focus on narratives, or the use of the construction of reality perspective, by many discourse analysts has been inspired by the sociology-based communications approach of British cultural studies (conceived by Stuart Hall [1980]). In Chapter 10, Sorley presents the fact that such an approach deconstructs the narratives of the leading Canadian financial newspapers. He illustrates the approach of the Glasgow Media Group and the Birmingham School in investigating journalistic bias (ideological and political functions of the media) through linguistic analyses of how the media—newspapers, television, broadcasting, and photography—treated various linguistic-processing subjects (e.g., reality construction in relation to women or minorities) (Hariman, 1995). The language of news reports by various newspapers, radio stations, and television channels was compared, sometimes in combination with other sources of information, such as interviews, surveys, and public reports.

The Philosophy of Language

The importance of the philosophy of language for the development of political language studies is mostly indirect. For instance, the connection between Chomskian linguistics and Noam Chomsky's sociopolitical attitudes—a widely discussed issue—is very doubtful. There are exceptions, however, with more direct foci, such as modern structuralism and the school of general semantics. These represent two distinguished paradigms within linguistic philosophy. The merits of the School of General Semantics (of which Korzybski's 1933 publication, *Science and Sanity: An Introduction to Non-Aristotelian Systems and General Semantics*, marks the beginning), can be derived from the fact that it draws one's attention to the possibilities of linguistic operations. It cannot be denied, however, that the school's concept of language as a dominant power, both positively and negatively, in causing neuroses and in preventing war is exaggerated and old-fashioned.

This is not true for Sapir's (1921) and Whorfs's (1956) influential linguistic relativity hypothesis, the paradigm that is the basis of the school's concepts. Their research conducted among the Hopi led to the observation that time does not exist as a notion when this notion is not present in the language. Linguistic relativism also influenced analytic philosophers, such as Ludwig Wittgenstein, and classic Marxist philosophers of different origins, such as Jürgen Habermas (Frankfurter Schule) and Adam Schaff (School of Philosophical Semantics). It essentially led to the conclusion that meaning depends on the use of language and upon the user's context. The relevance of this thought for political language studies is that semantics, which focuses on the relation of the text to the real world, should be preferred over semiotics, which focuses on the structure of a text (Ricoeur, 1975: 274).

Postmodernism

The philosophical-linguistic visions detailed in the preceding paragraph differ from structural linguistics, another paradigm. This paradigm, which lies at the basis of discourse analysis, considers discourse in itself a meaningful power process. Moreover, modern versions of structural linguistics (modernism, postmodernism, poststructuralism, deconstructionism) are still based on the ideas formulated by Ferdinand de Saussure (1916). This linguistic philosopher made the distinction between language as a system (*langue*) and language spoken by individuals (*parole*). The resulting idea that language can be studied while neglecting the social context has been increasingly criticized.

Modern structuralism, starting with Roman Jacobson and the Prague School, tried to counter this criticism, but this intellectual movement is still being attacked for the vagueness of its concepts and for the ideological confusion that it causes (Schaff, 1978: 22–23). The success of the newly formulated structuralism started during the late fifties in France (influential philosophers are Michel Foucault, Jacques Derrida, Roland Barthes, Jean-François Lyotard, and Jean Baudrillard) (Rosenau, 1992). Since the late seventies, modern structuralist ideas gained importance all over the world (Shapiro, 1982, 1984, 1989). Beer and Hariman (Chapter 15) represent the American postmodern approach in this volume. In addition, Beer and Hariman deal with international relations, a promising field for political discourse studies, about which the authors question the whole of scientific theory. Promising indeed, as Bell, in his article, "Political Linguistics and International Negotiation" (1988), had already concluded that language not only serves as the medium for the verbal interactions that constitute the process of negotiation but underlies the entire phenomenon. In a globalized world, negotiations and language become more important. John F. Kennedy and Nikita Krushchev translated each other, from procedural

(U.S.) to processual (Russian) knowledge structures and representations, so that successful negotiation of the Limited Test-Ban Agreement (August 5, 1993) was possible and nuclear conflict could be avoided (Bonham, Sergeev, & Parshin, 1997).

CONCLUSION

The intent of this chapter is to clarify the vagueness that surrounds the terminology and concepts within the political discourse area. But, more important, this chapter introduces political semantics, the concept that gives equal attention to language and politics. This concept is used as a guideline for exploring the broad area of study on political discourse. The area shows an extraordinary variety, both in scientific origin and in method.

Disciplines range from political science, political psychology and philosophy (both political philosophy and the philosophy of language) via sociology, anthropology, history, mass communications, and linguistics to public administration and even law science (both comparative and international). Methodology ranges from theoretical-philosophical via empirical-analytical to heuristic-descriptive; techniques used are quantitative as well as qualitative, or a combination of both; and theoretical directions range from functional-structuralistic via cognitive-psychological to Marxist and neo-Marxist approaches.

The chapters in this book reflect both this variety in the field and the political-semantic focus. The book is also intended to contribute to the promising area of international studies of political discourse.

REFERENCES

Barthes, R. (1982). *De nulgraad van het schrijven, gevolgd door een inleiding in de semiologie* [The zero-degree of writing, followed by an introduction to semiology]. Amsterdam: Meulenhoff.

Bell, D. V. J. (1988). Political linguistics and international negotiation. *Negotiation Journal*, 4, 233–46.

Bloch, M. (1975). *Political language and oratory in traditional society.* London: Academic Press.

Bonham, G. M., Sergeev, V., & Parshin, P. B. (1997). The limited test-ban agreement: Emergence of new knowledge structures in international negotiation. *International Studies Quarterly*, 41, 215–40.

Bonnafous, S., & Willems, D. (1982). *Etat present des etudes sur le discours gaulliste* [Current perspectives on studies of de Gaulle's speech]. *Mots*, 4, 171–80.

Burkhardt, A., & Fritzsche, K. P. (eds.) (1992). *Sprache im Umbruch: Politischer Sprachwandel im Zeichen von "Wende" und "Vereinigung"* [Language in transition: Political language during change and unification]. Berlin and New York: Walter de Gruyter.

De Landtsheer, C. (1986). Language and ideology: A representation of the function of ideology in the political use of language. In M. Brouwer et al. (Eds.), *Political psychology in the Netherlands*. The Nijmegen Papers. Amsterdam: Mola Russa.

De Landtsheer, C. (1994). The language of prosperity and crisis: A case study in political semantics. *Politics and the Individual*, 4 (2), 63–85.

De Landtsheer, C. (1995). Political communication. *Politics, Groups and the Individual*, 2 (Special issue), 1–20.

de Saussure, Ferdinand. (1916). *Cours de linguistique generale*. Paris: Payot.

De Sola Pool, I. (1956). Variety and repetition in political language. In H. Eulau, Samuel J. Eldersveld, and Morris Janowitz (Eds.), *Political behavior: A reader in theory and research* (pp. 217–31). Glencoe, Ill.: The Free Press.

Dieckmann, W. (1975). *Sprache in der politik* [Language in politics]. Heidelberg: Carl Winter Universittsverlag.

Discourse and Society (1997). An interdisciplinary journal for the study of discourse and communication in their social, political, and cultural contexts. 8 (2).

Dubois, J. (1964). *Distribution, ensemble et marque dans le lexique* [Distribution, word-groups and sign-relations within the lexicon]. *Cahiers de Lexicologie*, 4, 5–16.

Edelman, M. (1974a). The political language of the helping professions. *Politics and Society*, 4, 295–310.

Edelman, M. (1974b). *The symbolic uses of politics*. Urbana: University of Illinois Press.

Edelman, M. (1977). *Political language: Words that succeed and policies that fail*. Orlando, Fla.: Academic Press.

Eroms, H. W. (1974). Zur analyse politischer sprache [The analysis of political language]. *Linguistik und Didaktik*, 5 (1), 1–16.

Eroms, H. W. (1988). *Die entwicklung der politischen sprache in der bundesrepublik deutschland* [Political language development in West Germany]. Ghent: Paper Higher Translater's Institute.

Fagen, R. (1966). *Politics as communication*. Boston: Little, Brown.

Frey, M. (1925). *Les transformations du vocabulaire français a lépoque de la Revolution (1789–1800)* [The changing political vocabulary during the age of the French Revolution]. Paris: n.p.

Graber, D. (1976). *Verbal behaviour and politics*. Urbana: University of Illinois Press.

Gruenert, Horst. (1974). *Untersuchungen zum Sprachgebrauch der Paulskirche* [Research on the discourse of the Paul's Church]. Berlin and New York: Verlag W. De Gruyter.

Hak, T., & Helsloot, N. (Eds.) (1991). *De taal kan barsten: Spanning tussen taalkunde en maatschappijwetenschap* [Language can burst: Frictions between linguistics and humanities]. Amsterdam: Krisisonderzoek.

Hall, Stuart et al. (1980). *Culture, media, language: Working papers in cultural studies, 1972–1979*. London: Hutchinson.

Hariman, R. (1995). *Political style: The artistry of power*. Chicago: University of Chicago Press.
Jaeger, H. (1971). *Politische Metaphorik in Jakobinismus und im Vormrz* [Political metaphors of the Jacobines]. Stuttgart: n.p.
Klaus, G. (1965). *Die Macht des Wortes: Ein erkenntnistheoretisch pragmatisches Tractat* [The power of words: A theoretical pragmatical essay]. Berlin: Deutscher Verlag der Wissenschaften.
Klaus, G. (1971). *Sprache der Politik* [Political language]. Berlin: Deutscher Verlag der Wissenschaften.
Korzybski, A. (1933). *Science and sanity: An introduction to non-Aristotelian systems and general semantics* (4th ed., 1958). Lancaster: International Non-Aristotelian Library.
Lasswell, H. D., & Leites, N. et al. (1949). *Language of politics: Studies in quantitative semantics*. New York: George W. Stewart.
Lasswell, H. D., Lerner, D., & De Sola Pool, I. (1952). *The comparative study of symbols: An introduction*. Stanford, Calif.: Stanford University Press.
Ludz, P. (1980). *Mechanismen der Herrschaftssicherung: Eine sprachpolitische Analyse gesellschaftlichen Wandels in der DDR* [Mechanisms of power establishing: A political-linguistic analysis of the changing DDR society]. Munchen, Wien: Carl Hanser Verlag.
Malinowski, B. (1944). *A scientific theory of culture*. New York: New York University Press.
Mannheim, K. (1960). *Ideology and utopia: An introduction to the sociology of knowledge*. London: Routledge and Kegan Paul.
Mills, C. Wright. (1940). Situated actions and vocabularies of motive. *American Sociological Review*, 5, 904–13.
Meadow, R. (1980). *Politics as communication*. Norwood, N.J.: Ablex.
Neuman, R., Just, M., & Crigler, A. (1992). *Common knowledge: News and the construction of political meaning*. Chicago: University of Chicago Press.
Nimmo. D., & Swanson, D. L. (Eds.) (1990). *New directions in political communication*. London: Sage.
Nimmo, Dan. (1978). *Political communication and public opinion in America*. Santa Monica, Calif.: Goodyear Publishing Company.
O'Barr, W., & O'Barr, J. (1976). *Language and politics*. The Hague: Mouton.
Orwell, G. (1949). *Nineteen eighty-four: A novel*. Middlesex: Penguin.
Orwell, G. (1950). Politics and the English language. In *Shooting an elephant and other essays*. London: Harcourt Brace.
Pelster, T. (1966). *Die Politische Rede im Westen und Osten Deutschlands* [Political oratory in West and East Germany]. Dusseldorf: Paed. Verlag Schwann.
Prost, A. (1969). Vocabulaire et typologie des familles politiques [Vocabulary and typology of the political families]. *Cahiers de Lexicologie*, XIV, 1.
Radike (1849). *Lehrbuch der demagogie* [Reader in demagoguery]. Leipzig: n.p.
Ramat, P. (1976). Aspects sémiotiques de la linguistique textuelle [Semiotic aspects of textual linguistics]. *Cahiers de Lexicologie*, II, 29.
Ranft, T. (1908). *Der Einflusz der Franzoesischen Revolution auf die Franzoesische Sprache* [The influence of the French Revolution on the French language]. Darmstadt, Germany: n.p.
Reich, W. (1983). *The mass psychology of fascism*. Harmondsworth: Penguin.

Ricoeur, P. (1975). *La métaphore vive* [The lively metaphor]. Paris: Editions du Seuil.
Roberts, W. R. (1954). *Rhetoric and poetics of Aristotle*. New York: Modern Library.
Robin, R. (1971). Histoire et linguistique: Premier jalons [History and linguistics: First steps]. *Langue Francaise*, 9, 47–57.
Rosenau, P. (1992). *Post-modernism and the social sciences: Insights, inroads and intrusions*. Princeton, N.J.: Princeton University Press.
Sapir, E. (1921). *Language: An introduction to the study of speech*. New York: Harcourt, Brace.
Sapir, E. (1962). *Selected writings in language, culture and personality*. Berkeley, Calif.: Mandelbaum.
Schaff, A. (1960). *Introduction à la sémantique* [Introduction to semantics]. Paris: Editions Anthropos.
Schaff, A. (1978). *Structuralism and Marxism*. Oxford: Pergamon.
Schmidt, W. (1969). Zur ideologiegebundenkeit der politischen Lexik. *Wissenschaftlich Zeitschrift der Paed. Hochschule Potsdam. Gesellschaftliche und Sprachwissenschaftlichte Reihe*, 13, 461–473.
Schmidt, V. (1977). Zur Bildlichkeit ideologiegebundener Wörter und Wendungen [Metaphorical power of ideological words and expressions]. *Zeitschrift für Phonetik, Sprachwissenschaft und Kommunikationsforschung*, 30 (1), 40–47.
Schnauber, C. (1972). *Wie Hitler sprach und schrieb: Zur Psychologie und prosodik der faschistischen rhetorik* [How Hitler spoke and wrote: Psychology of fascist rhetoric]. Frankfurt: Verlag.
Seidel, E., & Seidel-Slotty, I. (1961). *Sprachwandel im Dritten Reich* [Language of the Third Reich]. Halle: VEB Verlag Sprache und Literatur.
Shapiro, M. (1982). *Language and political understanding: The politics of discursive practices*. New Haven, Conn.: Yale University Press.
Shapiro, M. (Ed.) (1984). *Language and politics*. Oxford: Basil Blackwell.
Shapiro, M. (1989). Representing world politics: The sport/war intertext. In M. Shapiro & J. Der Derian (Eds.), *International/intertextual relations*. Lexington, Mass.: Lexington Books.
Stewart, C., Smith, C., & Denton, R. E., Jr. (1984). *Persuasion and social movements*. Prospect Heights, Ill.: Waveland.
Ullmann, S. (1959). *The principles of semantics: A linguistic approach to Meaning*. Glasgow: Jackson & Co.
Ullmann, Stephen. (1962). *Semantics: An introduction to the science of meaning*. Oxford: Blackwell.
Van der Meiden, A. (1988). *Propaganda*. Muiderberg: Dick Coutinho.
Whorf, B. L. (1956). *Language, thought and reality*. Edited by J. B. Caroll. Cambridge, Mass.: MIT Press.
Windt, T., & Ingold, B. (1987). *Essays in presidential rhetoric*. Dubuque: Iowa: Kendall/Hunt Publishing.
Witteveen, W. (1988). *De retoriek in het recht* [Rhetoric of law]. Groningen, the Netherlands: Tjeenk Willink.
Wittgenstein, L. (1963). *Tractatus logico-philosophicus* [Philosophical-logical investigation]. Frankfurt: Suhrkamp.

PART I

The Nature and Scope of Political Discourse

CHAPTER 2

The Pervasiveness of Islam in Contemporary Arab Political Discourse: The Cases of Sadat and Arafat

RAPHAEL ISRAELI

POLITICAL DISCOURSE IN THE ARABIC LANGUAGE

If, in liberal-democratic societies, political discourse is of paramount importance—in spite of the fact that in a system of accountability what ultimately counts are deeds, not words—it is much more so in traditional societies. In these societies, which are usually authoritarian, the statements of the leaders, who are the epicenter, the focus, and the essence of politics, are also usually the most definitive and the most updated words about what lies ahead. In the Arab world, all this is further amplified by the extraordinary impact of the Arabic word, which many students of the Arab psyche emphasize (Patai, 1973; Hamadi, 1960; Laffin, 1975). Indeed, Arabic speech, with its strength of expression, wealth of allusions, and emotional associations that it evokes, has contributed to the inclination of Arab statesmen to use speech to impress their people.

The power of speech, which had been vested with the *sha'ir* (poet) in pre-Islamic Arab civilization, won him the attributes of the "oracle of the tribe, their guide in peace and their champion in war" (Nicholson, 1907: 73). Modern Arab leaders, realizing the potentialities lying in Arabic speech, not surprisingly took over the function of the ancient poet and successfully combined it with the authority of the political chieftain. Because of the receptivity of the Arab public to what might sound like sheer bombast and bravado to Westerners, the impact of Arabic speech on the minds of Arabic-speaking people is remarkable, and their leaders make generous use of it. Hamilton Gibb remarked, "The words, passing through no filter of logic or reflection, which might weaken or deaden their effect, go straight to the head" (Gibb, cited by Laffin, 1975: 56).

When listening to President Anwar el-Sadat of Egypt (1970–1981) or to Chairman Yasir Arafat of the PLO (Palestinian Liberation Organization) (since 1965), or any other Arab leader-orator for that matter, non-Arabs might have been struck by what they viewed as redundant repetitions, unnecessary dwelling on detail, illustrations and anecdotes, slogan brandishing, a quick transition from formal speech in literary Arabic to storytelling in local vernacular, metaphors and analogies, and an abrupt passage from one issue to another. One writer remarked that "Arabs delight in playing with words . . . and in their tendency to fit the thought to the word or to the combination of words, rather than the word to the thought" (Shouby, 1951: 293).

In Arab tradition, illustrations and parables are effective means of pleasing the public, and switches from one subject to another are thought to keep fatigue from the audience, which readily applauds amusing edification and informative witticism (von Grunebaum, 1953: 227). Because of overstressing of details, to convey meaning in an ordinary speech it is necessary to repeat oneself several times through different words and, like the traditional Arab teacher, to instill the information into the pupil's head by repetition (Laffin, 1975: 60–61). Yet, there are unmistakable personal touches to these general patterns of speech: Sadat, for example, always used a didactic approach to his audiences. Whether in a popular gathering or in a press interview, he delighted in teaching, which he considered a part of his patriarchal function to oversee his family's education. His favorite devices were historical analogies and the exemplary precedents set by historical heroes, among whom he implicitly counted himself. Arafat, a revolutionary at heart and a frustrated nationalist, prefers to adopt abrasive speech, hurl bitter references at his enemies and the world, instigate his people to struggle and sacrifice, and repeat his own words and phrases in an endless string of sloganeering.

SADAT—THE FERVENT PREACHER

Sadat's religiosity and attachment to the holy *Qur'an* and to the basic tenets of Islam can be traced to his rural upbringing. In the village, the local imam held a predominant role in religious as well as educational and moral affairs. He was a subject of adulation and a model of emulation for youngsters who wanted to memorize entire chapters of the Holy Book, as he had done. Even though Sadat, the leader and statesman, seemed committed to revolution, modernization, and technological development, he could not divorce himself from Islam. The tension between the two traits was reflected in Sadat's slogan: "We must create a state of faith and science" (Israeli, 1985: 10). Intensely preaching across Egypt for this combination, Sadat used an entire arsenal of village-drawn images to drive his point. He spoke of arrows and targets, and invoked parables about animals and other images connected with plants, land and soil, light and fire, and parts of the body when he needed to emphasize a point or to illustrate an event (Israeli, 1984).

Thus, the emergence of unity in the Arab world was likened to the "growth of a tree and the ripening of a harvest." Conspirators against the regime were looked upon as "dropping one after another like autumn leaves," and Arab society was exhorted to "cultivate itself, to bloom and burgeon and take root in the land." Those who stood ready to take advantage of a situation were seen by Sadat as "picking the fruits" without "burning their fingers in the flame." Once, he exhorted the Arabs not to let the world behave like a jungle, because "we might not be among the strongest beasts there" (Israeli, 1984: 11–13).

These illustrations of Sadat's attachment to his peasant roots should not obscure the other pillar of his identity—Islam. Elements of the faith had shaped his view of the world and even sent him into the arms of the Muslim Brothers in the pre-Revolutionary period, preceding Gamal Abdel Nasser's takeover in 1952 and the overnight catapulting to power of a group of young and inexperienced officers, Sadat among them. Thereafter and until the 1967 war, when the Arabs were routed by Israel, Sadat was on the sidelines of Egyptian politics and did not express much of his thinking in public. But the trauma of defeat generated a process of soul-searching in Egyptian society. Sadat, who had been preoccupied before with a personal, friendly Allah to whom he drew close during his years in jail in the 1940s and early 1950s, awoke after the war to the embodiment of Allah in the community as a whole.

Indeed, somehow the trauma of 1967, coupled with the people's massive demonstrations after the defeat and resignation of Nasser, made Sadat equate *vox populi* to *vox dei*. Thereafter, he stood in awe of the masses, engaged in dialogue with them, drew inspiration from them, and created a mystical link between him and them. On more than one occasion he said to his people: "You are, after Allah, my source of encouragement, stamina and inspiration" (Israeli, 1985: 26). This close communion between the people and Allah was to acquire far-reaching implications for Sadat's sense of mission when he became president. For if he was elected by popular will and popular will was Allah-inspired, then his election to government took on the aura of a divine mission. He repeatedly spoke of his faith in Allah and his mission, and of destiny, which had entrusted him with the sacred duty of leading his community.

After 1967, Sadat became much more openly pious than before. If his village had certainly contributed to the makeup of his personality and his experience in jail had further shaped the image of Allah in his own mind, statecraft added yet another dimension to his piety. It marked a transition from passivity and resignation, in the face of Allah's will, to a militant and active striving, a search for manifestations of Allah, something like *Aides-*

toi, Dieu t'aidera (help yourself and God will help you). He no longer saw faith as an individual belief, a personal way of living, but now perceived it as society's source of strength and cohesion, a potent weapon in war, a tool for national and inter-Arab unity, and a rationale to explain historical events:

Allah has ordained us to believe. I order you to believe. We all need to fill our hearts with faith, in addition to the weapons we are carrying, so that we may enter the battle with faith, so that we reach the standard of responsibility and of the mission that Allah has ordained.... In battle, the Prophet Mohammed has equipped us with the most potent weapon—faith. It has always given us the upper hand.... We are motivated by faith and the mission that the Prophet had destined for us. (Israeli, 1985: 47–48; see also Israeli, 1978–1979; Israeli, 1980)

In consequence, Allah became omnipresent and immediate, not transcendental and remote. From now on, Sadat uttered the name of Allah more frequently and more noticeably. He hardly ever made a speech without mentioning the name of Allah somewhere or without beginning and ending with a citation from the Holy Book, the Word of Allah. He openly thanked Allah that the Saudi mediation between Iraq and Syria had succeeded, called his troops the "soldiers of Allah," and often prayed to Allah in his public addresses:

Allah, forgive us if we have forgotten or have been led astray.... Allah, do not overburden us the way you did to our predecessors. Allah, do not burden us with more than we can bear.... May be peace upon you, with Allah's compassion. (Israeli, 1985: 48)

After the 1973 war, Sadat exclaimed, "I was certain that Allah would be on our side, for he supports all devoted believers who seek his help." No wonder that the Egyptian army war cry during the October 1973 battles was *"Allah Akbar"* (Allah is the greatest); the eyewitness stories abounded in the Egyptian press from those who had "seen" the Prophet riding his white horse, crossing the Suez Canal with the Egyptian troops, and leading the way before him. Ecstatic Egyptian troops then defied Israeli fire; stormed Israeli defenses; and, under the cry *"Allah Akbar!"* hoisted the Egyptian flag on the shattered Bar-Lev line, the "Maginot Line" of the Israelis along the canal. Sadat had exhorted his troops, as the "soldiers of Allah" to strive for "Allah's victory" because "all victories emanated from Allah," and they delivered. Sadat, in fact, attested after the war that "Allah's presence hovered above us in October" (Israeli, 1985: 10–12, 26–30).

Sadat saw a link between the intervention of Providence and unfolding events. To be sure, Muslim thinking had always attributed everything to Allah. Even natural phenomena, such as sunrise and sunset, winter and summer, rain and drought, are credited in Islam to Allah's daily renewed will rather than to a preordained cycle of life, itself determined by Allah. But Sadat went further than that; he directly imputed to Allah's will any happening, good deed, sound policy, or turn of events that worked in his or his people's favor. Allah came to be perceived as a close overseer of everyday life; Sadat saw his successes and his sheer good fortune as daily evidence of Allah's involvement. If "Allah is 'free' to determine what he wills and one cannot help but conform to his will," as Sadat often put it, however, then one also has to accept his trials, tests, demands, and sacrifices. Preceding the 1973 war, Sadat saw his own predicament in this light. He had a mission to accomplish. It was also God-ordained; therefore, he had to endure all the humiliation, denigration, and doubt voiced against him. He asked his troops to undergo the same kind of martyrdom. He constantly urged his people to strive, to struggle, to withstand Allah's tests, for "we are required to sacrifice life in order to deserve life," as he used to say. The liberation of Egyptian land from Israeli occupation was a "holy duty" that required sacrifice and Arab unity, both supreme manifestations of faith (Israeli, 1985: 44–49).

After that fateful war, Sadat gathered strength, authority, and popularity, both domestically and worldwide. But the economic austerity also gave rise to the Islamists—the Muslim Brothers—that emerged from underground in full force and began to win wide constituencies through their widespread social welfare and educational activities. When discontent with Sadat became wide ranging and culminated in the food riots of January 1977, he came up with the stunning news that he was going to Jerusalem to tell the *Knesset* (Israeli Parliament) that a settlement was needed. He couched that revelation, which was bound to arouse anger among the Islamists, in religious terms: he was going to pray in the Aqsa Mosque, even if that meant entering the lion's den of Israel. His tightly controlled media hailed him as the hero of peace and dismissed all of his critics at home and abroad as "myopic" or "dwarfs."

Sadat made the trip to Jerusalem during the Muslim festival of *Id al-Adhha*, the Feast of Sacrifice, which commemorates the sacrifice made by Abraham of his son Ishmael in submission and obedience to Allah's command. In choosing this date, according to Hjarpe (1988: 554), Sadat was transmitting a message to the Islamic world: "This is a necessary sacrifice to undertake." Sadat came back to that theme in his speech before the Israeli Parliament in November 1977, when he referred to Abraham, the father of both Jews and Muslims, and his sacrifice. This feast belongs to the *Hajj*, the pilgrimage to Mecca. That day and the next three days constitute the period of lapidation of the Devil by the believers at the end of the pilgrimage to commemorate Abraham's valiant struggle against the Devil, whom he scared away with rocks rather than succumb to the temptation of disobeying God's command to sacrifice his beloved son. This commemoration is symbolized by the ritual of lapidating with rocks the three pillars that represent the Devil, while shouting "*Allah Akbar!*" Sadat indeed lapidated the Israeli Parliament with harsh words that were certainly directed to the ears of the Muslim world.

The world widely acclaimed Sadat when he achieved the Camp David Accords with Israel in 1978, followed by his signature of the peace accords on the White House lawn in February 1979, and when he received the Nobel Peace Prize in 1978 along with Israeli Prime Minister Menachem Begin (1977–1983). At home, however, more trouble awaited him. Coming under strong attacks by nationalists on the one hand and Islamists on the other for his deal with the hated enemy at the price of destroying Arab unity, ceding to American pressures, and isolating Egypt, he counterattacked. First, he made sure that the accords got an Islamic seal from the religious establishment of al-Azhar University in Cairo, which compared them to the *Hudaibiyya* Treaty that the Prophet Muhammed had signed with his enemies in Mecca, and later reneged on them. This signified that, domestically, Sadat had to defend himself from the Islamists and others by being as Islamic as them, or more so. He also tried to soothe Islamic public opinion by adopting a series of Islamic laws banning alcohol in public places and acknowledging *Shari'a Law* (the Islamic Holy Law) as a major source of legislation in his country. That process culminated in his passing through his rubber-stamp parliament the "Law of Shame," which drastically restricted patterns of behavior in public.

These steps only earned Sadat more enemies at home. He reacted in the classic way of all dictators. Ordering massive arrests left and right, he threw thousands of his political enemies in jail. But the fate of Sadat—he, the believer in fate—was sealed. On October 6, 1981, while he was watching the military parade commemorating, ironically, the October War, which he regarded as his victory, he was gunned down by an Islamist from the ranks of his own army.

Sadat's last book, titled *Wasiyyati (My Legacy)*, was published posthumously. The range of topics that Sadat addressed in his book amounted to a rather lofty commentary on such chapter titles as "Faith—The Gift of Security," "Love—The most Wonderful of God's Favors," and "The Spirit, the Mind and the Body." These themes accord well with the image that his family and friends had of him during his last few months as a dreamer and an eccentric, one who often isolated himself in his native village to fast and to lead a rather ascetic life. He often invoked his close communion with God and spoke of establishing on Mount Sinai a joint house of prayer for the three monotheistic religions. In one passage of his book, where he extolled the virtues of divine love, he exhorted his readers to "come and listen to a Sufi poet" who said:

> It is my Lord whom I worship
> It is my Lord whom I love

It my Lord for whom I want
To suffer and be tormented
And want to be in agony,
And for whom I want
To be split, to be torn and die. (Quoted in Israeli, 1985: 274)

ARAFAT—THE SKILLFUL MANIPULATOR

Yasir Arafat, a Palestinian who grew up in Cairo and spent most of his adult life wandering from one place to another in search of his lost Palestine, has also had some bouts of religiosity that go back to his association with the Muslim Brothers in Egypt during his early years there. Arafat is a pious Muslim, but in his role as head of the PLO, and especially as the President of the fledgling Palestinian authority, he uses Islamic themes, symbols, vocabulary, and rhetoric in order to cater to the spiritual needs of his people and to thwart the accusations of the Islamists against him. Moreover, unlike Sadat, who was well-established as a head of state, Arafat's struggle to gain acceptance, recognition, and legitimacy worldwide, at times drives him to appeal to wider circles and constituencies. Thus, he can coax Palestinian Christians by promising them a happy existence under the protective wings of Islam or assure the world that he is the best curator of all holy places, both Muslim and Christian, in Jerusalem. But, most often, he uses Islamic themes as a powerful mobilizing factor in the struggle against Israel.

The mainstream of Palestinian nationalism, best personified by Arafat and the PLO, like most local forms of Arab nationalism, makes use of Islam, as Lewis (1976) and Johnson (1982: 8–15) have shown, to characterize enemies, to imply modes of action against them, and to define the nature of the Palestinian community and its struggle, thus linking together key religious and secular concepts. Examples are the *Jihad* (Holy War), linked with the armed struggle of the PLO, and the commitment to fight imperialism, linked with the fight against Zionism, itself seen as an extension of imperialism, and both being a contemporary manifestation of the historical presence of the West in the Muslim world since the Crusades. When the PLO, notably Arafat, refers to its casualties as *shuhada'* (martyrs) and to its guerrillas as *fida'iyun* (self-sacrificing), it implies the redemption inherent in dying in the Muslim sense of the concept. When Jews, Zionists, and Israelis are mentioned by Arafat and others, often interchangeably, they are posited as the latter-day version of the Prophet of Islam's struggle against the Jews of Medina some fourteen centuries ago. Even the avowedly secular document of the PLO charter, whose every word and comma was either written by Arafat or approved by him, is interspersed with concepts that can be seen as Islamic: sacrifice or struggle. Article 16, for example, refers to the issue of Palestine as the Holy Land with religious sites.

That Arafat and the PLO manipulate Islamic symbols should come as no surprise, for Islam is too important a part of Palestinian culture to ignore. Indeed, Lewis (1976) has shown that Arafat's very *nom de guerre* (Abu Ammar), as well as his parlance (e.g., *Bismillah, Jihad, Hudaybiyya*, sacrifice, Jerusalem) have Islamic connotations, as do the names of the Palestinian Army's regiments (e.g., Al-Aqsa, Hittin, Ein Jalut, Qadisiyya), all named after famous battles in Islamic (not Arab) history. One could imagine the thrill of a prospective recruit in a Palestinian refugee camp, when he is told that he can join Fat'h (Arafat's group within the PLO, also meaning "conquest" for the sake of Islam) and become a member of one of its regiments—with names that invoke the glory of historical Islam—under the supreme command of Abu Ammar (also the name of one of early Islam's generals).

The mobilizing effect of such Islamic slogans and symbols hardly can be exaggerated. In the new era of Palestinian autonomy, Arafat has been trying to adopt the trappings of a state with international respectability and national responsibility, and he has toned down his Islamic militancy for a while. At the same time, however, he cannot let the fundamentalists, such as *Hamas* and *Islamic Jihad*, overtake him on the right.

In late 1995 and at the beginning of 1996, when Israel surrendered to Arafat's rule the major cities of the West Bank, Arafat came as a hero to all of them and delivered passionate speeches to the delirious crowds who awaited him. Most of the themes he used in those speeches were imbued with a rich texture of Islam. For example, he invariably invoked Jerusalem as a powerful unifying symbol. In every speech, he listed all the towns and villages so far liberated and vowed to "march into Jerusalem" or "pray in Jerusalem" at the end of the process. He referred to Jerusalem as *Al-Quds a-Sharif* (Noble Jerusalem) or *Al-Quds al-'Arabiyya* (Arab Jerusalem). In Bethlehem, on Christmas Day 1995, Arafat referred to "our blessed land," which "witnessed the birth of "our Palestinian Messiah." Thus, Arafat connected the blessed land to its messianic message, and widened the scope of his Islamic commitment to Palestine to embrace Christianity, as well, when he said that the Christians of Palestine are as Palestinian as the Muslims thereof since the Christ himself was Palestinian. But his *beau geste* of extending his loving care to Christianity in Palestine immediately resulted in the interpretation that he coveted, and had probably arranged, when the Greek Orthodox Patriarch of Jerusalem declared to a delighted Arafat, on the occasion of his triumphant entering Bethlehem: "Here is the successor of Sophronius welcoming the successor of 'Umar ibn al-Khattab."

No one present or watching on television could miss the parallel. Reference was made, of course, to the submission of the Byzantine Patriarch of Jerusalem, in A.D. 636, to the second Caliph of Islam, 'Umar, who formally conquered Jerusalem for Islam and put an end to centuries of Christian rule there, until this was reversed again when the Crusaders established their Kingdom of Jerusalem in 1099. But until then, the city would remain, uninterruptedly, part of the domain of Islam. The declaration of the Patriarch was so melodious to the ears of Arafat that he ordered all his media to publish it in their headlines, a sign that these images fitted perfectly within his political discourse.

This makes Arafat the latest link in the apostolic chain of great liberators of Jerusalem, which to date include 'Umar, and Salah Saladin, who recouped Jerusalem in 1189 and put an end to the century-old Crusader rule there. If one bears in mind the oft-made comparison in Arab and Islamic circles between the medieval Crusader state and contemporary Israel, one necessarily comes to the conclusion that exactly as 'Umar had occupied Jerusalem by peaceful means through the submission of its patriarch and Saladin had done so by force, so will Arafat repeat that feat, either by accepting the surrender of the Israelis, at least of East Jerusalem for now, or by pressing his call for *Jihad* in order to retrieve all of it. Many Palestinian groups, especially the fundamentalists, take delight in this parallel and are quick to draw conclusions from it. 'Umar and Saladin had been accepted as legitimate rulers of Jerusalem, and both had followed the oath of allegiance (*bai'a*) accorded to them by the populace in the traditional Arab/Muslim manner. Then, in 1995, as the loudspeakers in Bethlehem enjoined the people to deliver the *bai'a* to Arafat, the parallel became neat, complete, and inescapable. History had come a full circle.

The all-important question of Jerusalem, which figures so highly and so frequently in Arafat's political discourse, is linked to quite another Islamic concept, to which Arafat often refers—the *Hudaybiyya* Treaty that Prophet Muhammad had signed with his enemies in Mecca. During a visit to Johannesburg, South Africa, in early 1994, Arafat addressed his fellow Muslims in a local mosque about the Oslo Peace Accords that he had signed with Israel merely six months earlier. He enjoined his audience to join *Jihad* in order to recover Jerusalem, mentioned the 'Umar-Sophronius precedent (discussed above), and compared the Peace Accords with the *Hudaybiyya* Treaty. Again, in live broadcasts to Palestinian audiences in Gaza, he hammered on the same themes of Jerusalem, *'Umar-Sophronius, Jihad* and *Hudaybiyya*, as he sought, in his statements, political precedents set by the most perfect of men, the Prophet Muhammad. In such a speech, broadcast on Palestinian television on January 1, 1995—*Mi'raj* Day (the Prophet's Ascension to Heaven)—Arafat said:

My brethren, we are a sacrificing and fighting nation.... A Jerusalem *hadith* (oral tradition related to the Prophet) says: "A group within my nation cling to my Faith and fight their enemies.... They cannot be harmed and they will win, with Allah's help. The Messenger of God was asked, 'who are they?' He answered: 'In Jerusalem ... in Jerusalem and its environs ... they stand at the forefront until the Day of Judgment....' " We are at the forefront, fighters at the forefront ... I said I saw the tunnel, and at the end of the tunnel are the walls of Jerusalem with its mosques and churches.... And today, the day Muhammad ascended to Heaven, we say: "Blessed be he who goes forth from the Mosque of Mecca to al-Aqua." We will enter the mosque and pray there, with Allah's help.

Allah does not break his promise. When the Prophet made peace with the tribe of *Quraysh* [at *Hudaybiyya*], 'Umar ibn al-Khattab said: "Stop! Had we known [of your future behavior] when we acclaimed you as Allah's Messenger, we would have never fought for you." 'Umar even called it the "despicable peace" ... we shall press on to Jerusalem.... Fighters in this revolution ... are the sons of Izz a-Din al-Qassam.... We renew our oath to the martyrs, and our oath of loyalty to Jerusalem, capital of our land in Palestine.... In the name of Allah the Merciful, we will redeem the downtrodden of the earth and make them leaders and heirs, and we will give them the land.

The same symbolism and vocabulary, repeated by Arafat in various gatherings, culminated in the Christmas ceremony at the closure of 1995 in Bethlehem. Taken together, they indicate the following patterns:

1. Arafat purports to abide by the precedent of the Prophet Muhammad in *Hudaybiyya* ("history is our best teacher"). This means that, as in the case of *Hudaybiyya*, peace with the enemies can be broken when convenient to the Muslims or likely to bring benefit to Islam.

2. The fact that 'Umar had dubbed *Hudaybiyya* "despicable," even when sanctioned by the Prophet himself, could justify *a priori* its breach, when circumstances so warrant.

3. Arafat learned from the experience of the *Hamas* that blood-and-sweat speeches, with promises of protracted struggles and endless sacrifices, are paradoxically more soothing, appealing, and credible to the masses than empty pledges of rosy life, easy victories, and plentiful peace. Because harsh language, of the kind seen in Arafat's political discourse, not only justifies, *post factum*, the departed martyrs but also mobilizes and encourages the new generations of *shuhada'*. The Islamic calls for *Jihad* and the certainty of divine retribution that goes with them were found by Arafat as more cajoling to the hearts of the populace, and he does not shrink from repeating them.

4. Jerusalem, the ultimate prize, the jewel of the crown of the Holy Land, is the best rallying war cry of the Muslims, from Johannesburg to Gaza, from Islamabad, Pakistan, to Rabat, Morocco. And this Jerusalem is primarily Islamic, secondarily Christian (Arafat said he saw in his dreams mosques and churches, not synagogues), which allows him to play the role of 'Umar, the Muslim leader and savior, while all manner of submissive Christians reenact the role of Sophronius.

5. All Palestinians are potential martyrs, that is, likely participants in the coveted *Jihad* of liberation. This sort of political discourse then allows Arafat to close ranks with *Hamas* and invite them to join his goal of liberating Jerusalem via *Jihad*, which is his, too.

Arafat's moments of dream and vision carry him to the heights of the Prophet Muhammad, whose policies he purports to articulate, and of 'Umar, in whose footsteps he wants to tread. But in his much more numerous moments of despair and frustration, he threatens, lashes out, and drives himself out of control, both in his discourse and demeanor. When the wings of vision transport him into the realm of the desirable and the coveted, *Hudaybiyya* is for him the quintessence of the Prophet's diplomatic and political success and Jerusalem is the peak of 'Umar's strategic and political blueprint, in both cases political wisdom and prowess having preempted war and violence. But when the feet of reality force him to crashland into the quagmire of the problems that stymie his very functioning and constrain the uplifting of his spirit, he impatiently embraces *Jihad* and reverts to his own self. After all, both the Prophet and 'Umar, his heroes, had resorted to *Jihad*, too, when there was no other recourse (i.e., when their enemies had refused to surrender to their wills).

The choice of the *Hudaybiyya-Jihad*-Jerusalem trio by an astute Arafat is not accidental but well-perceived. True to his Muslim conviction, he found common grounds between his beliefs and the deep chords he can play to instigate massive and passionate responses within his constituencies.

CONCLUSION—ARABIC DISCOURSE AND ISLAMIC LEGITIMACY

Whereas Sadat might be best characterized as a peasant-president, with his world of metaphors and images borrowed from the rural setting of Egypt (Israeli, 1984), Arafat can be best described as a roaming revolutionary, with roots nowhere, who borrows liberally from other revolutionary traditions to shape his analogies and draw his lessons. Nevertheless, one trait is common to both men—the profuse usage of Islam in matters of symbolism, historical precedent, and vocabulary. Both can be considered pious Muslims; therefore, their acquaintance with the faith, their organic and genuine handling of it, and their use of it to survive domestically and further their foreign policies externally have been unmistakable traits of their respective political discourses. Both had personal experiences with the Muslim Brothers prior to attaining prominence and power, and both, ironically, have been hunted down by Muslim fundamentalists, who murdered Sadat on October 6, 1981, and are now threatening Arafat's rule in the emerging Palestinian entity.

Alternately defying a vocal and well-organized Muslim opposition and placating it have been constants for both Arafat and Sadat in ruling their countries. On the one hand, they have attempted to herald democracy in their societies, but, on the other hand, Arafat is as aware today as Sadat had been in his time that an open democracy could mean the rise of fundamentalists, with their challenges to and even ultimate takeover of power, hence the continuous endeavors of these supposedly lay leaders to ascertain themselves and their legitimacy in Islamic terms. Certainly, the democratic game is there, with the trappings of participatory democracy (e.g., elections, referendums, state institutions), although everyone knows that the ultimate focus of power rests with the existing lay leader (Sadat then, Arafat now). Neither was, or is, in any mood to hand over power to the opposition. Like other Arab regimes who seek legitimacy in Islam, so did Sadat and so does Arafat.

REFERENCES

Hamadi, S. (1960). *Temperament and character of the Arabs*. New York: Twayne.

Hjarpe, J. (1988). La commemoration religieuse comme legitimation politique dans le monde Musulman contemporain [Religious commemoration as political legitimation in the contemporary Islamic world]. In P. Gignoux (Ed.), *La commemoration* [The commemoration]. Louvain-Paris: Peeters.

Israeli, R. (1978–1979). *The Public Diary of President Sadat*, 3 vols. Leiden: Brill.

Israeli, R. (1980). The role of Islam in President Sadat's political thought. *The Jerusalem Journal of International Relations*, 4, 1–12.

Israeli, R. (1984). The peasant-president: Sadat's world of images and metaphors. *Middle East Focus*, 7 (2), 4; 20.

Israeli, R. (1985). *Man of defiance: A political biography of Anwar Sadat*. London and Totowa, N.J.: Weidenfeld & Nicolson.

Johnson, N. (1982). *Islam and politics of meaning in Palestinian nationalism*. London: Kegan Paul.

Laffin, J. (1975). *The Arab mind*. London: Cassell.

Lewis, B. (1976). The return of Islam. *Commentary* (Winter).

Nicholson, R. A. (1907). *Literary history of the Arabs*. London: Unwin.

Patai, R. (1973). *The Arab mind*. New York: Scribner.

Shouby, E. (1951). The influence of the Arabic language on the psychology of the Arabs. *The Middle East Journal*, 5.

von Grunebaum, G. E. (1953). *Medieval Islam: A study of cultural orientation*. Chicago: University of Chicago Press.

CHAPTER 3

The Changing Political Language of Germany

CHRISTA LANG-PFAFF

INTRODUCTION

Contrary to other countries, Germany possesses an elaborate tradition in political language research. This chapter discusses problems involved with a systematic presentation of the concerned results. One issue is the struggle between two linguistic paradigms—"modern" and "context-based." The modern paradigm, which is rooted in the rhetorical system during the period between Aristotle and Machiavelli, considers rhetorical and political systems to be independent. The "context-based" paradigm, which follows the French and English revolutionary tradition, states that discourse coincides with the current political system, elite, and roles and with the according transformations, such as those caused by revolutions. The paradigm struggle influences the status of German political language research, a struggle intensified even more because the German political system has changed radically several times during the twentieth century. Seeing the context-based linguistic paradigm, Germany's different political systems (democratic parliamentarism, its breakdown during the Weimar Republic, the totalitarian Third Reich system, and the totalitarian German Democratic Republic) affected the essentials of political socialization and language research concepts. This context-based linguistic paradigm was attached to criteria of war or postwar generation, democratic or totalitarian socialization, marginal participation or entanglement in continual nation state debate and European discourse. Accordingly, scholars must decide between results to recognize and those to forget.

This chapter consciously focuses on the German contribution to the solution of the German question in Europe during the 1980s. It chooses only small examples from large quantities of text. These extracts of text, however, explain the particularity of the German situation, in which the executive branch liberated itself from the political traumas of twentieth-century German history and sought role models in the revolutionary tradition of the American Constitution and the French Revolution. The political public sphere remained trapped by its traumas, however, and thus lost its ability to conceive of completely new political developments.

The broad concept of the German question in Europe is historical, based within the first part of nineteenth century. This concept includes a pattern of long-term political, territorial, and ideological problems. Starting with the Carolingian division, it expressed the construction and arrangements of German history (Hildebrandt, 1985: 317–326). It concerned contradictory concepts, traditions, and political tensions between two models of nation building: the French model in the West and the German model in the middle of Europe. The German development was destined by the discrepancy between supranational ideas and goals of spaciousness and the difficult reality of political dissipation and particularism.

The narrow concept of the German question in Europe since 1945 focused on national and international problems of German division after World War II. It also focused on the fundamental regulations in the constitution of the Federal Republic concerning the demand of reunification. In every case both concepts touched the center of the historic idea and political claim of European equilibrium. They touched also the permanent dialectic between ideologies of identity and expansion in the German history and the continental European perception (Hillgruber, 1983: 3–15). The issues discussed in this chapter result from the differences of both concepts and their influence on the changing political language of Germany during the 1980s.

POLITICAL LANGUAGE RESEARCH IN TWENTIETH-CENTURY GERMANY

Since 1945, language research in Germany with respect to linguistics, political science, and sociology has been traumatic in three aspects: the world wars caused by Germany, the crimes committed under the rule of the National Socialists in the Third Reich, and the problem of the German question in Europe, with the existence of two German states on German territory: the Federal Republic of Germany, a civil and liberal state with a representative parliamentarian system and a federal system of state organization, and the German Democratic Republic, a communist, centralist state under the dictatorial rule of a single party system. Because of the (narrow) German question in Europe, which remained unsolved for forty years, both countries continued to be connected as nation states. At the same time, they laid down their political systems within opposing alliances, hostile to each other (North Atlantic Treaty Organization (NATO) versus the Warsaw Pact), and concentrated on fierce ideological and military-technological competition.

Within the respective dependency of both German states on political and alliance systems, political language researchers took these traumatic conditions into account. Therefore, in spite of the liberty of research guaranteed by the constitution of the Federal Republic, language research was not free in the political sense; it was concentrated on the language of national socialism, the history of concept, language criticism, ideological criticism, and rhetoric. Further, a series of publications followed the periods of political climate change from warm to cold to the thaw during the cold war. Many studies concentrated on questions concerning identity, political culture, and characteristics of the language dispute during parliamentary elections in the Federal Republic, as well as on questions concerning the culture and identity of the German Democratic Republic.

Other studies focused on the semiotics of the parliament, as well as on the language of politicians as a problem of informal language activity. The studies dealing with parliament concentrated on and dealt with the Federal Republic and the German *Bundestag* and, after 1990, with the People's Chamber of the German Democratic Republic. The *Bundesrat*, the common federal organ of the executive powers of the Federal Republic states (Bundesländer), has been completely left out of the research perspective.

In 1990, the solution of the German question in Europe and German unification overwhelmed the research situation outlined above. Political language researchers were completely surprised by this development, in particular because, from the scientific point of view, they got along well with the German division and had expressed their political dependency as linguistic, ideological, and political criticism. In view of the nation-state clamp between the two German states and the traumas outlined above, language researchers defined its scientific and political task in the old Federal Republic as that of a guardian of democracy which, at the same time, must keep some research bridges open to the German Democratic Republic.

In this situation, political language researchers in Germany took advantage of the period from 1990 to 1994 (1994 was the year in which, in my opinion, they also completely freed itself from the political point of view) to orient their research in a new direction. Two groups of publications are of special value: (1) those concerning German language history, controversial concepts, guiding vocabulary during the Konrad Adenauer era, language in conflict, and language in upheaval and (2) those concerning the question of public sphere and public opinion.

Although both groups must be considered as distinct with respect to their specialized scientific subjects, and although they can be regarded only partially as transdisciplinary, they are discussed below under the common heading, "Language, Politics, and Policy—Public Sphere." Even if one must presume that both large groups of researchers take (and took) note of each other in only a limited way, they should be brought together for an analysis of politics and policy, language, and public sphere.

LANGUAGE, POLITICS, AND POLICY—PUBLIC SPHERE

Following German unification, political language researchers, emerging from their two segments began to spread throughout all regions of the new and unified Federal Republic. Also, the development of research into the public sphere (sociology of the public sphere and political science of the public sphere) began at that time.

In 1992, there appeared *Language—Politics and Policy—Public Sphere*, a series of scientific publications jointly edited by linguists, political scientists, and sociologists. Although scholars from various German universities now had a forum for German transdisciplinary political language research, they faced the following problem of coming from two political alliance systems. The title of the series continued to describe the objects of their research, but, within a year, the issues had been dramatically radicalized.

A series of comprehensive publications in the 1990s throws light on these scientific discussions of the public sphere and its concepts, functions, and structures. The collection by Burkhardt & Fritzsche (1992), which presented the most up-to-date results of research, represented completely different political public spheres. Although the book was an attempt to exercise political influence, it was too far behind the events themselves.

In the united Germany, political language researchers of West and East were swept into a whirlpool of irreversible political events and decisions that particularly affected scientists from the former German Democratic Republic. They were made personally responsible for the results of research they had done until that time. Shortly before unification, political figures, opinion formers, and the mass media in both German states were extremely shaken and their forms of expression oscillated rapidly between political euphoria on the one hand and anxious euphemisms and incantations of stability on the other. The politically restrictive socialist public sphere had shown itself to be malleable when people began to "vote with their feet" in the German Democratic Republic in 1986. The political ideological system turned out to be surprisingly shaky. By 1989/1990, it had reached a revolutionary and plebiscitary state that exceeded, by far, that of the civil public sphere in the Federal Republic. Uncertainty and skepticism overcame even the politically alert public sphere in Berlin, which now suddenly included both public spheres as a consequence of unification. The transformation of the socialist public sphere had destroyed the systematic clarity of public sphere concepts in the German Democratic Republic after 1986 and in the Federal Republic of Germany after 1989 (Löcher & Blaum, 1983: 542–46).

Schroeter's (1994) publication is another example of the confusion in German political language research following 1990. It was (according to the publishing house's publicity material) intended to "contribute to the clarification of the relationship between language and society and/or language and ideology, taking the GDR as an example." The German Democratic Republic, however, no longer existed; despite some public declarations to the contrary, the world could see that the East Germans had little interest in reviving it. Thus, Schroeter's work was up to date but also an anachronism. It made the reader aware of that which is transitory and that which, politically, has ceased to be or has reemerged as dangerous.

The political language of Germany had not only changed but turned around; this has occurred eight times during the twentieth century. The withdrawal of the Allied troops from Germany in August and September 1994, as described below, marked the most recent turnaround.

In a few weeks the last Russian soldiers will leave our country—50 years after the Red Army arrived in the German Reich. The soldiers arrived in late autumn 1944; at that time, they were Soviet troops and the agreement on their withdrawal was entered four years ago with the Soviet President Mikhail Gorbachev. The Russian troops are leaving Germany today, and the Russian President Boris Yeltsin is present at the leaving ceremonies. They are not leaving our country as an occupying power, but as our partners and, hopefully, as our friends now and in the future. For me [Chancellor Helmut Kohl] personally, a dream has come true. (*Bulletin*, 1994: 585)

POLITICAL RHETORIC VERSUS POLICY AND POLITICS

Before this event, international rhetoric is contradictory. Scholars should be aware that excessive discussions of the German question within the public sphere (particularly 1984–1987 rhetoric) at the national, bilateral and European levels, do not reflect the actual politics and policy of the 1980s.

During 1984–1985, one finds some extremely contradictory discourses between the Federal Republic and the German Democratic Republic and between these two states and the former Allies. The official visits of the presidents of Sweden, Greece, France, and Italy, as well as the visits of the foreign ministers of France, Britain, Belgium, and Austria and the Austrian chancellor to East Berlin, are in contrast with the failure of attempts by the Federal Republic to arrange an official visit to Bonn by Erich Honecker, general secretary of the central committee of the Socialist Unity Party (SED) and chairman of the Staatsrat of the German Democratic Republic. Honecker had made diplomatically successful journeys to Norway, Sweden, Greece, Italy (including an audience with the Pope), Finland, and Yugoslavia. The foreign minister of the German Democratic Republic, Oskar Fischer, had officially visited Austria, Denmark, and the Netherlands. Central

European countries were putting diplomatic pressure on the Federal Republic regarding its policy on Germany.

Ten days after the official rejection of a visit by Honecker to the Federal Republic in September 1984, Italy's foreign minister, Giulio Andreotti, caused a massive political dispute at the national, bilateral, and European levels. This dispute was picked up rhetorically and politically in the old Federal Republic and in all neighboring European states. In front of members of the Italian Communist Party and mass media in Rome, Andreotti stated: "We all agree to the necessity of a good relationship between the two German states, . . . but we should not exaggerate. The Pangermanism has to be overcome. There are two German states and two states should remain in force" (Archiv der Gegenwart, 1984: 28145). In consequence of Andreotti's rhetoric linkage between the concept of Pangermanism and postwar policy of the Federal Republic, Andreotti revocated his manifestation (September 17, 1984) (Archiv der Gegenwart, 1984: 28146). The dispute over the German question in Europe (whether it was open or closed) determined politics and policy until 1989 (even after Honecker's visit to Bonn on September 7–11, 1987).

Another example concerns post-1985 German-Soviet relations. West Germany's Chancellor Helmut Kohl caused a dispute when, in a *Newsweek* interview (October 27, 1986), he chose to compare Gorbachev to Joseph Goebbels (propaganda minister under the National Socialist regime). Long after Kohl's apology to Gorbachev and the Soviet reply concerning the German "caveman," this comparison affected the public sphere in the Federal Republic. A deterioration in German-Soviet relations was expected. As it happened, there was no deterioration. Gorbachev decided to teach the West Germans a lesson. Even though Gorbachev assumed that the two German states would continue to exist (Chernaev 1993: 144), there was a significant improvement between them in 1987. In October 1988, exactly two years after the Goebbels comparison, Kohl visited Moscow, on October 28 (at a talk between Gorbachev and Kohl in the Kremlin), "a turnabout in relations" took place (Chernaev, 1993: 228).

Politics and policy did not echo the exaggerated rhetoric. This was true in all cases where bilateral policies formed part of a European policy (which was either conceptual or actually followed). The discourse regarding the conflict-ridden relations between Germany and Britain and the British rhetoric on the German question in Europe followed a similar pattern.

The semantic dispute, however, seems to be system-dependent. The general political discourse concerning Europe was determined by the political alliances of the cold war, whereas the various discourses on Europe depended on bilateral politics. Also, the dispute changed after 1990 under the influence of German unification and Western Europe's commitment to the European Union and against the backdrop of political changes on the European continent in general.

Significant to the latter is the Charter of Paris for a New Europe (joint declaration of November 21, 1990 of the 22 NATO and Warsaw Pact states that made partners out of hostile alliances) (Wagner, 1990: D656–D664). From this strand had to be separated the element that referred to the two German states and their relations to the former victorious powers of World War II. The question whether there was a direct or an indirect dependency on the victorious powers became crucial in order to distinguish European concepts from bilateral policies. This culminated in the Two-Plus-Four Negotiations and the German-Russian Treaties of 1990, as well as in the new German East Treaties of 1991 and 1992.

Under these complex conditions, one should approach with great care the challenging and symbolic appearances and speeches by the American and French presidents (Ronald Reagan and François Mitterrand, respectively) at several locations within a diplomatically well-contrived geography. Lowering of the Germans' status and their partial diplomatic "punishment" are part of a nationally staged rhetoric. Indeed, the policies of 1985–1995 differ from the rhetoric of memorial days during this period: D-Day celebrations of the Allies' landing on the Normandy beaches, the symbolic repetitions of the victory celebrations and inferiority rituals commemorating May 8, 1945 (the end of the war in Europe), and the symbolism of the Russian-American encounter at the Torgau bridge.

Traditional national images of the enemy are part of rhetorical crusades held at national and revolutionary American, French, British, and Soviet/Russian memorial days. At the same time, the heads of state and governments of the former victorious powers (insofar as they had become "protecting powers," in particular for Berlin) made gestures of reconciliation and declarations of sovereignty. Diplomatic upgrading of the Germans' status was performed via bilateral acts. This pattern changed in the years 1994–1995 when the Federal Republic, for the first time since 1945, enjoyed full sovereignty. The last semantic and political disputes between Germany (as a whole) and the former victorious powers occurred in 1994. These were disputes over their equal value, in particular that of the Russians, and over the timing of the withdrawals of Russian troops from Germany, as well as over the location of the leave-taking ceremonies and whether they should be conducted at the same or different places (i.e., in Berlin and/or Weimar, cities with different historical and political contexts).

AVANT-GARDISTIC DISCOURSE VERSUS PUBLIC SPHERE

The German discourse corresponds only slightly with that of other Western states. As a consequence of the manifold breaks between systems in twentieth-century Germany and the division into two states, the Federal Republic was "sentenced to be a kind of role model for liberal development" (Stern, 1987). The Federal Republic was forced to develop its own political concepts and rhetoric and to find corresponding models that supported its long-term national political targets. This had to happen independently of the question to what extent those targets were accepted or criticized by the German public.

In this respect, one is confronted with the development of a problematic political sphere in the old Federal Republic. It was not only different from political spheres in other Western states, but it fulfilled its role model function in all relevant political questions as required by the Federal Republic. This role model function characterized the German Constitution, the Basic Constitutional Law of 1949, and the phases of the drawing up of the constitutions of each of the states (Bundesländer). It was, however, a backward-looking view, the image of the disastrous twentieth-century Germany, that determined the German public sphere in general. It even adhered to this view in those years during which the victorious powers and most of the European neighbor states had politically, but not always rhetorically, left those views behind. As a consequence of this negative fixation, the citizens of the Federal Republic were unable to achieve a differentiation between the novel German-Soviet policy of the 1980s and the policy of past decades.

The public sphere did not understand the actual policy by the Federal Republic at national and European levels. This policy was based on a subordinated role of Germany (instead of an equal relationship between nation-state and European politics and rhetoric). Consequently, the public sphere was taken by surprise, in a dangerous way, in the autumn of 1989, as were the presidents of the States (Bundesländer) who were bound to their political parties. The political executive of the federation formed an avant-garde; it was no longer followed by general and parliamentarian discourse.

From 1986 to 1989, the public sphere in the Federal Republic had discussed the policy in a generally backward-looking and almost timeless way. The federal chancellor and parts of the federal government, however, developed an up-to-date time frame based on new European concepts.

After 1987, within a short period of time, the federal government had succeeded in achieving its nation-state targets that had been originally planned as long-term targets. The secret of its success was that nation-state and European politics and rhetoric were carried out simultaneously. Oriented in the same direction, they gave preference to the rhetoric of Europe over the rhetoric of the nation-state. The Federal Republic achieved the national target of unification. In a series of high-ranking dialogues and mutual visits, it had convinced the leaders of the Soviet Union that its concept concerning German unification was a future-oriented security concept for the whole of Europe (the "continent Europe") and that the real threat for the Soviet Union emanated from the division of Germany. In an interview in *Der Spiegel* (October 2, 1995: 66–81), Gorbachev paid tribute to German Chancellors Adenauer, Willy Brandt, Helmut Schmidt, and Kohl for their respective preventive achievements in furthering German-Soviet understanding. If public discourse in the Federal Republic is compared with Gorbachev's statements from an originally Soviet point of view, one can see that they are exactly opposite.

The federal government adapted its nation-state rhetoric and politics to European rhetoric and politics. Thus, it politically subordinated them to European ideas and placed them within the European Enlightenment tradition. It succeeded in connecting its "priority for freedom in Europe" with the traditions of the American Constitution and the French Revolution. This can be learned from the speech by Chancellor Kohl to President Reagan in front of the Brandenburg Gate in Berlin on June 12, 1987:

"Certainly, we have not always had the same opinion, because the interest of our countries and our peoples, as everybody understands, demands a careful approach to the problems. This is normal. However, we will never forget that a different opinion on one question or another does not change that which we have fundamentally in common, that means, our commitment to freedom, our common heritage and our nations' civilization which is based on the principles of democracy, personal freedom and the rule of law.... These democratic ideals were set out exactly 200 years ago in the American Constitution. The citizens of your great country can be proud of the 200 years of their democratic constitutional order.

The history of the United States proves that democracy can weather the storms of time. Just as the fathers of the American Constitution could build on the ideas and philosophies of the old world, we Europeans have been able to and can participate in your 200 years' experience of the rule of your Constitution. (*Bulletin*, 1987: 535)

The semantic identification of German and European politics was perfectly tailored to the Soviet state leadership. It accommodated the wish of the Soviet Union to define itself politically as a self-confident part of this 'entire Europe' (a Europe stretching from the Atlantic to the Urals) and, at the same time, to come closer to another democratic European revolution. At the Kremlin in Moscow on July 6, 1987, President of the Federal Republic von Weizaecker formulated this as follows:

Our wish for good neighborly relations with the peoples of the Soviet Union is heartfelt. We are in a phase of historical significance for East and West. Comprehensive agreements have come within tangible reach. In this respect, it is very important to make decisions now in the light of a long-term perspective for the future. How do we imagine the relationship between East and West in the year 2000? Which concepts do we have for Europe as a whole at the transition to the next century? . . . Approaching the next century we should leave the idea of blocks and the borders between them. It is more important to recognize clearly the unity of Europe and to turn it into political reality. Europe is politically divided, but it is undivided and indivisible in its spirit. All peoples, from the Atlantic to the Urals, have rendered a unique contribution which has enriched all Europeans. What connects us, is our common history, the unity in the plurality of our national cultures and our interwoven fates in a small space. We are all dedicated to the European Enlightenment with its confidence in rationality and its noble respect for the dignity of man living in freedom and peace. The young Karl Marx was also touched by this spirit.... I think, Mr. President, that it is worth developing a European cultural consciousness which corresponds to our political goals. This can become a spiritual basis for common actions. European culture without Russian literature and the dedication of your people to reading, or without their music and fine art, without theater, dance and film from the Soviet Union is unthinkable. (*Bulletin*, 1987: 627–629)

In Bonn on July 10, 1987, Chancellor Kohl confirmed the willingness to base the relations between Germany and the Soviet Union on a new, solid, long-term foundation, in view of the year 2000:

Continuing their tradition and history German-Soviet relations can reach a new dimension if we do not restrict our vision to bilateral relations, but look at an encounter with Europe as a whole. Therefore, I would be happy if General Secretary Gorbachev could realize his visit to the European Communities during our Presidency in the first six months of 1988. Then we could talk together about European realities as the century comes to a close.... We could talk about what we mean when we pay tribute to the German-French reconciliation as the great historical achievement of the post-war period and take this as a role model for our relationship with our neighbors to the East, because in our opinion, borders should not divide but connect people in the Europe of tomorrow. This is precisely the core of our politics in the divided Germany. (*Bulletin*, 1987: 617f)

As can be learned from the former text examples, the Federal Republic, in talks with the Soviet leadership, addressed core questions of peace and security of bilateral and European cooperation and of the unity as a nation. As a result, Kohl was able in 1991 to address the following declaration to the German Bundestag:

With the unification of our fatherland Germany entered a new epoque. After 200 years the struggle for the political shape of our fatherland, its internal order and its place in Europe has come to a happy end. (Deutscher Bundestag, January 30, 1991: 90A) (*Der Spiegel*, 1995)

CONCLUSION

Political language research and ideology criticism in Germany after 1945 are characterized by the Nazi-Complex (Stötzel & Wengeler, 1995: 355–382) and by dichotomous attitudes toward rhetoric. Without a more detailed examination, one also assumes that classical rhetoric has survived across all systems (almost as if purged by many centuries of human and political experience). Rhetorical analysis is seen to be still profitable for political language and text analysis, whether one is dealing with Pericles, Winston Churchill, Otto von Bismarck, Adolph Hitler, Walter Ulbricht, Adenauer, or Brandt.

I believe this assumption is questionable with respect to scientific analysis because the general analytical potential of classical rhetoric in its bivalent basic structure leads to distortions when we are confronted with bivalent political systems and their respective political theories. Classical rhetoric, on the one hand, seems to provide a means to conceal confrontations and breaks between systems, but, on the other hand, it also seems to have an additional polarizing effect if opposing political systems are examined.

The case study on the German question in Europe during the 1980s (within the warp and woof of relations between the old Federal Republic and the German Democratic Republic, on the one hand, and the four victorious powers, on the other hand) indicates that dichotomous rhetorical concepts became less important after 1986. From then on, multivalent orientations drawing on Western revolutionary traditions gain importance. This conclusion is attractive because it should lead to a reconsideration of the fundamentals of interpretation concerning German political language during the twentieth Century.

REFERENCES

Archiv der Gegenwart [Contemporary archives]. (1984). October 14, 28145–47.
Becker, J., & Hillgruber, A. (Eds.). (1983). *Die Deutsche Frage im 19. und 20. Jahrhundert* [The German question in the nineteenth and twentieth centuries]. München: Ernst Vögel.
Bulletin. (1984). No. 105, 934.
Bulletin. (1987). No. 61, 533–35.
Bulletin. (1987). No. 62, 541–48.
Bulletin. (1987). No. 72, 617ff.
Bulletin. (1987). No. 73, 625–32.
Burkhardt, A., & Fritzsche, K. P. (Eds.). (1992). *Sprache im Umbruch: Politischer Sprachwandel im zeichen von "Wende" und "Vereinigung"* [Language in upheaval: Political language in function of change and unification]. Berlin: Walter de Gruyter.
Chernaev, A. (1993). *Die letzten jahre einer weltmacht. Der Kreml von innen* [The last years of a world power: The Kremlin from within]. Stuttgart: Deutsche Verlegaustaft.
De Landtsheer, C. (1992). The language of unification: Specification of a coding process as a basis for observation. In A. Burkhardt & K. P. Fritzsche (Eds.), *Sprache im Umbruch: Politischer Sprachwandel im zeichen von "Wende" und "Vereinigung"* [Language in upheaval: Political language in function of change and unification]. Berlin: Walter de Gruyter.
Deutscher Bundestag. (1991). Stenografische Berichte zur 12. Wahlperiode [German Bundestag (1991): Stenographical proceedings of the twelfth electory period], January 30. *Der Spiegel* (October 2, 1995), 66–81.

Hildebrandt, W. (1985). Die geschichtliche Dimension der Deutschen Frage [The historic dimension of the German question]. *Deutsche studien: Viertel jahreshefte der Ost-Akademie Lüneburg*, XXIII (December), 317–26.

Hillgruber, A. (1983). Die Deutsche frage im 19. und 20. jahrhundert—Zur Einfuhrung in die nationale und internationale Problematik [The German question in the nineteenth and twentieth centuries—Invention in national and international problems]. In J. Becker & A. Hillgruber (Eds.), *Die Deutsche Frage im 19. und 20. Jahrhundert* [The German question in the nineteenth and twentieth centuries] (pp. 3–15). München: Ernst Vögel.

Locher, W., & Blaum, V. (1983). Offentlichkeit [Public sphere]. In W. Langenbucher, R. Rytlewski, & B. Weyergraf (Eds.), *Kulturpolitisches worterbuch bundesrepublik Deutschland/DDR im vergleich* [Comparative dictionary of East and West Germany] (pp. 542–46). Stuttgart: J. B. Metzler.

Newsweek. (1986). October 27, 19–20.

Rytlewski, R. (1987). Soziale kultur als politische kultur: Die DDR [Social culture as political culture: The DDR]. In D. Berg-Schlosser & J. Schissler (Eds.), *Politische Kultur im Deutschland: Bilanz und Perspektiven der Forschung* [Political culture in Germany: State of the art and perspectives in research]. Opladen: Westdeutscher Verlag.

Schroeter, S. (1994). *Die Sprache der DDR im Spiegel ihrer Literatur: Studien zum DDR-typischen Wortschatz* [The language of the DDR from the view of literature: Studies on DDR vocabulary]. Berlin: Walter de Gruyter.

Stern, F. (1987). Gedenken an den 17. Juni 1953 in der Sitzung des Deutschen Bundestages am 17. Juni 1987 [Memory of June 17, 1953 in the German Bundestag on June 17, 1987], *Bulletin*, no. 62, pp. 541–48.

Stötzel, G., & Wengeler, M. (Eds.) (1995). *Kontroverse begriffe des öffentlichen sprachgebrauchs in der Bundesrepublik Deutschland* [Controversial concepts in public speech of West Germany]. Berlin: Walter de Gruyter, pp. 355–382.

Wagner, W. (Ed.). (1990). *Europa-archiv*: Zeitschrift fur internationale politik [Archives on Europe: Journal for international politics]. *Folge*, 24, D656–64.

CHAPTER 4

The Political Language of Japan: Decoding What Politicians Mean from What They Say

OFER FELDMAN

This chapter describes and details the principal characteristics and nature of the political discourse among high-level members of the Diet, Japan's Parliament, including the prime minister, the chief cabinet secretary, and leaders of political parties. It also reviews the discourse of government officials in *Nagatacho*, the Tokyo district that is the center of the nation's political sphere, where the Diet itself, the prime minister's official residence, offices of Diet members, and headquarters of the major political parties are situated. By illuminating central aspects of political language in Japan, their background, and their functions, this chapter also examines how the circumstances and intended visibility of an event affect the content of political discourse. Moreover, this chapter also illustrates how the relationship of social influences, the political culture, and the nuance and tone of the language of politics and government affect the delivery of information and the way that information is interpreted by the audience.

FACE AND OBVERSE IN POLITICS IN JAPAN

The talk of Japanese politicians and government officials is characterized by two distinctive features: *honne* and *tatemae*. *Honne*, meaning the honest feeling, is the *ura*—the obverse, or the actual, genuine intent, which sometimes means the hidden side of a subject. This is *watakushi*, which means being private, informal, and nonceremonial. *Tatemae* is the surface pretense, or the face of a subject. This is the formal, or presented truth, and the visible circumstances of a given issue. This is the *oyake*, which means being public, formal, and ceremonial.

The two concepts of *honne* and *tatemae* reflect different attitudes of a person conversing on a given issue. When the speaker tends to disclose the real meaning of an issue, to reveal all and to openly disclose true feelings—regardless of the reception those feelings receive—it is *honne*. In contrast, when everything said is carefully expressed in order to restrict the conversation to official positions or when one speaks in generalities, avoids direct opinions, and avoids display of any personal feelings through the use of euphemisms, ambiguous generalities, or lack of clear expression, it is *tatemae*. *Tatemae* is the most commonly used form of public speaking in Japan because it is not socially acceptable to express personal feelings or opinions in a public forum, nor is it appropriate to interject personal opinions in what is regarded as public affairs. The distinction between public obligation and private matters must always be made clear (Yoneyama, 1971).

For Diet members, leaders of political groups, and government officials, the difference between the two concepts of *honne* and *tatemae* ultimately distinguishes public disclosure from private discretion. This enables a politician or a government bureaucrat to speak in general terms, giving only the official line of the administration, the party, or other official position, without seeming to take a stand. It also enables the speaker to avoid being concrete about anything and getting pinned down later for what could be construed as an indiscretion. The opposite can also work. The speaker can go into elaborate detail and load the talk with professional jargon to an extent that it becomes difficult for the listener to understand the real thread of the speech. Again, the speaker is able to appear to say a lot without revealing personal opinions and to phrase the comments in a way that makes it impossible to determine where the speaker stands on the issue at hand (Arthy, 1996).

One linguistic trait peculiar to such public statements is the ability of the speaker to avoid using vocabulary that in any way seems to pass judgment or to make a commitment to a position. Speakers in such circumstances often hedge their comments with such words as *tabun* (literally "probably"), *osoraku* ("perhaps"), or *hyotto shitara* ("possibly"). They frequently use such terms as *maemuki ni* ("positively" or "constructively") and thus give the impression that there might be some intended move on an issue in the distant future, although there are no immediate prospects; *eii* ("assiduous" or "energetic"), used when prospects are poor, although the speaker wants to convey a sense of having made an effort; *jubun* ("fully" or "thoroughly"), used when stalling for time; and *tsutomeru* ("to endeavor" or "to make efforts"), which means taking no personal responsibility.

There are at least three plausible explanations for the common tendency to avoid revealing real feelings or expressing any kind of commitment and to disclose only the official view, often in an ambiguous manner. The first is that, ordinarily, to avoid giving offense or to avoid "the loss of face," which means the loss of self-respect and dignity for both the speaker and the listener as a result of public humiliation and embarrassment, Japanese refrain from expressing definite opinions. They shy away from taking any clear-cut position on issues and from demanding, rejecting, asserting or criticizing directly. Vagueness in language choice is thus designed presumably to maintain harmonious relations in Japanese groups by avoiding conflicts (Nakane, 1972). Tsujimura (1968; 1977) astutely noted that the tendency to use indirect expressions rather than direct ones in communication is, along with the tendency to be taciturn, the most important characteristic of the Japanese. In this respect, the spiritual aspects of *ishindenshin* (or *haragei*, literally "stomach act") dictate communication of thoughts from one mind to another without anything actually being verbalized. Racial and linguistic homogeneity further holds that Japanese can understand each other easily with few words because they are linguistically and racially homogeneous.

The second explanation is that Diet members and government officials avoid concrete evaluations because of the way political activities in Japan are managed. In the broad sense, the two concepts of *honne* and *tatemae* reflect the bifurcated quality of Japanese polity, in which everything has a front and a back. The obverse is the arena in which the real deal-making and decision-making process is conducted in government and the bureaucracy. The action is in the back rooms. Only the outcome is shown publicly. As noted elsewhere (C. Johnson, 1980), all politically organized societies reveal a discrepancy between the formal and the actual functioning of their political institutions. The proverb, "To say is one thing, to practice is another," illustrates that the gap between the two concepts is universal. In the Japanese case, however, for historical reasons, the expected discrepancy is a structural feature around which the polity has evolved. Thus, the discrepancy between the face and the obverse, found in all societies, is more pronounced in Japan and is, perhaps, the single most important benchmark for any political analyst.

Diet proceedings, for example, constitute the face of the political process. This is where speeches on social and political issues are made, and procedures concerning the routine work of both chambers of the Diet are usually decided on by a vote in the plenary session. In fact, though, such votes merely ratify decisions already reached in negotiations between leaders of political parties and their representatives before the session began. Such negotiations, conducted far from the public's eye, are the back side of the Japanese political process. In these capacities, leaders of political groups meet and discuss, for instance, how each party will be represented in leadership posts, the duration of an extraordinary or special Diet session, and where each party's Diet members will be seated. Some bills introduced in the Diet are also first negotiated by representatives of the various political parties and are jointly endorsed by all the political parties involved (Kishimoto, 1981).

Leaders of political groups or their aids conduct the *misshitsu seiji* ("political decisions made behind closed doors") or *machiai seiji* ("behind-the-scene politics"). This involves secret political consultations among the various partners in the political game. There, representatives of political groups quietly present to each other their stances on specific issues, express support for or objections to the views held by other members on these topics, and try to resolve conflicts of opinions by involving all the relevant parties in the decision-making process.

In order to avoid a direct and open clash of ideas or wishes and to achieve a mutual understanding among all participants, to resolve differences of opinion, and to maintain harmony, each individual's opinion is usually adjusted informally in a kind of groundwork before the formal meeting takes place. This is the *nemawashi* ("trimming of a tree's roots prior to its being transplanted"), the process of prior informal negotiation and persuasion among concerned parties before a proposed matter is formally presented. Through careful personal interaction, politicians and government officials alike try to improve empathy and cooperation among all members of the different groups and obtain complete support for a certain issue (Hashiguchi et al., 1977). In the *nemawashi* process, each individual is rarely forced to change his or her opinions. Individuals are informed only of others' positions. If there are differences of views, they feel obliged to make some adjustments in their stands. When consensus is reached, all concerned feel that their views are equally reflected in the final decision.

Frequent negotiations also exist among Diet members, cabinet officials, and economic leaders who present to each other their views regarding various issues, listen to each other's arguments, and endeavor to resolve differences of opinions to achieve, through concessions and bargaining, a mutual stand that will be accepted by everyone. Diet members and government bureaucrats also have regular meetings. Although most bills originate within government bureaus, preliminary negotiations and approval by the political parties constitute a necessary step in the process. To ensure smooth passage of bills, senior bureaucrats of various ministries present their proposals to influential Diet members and explain their content and objectives. Through these contacts, some needed adjustments are made. To win complete support for a certain bill, Diet members from the various political parties and government bureaucrats then conduct informal meetings to discuss the manner and date for the introduction of a bill (Craig, 1981).

In sum, because of the constant need to know the desires and intentions of the other participants so as to prevent a clash of ideas over leadership positions or over the presentation of a bill in the Diet, subtle negotiations and lengthy lobbying sessions go on behind closed doors and include all political participants. As these negotiations always require concessions from the sides involved in order to reach formal agreement, they are often complicated and sensitive. Because of the fear that even a casual comment might interfere with the process and cause inconvenience to one partner, the involved parties may not wish to remark on these negotiations until a final decision has been achieved. Thus, Diet members may prefer to refrain from talking on pending issues or to pass no more than vague comments on the issues being negotiated. In such a process, they are careful not to break the atmosphere in which the negotiations take place. In other words, as long as an issue is still pending and being negotiated, neither politicians nor officials are likely to reveal any detail or their real thoughts that could interfere in the process of achieving a consensus.

No less important is the third explanation for the tendency of Japanese politicians to avoid making clear-cut public statements on various issues. In a society such as Japan, in which the striving for and preservation of social harmony, consensus decisions, and conformity with the group are major objectives in both public and private behavior (F. A. Johnson, 1993), Diet members, especially those in leading positions or those who are pursuing higher positions, constantly seek the sympathy and support of members of diverse groups. Although some of these groups might have opposing opinions about many issues, it is necessary to secure their support. So, it is important to these Diet members to be perceived as neutrals who do not identify with or advocate a certain issue or idea. They therefore try to be *happo bijin* (liked by everybody) and, in turn, to receive support for their goals and activities.

These Diet members do not really value fixed and durable clear policy positions. Rather, they much prefer loose statements of philosophy that can be interpreted in a variety of ways, whereby they can preserve their image of neutrality on any sensitive issue. To avoid making anybody angry or provoking criticism from other Diet members, these individuals tend to express in public the officially accepted opinions or, in other words, the least controversial views. They avoid passing judgment and speak in such a way that they will not embarrass those who have different views. They hope that they will be accepted and liked—and consequently supported—by as many people as possible.

Talking in *tatemae* euphemisms is perhaps the safest way for members of the Diet and the bureaucracy to express themselves and still get along within the political labyrinth. In this way, either by blurring their opinions or by presenting only the official, broadly agreed-upon views, they limit the risk of giving offense to those with different views. At the same time, they can be seen as neutral or at least distanced from any specific point of view or interest of any particular group. This, in turn, makes it more likely that they will be accepted by a larger number of groups with different views.

THE CONCEPTS OF *TATEMAE* AND *HONNE*

By presenting their views openly (*honne*) or in general terms (*tatemae*), leading members of the Diet or government bureaucracy can adjust, as suggested by Feldman (1996), to the circumstances or the degree of visibility of the circumstances in which they address or avoid addressing certain subjects. They use buzzwords, abstractions, and metaphors when speaking before big crowds, but they are less vague when talking with smaller groups. In certain circumstances, such as political fund-raisers or press conferences, high-level politicians and political leaders usually do not express anything beyond the official, broadly accepted view, nor do they utter more than the most vague of opinions. In short, when they speak in public gatherings, *tatemae*, not *honne*, dictates the tone of the talk.

Typical examples are found in the speeches of prime ministers before the Diet or in press conferences. To the representatives of the news media, press conferences with the leaders of the nation, including the chief cabinet secretary, who is usually also the chief spokesman for the administration, and the prime minister himself, represent useful channels for drawing out the formal positions of officials—the pure statistics, rather than the circumstances of events.

Press conferences are usually carefully stage-managed events. High-level Diet members would never disclose in detail their real opinions on any "hot" domestic or international issue. In many such press conferences, especially those broadcast live on television, reporters have to pool their questions before these conferences and let the leading Diet member know in advance the precise questions that they are going to ask. Reporters are often asked to omit sensitive questions or to change the wording of others. Key Diet members try to keep the press focused on a defined set of issues. They are able to anticipate questions and to limit the risk of being drawn into uncharted waters, which require an expression of *honne*.

Politicians and government officials disclose their real intentions when meeting with a small group of people in the silent corridors of the Diet, in headquarters of political parties, in their private offices, or in their private residences. One example of such meetings is an effort to resolve differing opinions held by political groups when they meet behind closed doors to present plainly and clearly their varying opinions and positions on certain issues. Diet members also disclose their *honne* during seminars or study sessions organized with colleagues from the same political group. These seminars aim to give members of a group the opportunity to socialize together, perhaps in a relaxed atmosphere during a weekend or holiday in a resort area far from Tokyo, and to discuss informally issues of common interest.

Diet members will also talk *honne* when they meet in their offices with a limited number of media representatives, such as ten to fifteen reporters from national newspapers and major television channels, for a friendly, relaxed background briefing (*kondan*). In such a gathering, politicians explain and detail issues related to their work—"the stories behind the stories" and other information—that they would not reveal in a press conference setting. High-echelon Diet members also talk *honne* when they meet reporters outside their workplace or in their residences. Meeting leading Diet members in a home living room provides an intimate and relaxed atmosphere for conversation. During this friendly meeting, which might include drinks and snacks, reporters have the best chance to gather real information about political events and personnel matters.

Revealing the *honne* to a close circle of people reassures a speaker that it will remain among friends and will not leak to outsiders in a way that could cause them inconvenience. As a rule, in Japan, the real feelings and opinions on politics and politicians are not supposed to erupt in the "front world," where things have to be kept calm, relaxed, and under control. If they do, the expressed feelings can bring criticism and even cause political chaos, with the result that a speaker is not appreciated or respected. When public figures cannot conceal their feelings or cannot restrain their verbal behavior to only the back side of politics, their remarks are usually classified as a *hogen* ("indiscreet remark"), *bogen* ("violent language"), or *shitsugen* ("slip of the tongue").

SLIP OF TONGUE OR POLITICAL *HONNE*

When Diet members speak too frankly about what they believe and find themselves being reprimanded for such comments later, reporters define such indiscretions as a "slip of tongue." At such times, they often find themselves criticized by their opponents, by certain groups of the public, and even by colleagues from their own political parties. Several Diet members who were criticized regarding remarks made in public had to take responsibility for the remarks and apologize to the offended people (Konno, 1995). On other occasions, Diet members resigned voluntarily or were forced to resign from their posts in order to assume responsibility for their indiscreet public remarks.

In another example, while answering an opposition question in a meeting of the lower house's most powerful committee, the budget committee, in March 1953, former Prime Minister Shigeru Yoshida said, "*Bakayaro!*" ("You stupid fool"). The opposition quickly moved to discipline the prime minister. The motion was carried, and the plenary session then passed a nonconfidence resolution. Prime Minister Yoshida, in what is termed *bakayaro kaisan* (you stupid fool dissolution), chose to dissolve the lower house rather than resign.

In February 1988, during a televised debate session of the lower house budget committee, Chairman Koichi Hamada accused Kenji Miyamoto, the supreme boss of the Japanese Communist Party, of being a "murderer." Hamada was referring to the infamous prewar incident in which a group of communist leaders allegedly lynched a suspected police spy. The impromptu remark moved the leaders of the opposition parties to demand

Hamada's resignation; he later resigned his post as the chairman of the committee. In 1993, Keisuke Nakanishi, the director general of the Defense Agency, was forced to resign from his ministerial post to resolve a Diet deadlock over his controversial remark in which he called for a revision of the war-renouncing constitution. The remark was taken as a call to give the Self-Defense Forces a more active role in United Nations peacekeeping operations by amending Article 9 of the constitution, which bans the use of force to resolve international conflicts.

Because Japan's political culture for the postwar period has remained polarized over the issues of defense and alliance with the United States, two former prime ministers, Zenko Suzuki and Yasuhiro Nakasone, were chastised for remarks they made on different occasions. After his official talks with President Ronald Reagan in May 1981, Suzuki was reproved for issuing a communique that included the word *domei* (alliance). Suzuki's foreign minister, Masayoshi Ito, resigned in disagreement with the prime minister's refusal to admit that there was a military intent in the alliance referred to in the communique.

In January 1983, Nakasone was criticized following several phrases he uttered while referring to defense issues during his meeting with Reagan. On one occasion, Nakasone claimed that Japan should aim for "complete control" of the strategic straits controlling the sea of Japan "so that there should be no passage of Soviet submarines and other naval activities in time of emergency." In an interview, he referred to Japan as an "unsinkable aircraft carrier" (*fuchin kubo*), to prevent penetration of the Soviet Backfire bombers into Japanese airspace. To many opposition party members and a great number of Japanese, this expression evoked negative images of Japan as a military fortress (Sakonjo, 1983).

On another occasion, in May 1994, Ichiro Ozawa, leader of the *Shinshinto* (New Frontier Party), was also criticized by women's groups for saying, "One is free to sleep with the woman of one's choice." The remark was allegedly made over the Social Democratic Party of Japan's departure from the ruling coalition. Comparing the unified parliamentary ruling alliance in the lower house, which prompted the Socialist Party to quit the coalition, to an extramarital affair, Ozawa reportedly told reporters in the Diet building, "It doesn't matter which women you sleep with.... If the Socialist Party felt jealous of the new alliance, they have only to come and join us."

Often, an inappropriate remark made by a Japanese politician has also provoked criticism from foreign countries and groups outside Japan. Two topics in particular have resulted in such responses. The first gained the attention of minorities for discriminatory comments that politicians had made in praising the "homogeneity" of Japan's population. For example, while addressing a party seminar in September 1986, former Prime Minister Nakasone made a remark about the achievements of the Japanese as a "high-level information society." He praised Japan's average level of education by contrasting it with America's, which he declared was dragged down by the many minority groups within the population:

And there is no country which puts such diverse information so accurately into the ears of its people. It has become a very intelligent society. Against the likes of America it is by far so, when seen from averages. In America, there are many blacks, Puerto Ricans, and Mexicans, and seen on an average, America's per capita level of intelligence, as gained through education and the mass media is still extremely low.... Japan is such a dense, vibrant society, a high-level information society, a highly educated society, a society in which people are so vibrant. (Quoted in Akasaka, 1986)

In July 1988, Michio Watanabe, chairman of the ruling Liberal Democratic Party's Policy Research Council, revealed at a party-sponsored seminar that many Blacks in the United States who often use credit cards are quick to declare bankruptcy, thus implying that they walk away from their debts. In September 1990, Justice Minister Seiroku Kajiyama compared prostitutes in Japan to black Americans who "ruin the atmosphere" of neighborhoods they move into. He made the remark to explain to reporters his impressions after observing a police crackdown on foreign women allegedly soliciting customers for sex on Tokyo's streets.

Likewise, in January 1992, at the gathering of his supporters, House of Representative Speaker Yoshio Sakurauchi, who had once served as foreign minister, said that even though American workers were lazy and unproductive, they wanted high pay. He was discussing a pledge by Japanese carmakers to sharply increase purchases of U.S.-made auto parts. Japanese manufacturers had complained that car components produced in the United States were of inferior quality. "The root of the problem is the deteriorating quality of American workers," Sakurauchi said. "The American labor force doesn't work enough. They want to receive high salaries without working fully." Casting doubt on the quality of U.S. goods, he also stated that about 30 percent of the U.S. labor force was so illiterate that work instructions could not be given in written form.

And, in March 1993, a local Prefectural Assembly member made discriminatory remarks against Blacks and other foreigners when he said:

I realize that there are some stupid Japanese women who would marry those useless people (foreign workers in Japan).... I feel strange when I go somewhere where more than 10 Pakistanis or Indians have gathered.... Have you ever shaken hands with a black person? When I shake hands with a black person I feel like my hands are turning black.

Yet another topic that Diet members address and one that has resulted in considerable and slanderous remarks concerns World War II and Japan's role in it. As a result of apparently nationalistic arrogance and ignorance of history, several intentional misinterpretations of historical facts of Japan's invasion of Asian countries have occurred in recent years and stirred criticism from these countries.

For example, in September 1986, Education Minister Masayuki Fujio committed the blunder of angering South Korea after saying that it bears some responsibility for Japan's colonization of the Korean Peninsula between 1910 and 1945. Similarly, in April 1988, National Land Agency Director General Seisuke Okuno attempted to justify Japan's military actions against Asian countries during World War II by saying, "Japan fought the war in order to secure its safety. . . . Asia was colonized by Caucasians at that time. Japan was by no means a nation of aggression."

In May 1994, Justice Minister Shigeto Nagano told reporters of the daily *Mainichi*:

It was wrong to define the Pacific War as a war of aggression on Japan's part. . . . Japan stood up for survival because it was in danger of being crushed. . . . Japan thought seriously about liberating colonies . . . allied powers should be blamed for having driven Japan that far. The aims of the war were fundamentally permissible and justifiable at that time.

Nagano also added that the 1937 Nanjing Massacre, during which, according to Chinese estimates, the Imperial Japanese Army troops slaughtered more than 300,000 Chinese civilians following the invasion of Nanjing in December 1937, was "a fabrication."

Also, in November 1995, Takami Eto, director general of the Management and Coordination Agency, commented that "Japan did some good" during its 1910–1945 occupation of Korea, "including planting trees and building roads."

Following their public statements regarding wartime Japan—amid an uproar caused by these remarks from foreign countries and domestic groups—Fujio, Okuno, Nagano, and Eto all had to step down from their ministerial positions.

CONTROLLING THE INFORMATION

Obviously, Japanese Diet members have to pay a great deal of attention to what they say in public because speaking inappropriately on the front side of politics can cause them harm. To prevent embarrassment, public debate, and criticism over what they might say, high-level Diet members and other public officials often conceal in public their real thoughts and opinions. Instead, they prefer to comment in a formal manner or to remark vaguely on a given issue. Ordinarily, to avoid criticism for using indiscreet language, they try to control the information they disseminate to the public through the news media in several ways.

First, they tend to volunteer more information and disclose their real intentions to only a selected and limited number of reporters who are invited to attend informal meetings. In most of these meetings, information passed to reporters is classified as off the record. Reporters are thereby prohibited from publishing such comments verbatim. The content of the remarks can be used only as data to explain the background of another story. Sometimes reporters are given permission to publish portions of the *honne* they heard on condition of anonymity and lack of attribution. This forces reporters to resort to a jargon intended to disguise the actual sources; information is attributed to "a top government official," "a political party leader," or a "source close to the prime minister," which assures the sources that there will be no reaction aimed directly at them for what they said (Feldman, 1993). By limiting the number of reporters at an off-the-record session, it is easy for the source to determine which reporter did not respect the request and used the information simply by looking at the next edition of a newspaper.

Second, high-echelon Diet members carefully select "safe" issues as speech topics and leak information that supports their own objectives, while they distract attention from other more troubling issues, often to encourage discussion and to promote stories on pet issues that they want high on the national agenda. Frequently, they explicitly express the desire to see a related story in the newspapers or in a television report, thus having reporters write *yarase kiji* (literally, compulsory articles, but more euphemistically regarded as invited articles) that spotlight their own activities and achievements. As discussed, to keep the news media focused on a set of safe issues and limit the risk of being "forced to the corner," in which they would have to disclose the *honne*, Diet members and officials ask reporters to pool their questions before important press conferences to prepare themselves for possible questions.

Moreover, Japanese politicians and officials try to influence the formation of public opinion and national consensus by creating *kuuki* (air, mood, or atmosphere requiring compliance). *Kuuki* requires an individual or a group to accept the dominant atmosphere and comply with it, thus making those who do not agree with it silent or reluctant to speak. The process of creating *kuuki* can be "unconscious, unintentional, and spontaneous," but at times "artificial *kuuki*" is created (Yamamoto, 1977: 21) to evoke a certain public opinion. Through the use of words, government official and Diet members try to produce certain moods, such as optimism, patriotism, encouragement, and community, and spur or guide action.

For example, *kuuki* is created with slogans used by political leaders, especially prime ministers (Takase, 1993). Former prime ministers who used slogans include Hayato Ikeda, *shotoku baizo keikaku* (income-doubling plan); Kakuei Tanaka, *Nippon retto kaizoron* (remodeling the Japanese archipelago); and Nakasone, *sengo seiji no sokessan to kokusai kokka nippon* (the final settlement of postwar politics and the internationalization of Japan). They also used other media-oriented appeals to raise the rate of support for their governments in the opinion polls. To produce mood of community, former Prime Minister Noboru Takeshita introduced in 1988 the slogan of *furusato sosei* (revive the hometown), meaning "let's cherish our hometowns and home villages." In his first policy speech in the Diet after being elected as prime minister in May 1994, Tsutomu Hata reiterated his slogan of *futsu no kotoba no tsujiru seiji* (plain-language politics). Prime Minister Tomiichi Murayama proclaimed in his first speech in July 1994 his slogan to be *hito ni yasashi seiji* (a government that cares about the people). In his first policy speech as prime minister in January 1996, Ryutaro Hashimoto indicated the goals of his cabinet by using the slogan of *kaikaku to sozo* (Renovation and Creation).

Because Diet members try to control the content of the news and, through this control, to dominant public opinion, certain information rarely appears in the media. Examples include detailed stories on disagreement among Diet members and stories on ongoing negotiations between the ruling and opposition parties and on differences of opinion between government bureaucrats and leading Diet members. Such information is considered the *ura* (the back side) of Japanese politics. Stories on these topics, if they do appear, show the face of politics, exposing a *kuuki* that both politicians and the news media would like to avoid in a society like Japan's, in which the struggle for consensus decisions and preservation of social harmony is the major objective in both public and private behavior (Feldman, 1997).

Conversely, political stories in the national daily newspapers and on television networks are dominated by coverage of the routine activities of high-echelon Diet members, including leaders of political parties and particularly the prime minister. Questions about what these leading people did, who they met with, and what they talked about form the heart of political coverage. This is the formal, the *tatemae* side of Japanese politics. Such stories are safe for politicians because they are descriptive and rarely detail personal opinions, evaluations, or direct statements. The public is thus left with the choice of trying to read between the lines to fathom the real points. The public is on its own in attempting to understand the dynamics of the political process and the will of the leadership, and to decipher beyond what the Diet's key members and the bureaucracy's key officials allow to slip through the cracks.

REFERENCES

Akasaka, T. (1986). *Nakasone shitsugen mondai no yukue* [The whereabouts of prime minister Nakasone's slip of tongue]. *Bungei Shunju*, 11, 162–66.

Arthy, I. (1996). *Oeragata seikanzai no kokugojuku* [The establishment's language school]. Tokyo: Chuo Koronsha.

Craig, C. M. (1981). Functional and dysfunctional aspects of government bureaucracy. In E. F. Vogel (Ed.), *Modern Japanese organization and decision-making* (pp. 3–32). Tokyo: Charles E. Tuttle.

Feldman, O. (1993). *Politics and the news media in Japan*. Ann Arbor: University of Michigan Press.

Feldman, O. (1996). *Seiji genjitsu to genjitsu sozo: Nihon ni okeru seiji gengo no kenkyu* [Political reality and the creation of reality: A study of political discourse in Japan]. *Naruto Kyoiku Daigaku Kenkyu Kiyo*, 11, 97–111.

Feldman, O. (1997, August). *A Japanese version of "conflict behavior:" The role of the news media in creating and manipulating political conflict and harmony*. Paper presented at the 17th World Congress of the International Political Science Association, Seoul, Korea.

Hashiguchi, O., Takeshita, T., Sugiura, K., & Murayama, T. (1977). *Taikenteki nemawashiron* [Empirical study of "Nemawashi"]. *Jichi-Kenshu*, 203, 2–17.

Johnson, C. (1980). *Omote* (explicit) and *ura* (implicit): Translating Japanese political terms. *Journal of Japanese Studies*, 6, 89–115.

Johnson, F. A. (1993). *Dependency and Japanese socialization: Psychoanalytic and anthropological investigations into amae*. New York: New York University Press.

Kishimoto, K. (1981). Diet structures, organization, and procedure. In F. R. Vales & C. E. Morrison (Eds.), *The Japanese Diet and the U.S. Congress* (pp. 39–59). Boulder, Colo.: Westview.

Konno S. (1995). *Seijikara no hatsugen to sono sekinin* [Politicians' verbal behavior and their responsibilities]. *Jiyu*, 2, 44–52.

Nakane, C. (1972). *Japanese society*. Berkeley: University of California Press.

Sakonjo N. (1983). *Nakasone "fuchin kubo" ron wo toku* [Solving the dispute over Prime Minister Nakasone's remark on "unsinkable aircraft carrier"]. *Chuo Koron*, 3, 152–56.

Takase J. (1993). *Soridaijin enzetsu no komiyunikeshon sutairu bunseki* [Analysis of the communication style of prime ministers' speeches]. *Waseda Daigaku-Okuma Kinen Shakai Kagaku Kenkyujo Shakai Kagaku Tokyu*, 39, 721–46.

Tsujimura, A. (1968). *Nihon bunka to komyunikeshon* [Japanese culture and communication]. Tokyo: Nihon Hoso Suppan Kyokai.

Tsujimura, A. (1977). *Nihonteki komyunikeshon no tokushitsu to shinbun no arikata* [Characteristics of Japanese communication and the function of the press]. *Senmon Shimbun*, 1, 7–24.

Yamamoto, S. (1977). *"Kuuki" no kenkyu* [A study of "kuuki"]. Tokyo: Bungei Shunjusha.

Yoneyama, T. (1971). *Nihonteki shakai kankei ni okeru "kihongainen-gun"* [Basic concepts in Japanese social relationship]. *Kikan Jinruigaku*, 2, 56–76.

CHAPTER 5

The Rhetoric of Jewish Cohesion and Territorial Attachment in Rabbinic *Midrashim*

CAROL B. CONAWAY

How did rabbis in late antiquity—political and spiritual leaders of world Jewry—transmit their beliefs on Jewish nationalism to generations of Jews for centuries to come? In the case of secular political elites, speeches, appeals, declarations, and other sources reveal much about the belief systems of leaders and serve as texts for analysis. But when religious leaders are also political leaders, rhetorical analysis can be more elusive than analysis relating to secular leaders because the sources of evidence might not be the standard fare. This is certainly the case with Jews in the early centuries of the Common Era after the Roman conquest when the previous Jewish political structure, the High Priesthood, had collapsed under the occupation. Rabbinic messages about Jewish national identity and claim to Israel as the eternal homeland are found in theological texts as interpretations (*midrashim*) of the Torah.

TORAH AND *MIDRASHIM*

The Torah is the most sacred text in Judaism. Its five books related the Jewish creation myth, early Jewish history, and the laws and commandments that govern the lives of observant Jews. In addition to being theological, the Torah is also a political text. As such it deals with Israel's incorporation as a nation; its international relations and conflicts; the years of slavery in Egypt; and the conquests that led to its triumph over rival states, thereby enabling its armies to take possession of a homeland; and similar subjects.

Rabbinic interpretations of the Torah are called *midrashim*. They were the most important undertaking of all Jewish writing until the modern periods. The word *midrash* (plural, *midrashim*) derives from the Hebrew root "to search out." *Midrash* is the process of interpreting as well as the interpretation. In the process of *midrash*, rabbis and sages attempted to fill in any lacunae in the Torah text. For example, the Torah tells the events related to Moses leading the Jews out of slavery in Egypt, but *midrashim* on those verses in the Torah might explain what Moses was thinking as he left Egypt. That information is not in the Torah. In the process of interpreting one verse in the *Torah*, the rabbis provide information on Moses's thoughts and feelings—information that completes what they understand to be lacunae in the Torah text.

Because observant Jews believe that all *midrashim* were in God's mind when he dictated the Torah to Moses, *midrashim* are considered divine revelations and are sacred texts. Thus, rabbinic interpretations were, and are, taken quite seriously by believers. When believers study these texts, they see how the rabbis explained or interpreted various contemporary events or problems of the Common Era in terms of the Torah. For them, the Torah was, and is, applicable to all situations for all time. This is made possible by the process of interpretation, *midrash*.

How then did this theological rhetoric become political rhetoric? When the Torah addresses political issues, an interpretation might also be political, especially if contemporary problems in the society warrant both an explanation and demonstrations that the Torah is relevant to those issues. In some cases, the Torah text might not be political at all, but the rabbinic *midrashim* explaining, interpreting, and embellishing the Torah text might be very political in tone and content. In both cases, what made the rabbinic rhetoric valid and sacred to believers was the idea that *midrash* was divine revelation. What a rabbi or sage said in his exegesis was holy to believers. Believers made no distinctions between theological and political when they were exposed to the *midrashim*.

Furthermore, rabbis supported their arguments in the exegetical *midrashim* by referring to other parts of the Bible that shed some light on, or agreed with, the rabbinic interpretation. This validated the *midrash* even more. In addition, the supporting evidence made the original interpretation clearer in the mind of anyone exposed to the *midrash*, thereby making it easier to remember. This is how the beliefs of the rabbis became the beliefs of the individuals studying the text, hearing it, or memorizing it.

The present study analyzes the embedded messages within some rabbinic interpretations of the most sacred text in Judaism, the Torah. One of the results is evidence of messages that are clearly more nationalistic than theological. This is important because it is evidence of how rabbis interpreted the Jewish loss of the Land of Israel and the subsequent Diaspora, understood the Jews as a unique people with a unique destiny as a nation, and made their claim to an eternal homeland, Israel.

So the real significance of the Torah on Jewish nationalism lay in how its texts were interpreted by the rabbis and passed on to successive generations of Jews worldwide for centuries by *midrashim* in sermons to congregations, at the rabbinic academies to students and disciples, and in written compilations that were studied and memorized.

In the early centuries of the Common Era (C.E), a time when the Jews no longer held sovereignty over the Land of Israel and there was a vast Diaspora, rabbis and sages interpreted and compiled *midrashim* on the biblical book of Genesis, the story of the creation of the world and the early history of the Jews, including their incorporation as a distinct people, and the divine promise of an eternal homeland.

The exegetical *midrashim* on Genesis are called *Genesis Rabbah*, the great commentary on Genesis. The *midrashim* were compiled in the fourth and fifth centuries of the Common Era. From the analysis of *Genesis Rabbah*, the argument can be supported that some of these interpretations of Genesis reflect a very clear, systematic rabbinic belief system on Jewish nationalism that, taken together with the Torah, passed on rabbinic nationalism from the fourth century of the Common Era to successive generations of observant Jews. The reason is because these texts were studied, memorized, and believed. This belief system was cultivated by rabbinic rhetoric on nationalism, discourse that both consolidated rabbinic political leadership over worldwide Jewry and established a rabbinic theory of Jewish nationalism.

Midrash flourished most dramatically in the Land of Israel during the periods of the Tannaitic and Amoraic sages, 70 C.E. to 220 C.E., and 220 C.E. to 400 C.E. respectively (Strack and Stemberger, 1992). After the destruction of the Second Temple in 70 C.E., however, these *midrashim* were compiled, redacted, and written down, probably with the aim of preserving them more carefully. In view of the fact that the rabbinate was attempting to show how the scripture of old explained contemporary life, the *midrashim* appear to have been a creative reaction to the upheavals suffered by Israel during the Tannaitic and Amoraic eras. At this time, rabbinic thought was highly nationalistic and land-based. For fourth and fifth century rabbinic elites, however, there was no call for physical revolt. Instead, they spoke to their constituencies, through the *midrashim*, about the arrival of redemption and restoration—a world with Jerusalem as its capital and the people Israel as its primary citizens.

The rhetorical cases discussed in the study reveal that two broad concepts of cohesion and territory were espoused by the rabbis: (1) Jews were a distinct and holy people with a unique relationship with God that no other nation possessed and (2) the Land of Israel was given by God to the Jewish people as part of an eternal covenant with the Patriarch Abraham.

METHOD

The study analyzes the Soncino edition of *Genesis Rabbah* (*Bereshith Rabbah*), an authoritative English translation of the rabbinic commentary on Genesis. The Soncino edition comprises approximately one thousand *midrashim* that interpret the verses of Genesis. They vary in length from a brief paragraph to several pages. The number of *midrashim* that are pertinent to cohesion and territorial attachment is approximately 10 percent of the total. The study focuses on revealing, exposing, and explaining both the superficial and embedded meanings within the *midrashim* that address the subjects of collective identity and territory. Because of space limitations, I discuss only two examples in this chapter—one on the Jews as a unique people, and the other on the Land of Israel as the eternal homeland of the people Israel.

MIDRASHIM ON THE THEME OF ISRAEL'S COHESION AND PERMANENCE AS A DISTINCT PEOPLE

Various rabbinic interpretations of verses in Genesis address the subject of collective identity. The loss of the Land of Israel with its subsequent Roman occupation and the Christians' contention that they, not the Jews, were the chosen people posed an enormous challenge to Palestinian Jewry. One way in which rabbinic elites could defend the people Israel from these assaults was with the *midrashim* because of the authoritative status accorded rabbinic revelation. Exegesis permitted the rabbinate to interpret verses of biblical Genesis to be relevant to the concept of Jewish collective identity. Thus, while superficially a verse might appear to have one meaning for its audience, the rabbinate attributed an ethnocentric meaning to the same verse. An example of this is the *midrash* that follows from *Genesis Rabbah* 41:9.

In the biblical verse, God speaks to the first Patriarch of the Jewish people, Abraham, telling him about the future people, Israel. God says, "And I will make thy seed as the dust of the earth; so that if a man can number the dust of the earth, then shall thy seed also be numbered" (Genesis 13:16).

How do the rabbis interpret this verse? Their interpretation is that Israel will be a great nation, too numerous to count; that it will be blessed; and, as a nation, exist forever. How is this interpretation accomplished?

They begin by saying, "Just as the dust of the earth is found from one end of the world to the other, so shall thy children be found from one end of the earth to the other; and as the dust of the earth can be blessed only through water, so will thy children be blessed only for the sake of the Torah, which is likened to water." This statement alludes to passages in Isaiah, the prophet. Thus, they interpret one statement in terms of another, the other being an older, revered text. This is an important technique that affirms the validity of the interpretation.

The rabbis continue their interpretation by positing that the people Israel will exist forever, an assertion not apparent in Genesis 13:16. They say, "As the dust of the earth wears out even metal utensils yet itself endures forever, so will Israel exist [forever] while the [other] nations of the world will cease to be."

If that is the case, however, they must explain Israel's present predicament as a nation under Roman occupation. Thus, they continue, "As the dust of the earth is trodden upon, so will thy children be downtrodden under the heel of [foreign] powers, as it is written, *and I will put it into the hand of them that afflict thee*; which means, those who make thy wounds flow." The italicized part of the above statement is a quotation from Isaiah 51:3, so scripture is interpreted again in terms of another scripture to explain the Roman occupation of the Land of Israel and Jewish subjugation.

Why have foreign powers come to subjugate Israel? To respond to this, the rabbis continue by saying, "Nevertheless, it is for [Israel's] benefit, for [foreign powers' subjugation of Israel] purify [Israel] of guilt, as you read, *Thou makest her soft with showers*, etc. (Psalm 65:11). *That have said to thy soul: Bow down that we may go over* (Isaiah 51:3)." So, Israel's current status as an occupied nation is explained by the rabbis as being a result of Israel's departure from righteousness. Again, this interpretation relies on the cited verse in Isaiah for its validity and affirmation.

Finally, how do the rabbis conclude their interpretation of "And I will make thy seed as the dust of the earth"? Now that they have posited Israel's numbers, status as being the blessed nation because of its devotion to Torah, and endurance, the rabbis conclude their interpretation by describing what has been done specifically to destroy Israel as a people, and how that has failed. They ask, "What did [foreign powers] do to [Israel]?" The answer: "[Foreign powers] made [Israel] lie down in the streets and drew ploughs over them. Rabbi 'Azariah said in Rabbi Aha's name: That [being forced to lie down in streets] is a good augury: as the street outlives those who travel on it, yet itself remains for ever, so shall thy sons [the people Israel] (said God to Abraham), outlive the nations of the world while they will remain for ever." The rabbis are saying that Israel will outlive the nations that persecute it, because those nations are doomed to perish.

Therefore, the rabbis have developed a four-part interpretation to the question of what is the meaning of "I will make thy seed as the dust of the earth." Israel will be as numerous as the dust, will be blessed, will be persecuted for its wrongdoing, but will endure forever, despite its persecution. The second, third, and fourth parts of that interpretation are not present in a literal interpretation of Genesis 13:16. Instead, this verse has provided an exegetical opportunity for the rabbis to develop their concept of the eternal character and cohesion of the people Israel, despite contemporary hardship, persecution, and Diaspora. The exegesis is a statement in ethnocentrism and comprises an ancient nationalism.

MIDRASHIM ON THE THEME OF ISRAEL'S HOMELAND, THE LAND OF ISRAEL

Numerous *midrashim* in *Genesis Rabbah* address the theme of a permanent Jewish homeland—one that was given to Israel as part of God's covenant with the Patriarch Abraham quite early in biblical Genesis. In these, Israel is a polity with God as its king and takes possession of the Land of Israel as its eternal homeland. In their rhetoric on this subject, the rabbis contend that only Israel has acknowledged God's kingship over all the earth; other nations, when presented with the same evidence, have rejected that concept, and they have lost their lands and the knowledge of their origin to the nation, Israel.

In the following example, the verse that is interpreted is the familiar opening sentence of the biblical Genesis: "In the beginning God created the heaven and the earth" (Genesis 1:1). How do the rabbis interpret what superficially appears to be a very simple statement?

In *Genesis Rabbah* 1:2, first, Rabbi Joshua of Siknin quotes in Rabbi Levi's name: "[This verse of Genesis means that God] hath declared to His people [Israel] the power of His works in giving them the heritage of the nations (Psalm 111:6)." What does Rabbi Joshua mean by his statement? If we examine Psalm 111 from which he has quoted, verse 7 explains that the works of the Lord are "truth and justice." Rabbi Joshua interprets "In the beginning . . ." to mean that the divine King has revealed the story of the Creation (truth) to Israel, and given the lands of various peoples to Israel (justice). Verse 9 of the Psalm states, "He hath sent redemption unto His people; He hath commanded His covenant forever." Allusion to the covenant and redemption refers to the unique relationship that God has with Israel.

But what is the exegetical motivation for Rabbi Joshua to link Israel with the Creation? We learn the reason by continuing his exegesis: "Why did the Holy One . . . reveal to Israel what was created on the first day and on the second day, etc.? So that the nations of the world might not taunt Israel and say to them: 'Surely you are a nation of robbers [who have stolen the Land of Israel]. . . . ' " Here Rabbi Joshua directly addresses the charge by rival ancient peoples and the Christians that Israel is not entitled to its claim to the Land of Israel. He interprets the first verse of Genesis to mean that Israel is being told the history of Creation so that it will be able to explain and justify both its origin in history, *and* its claim to the specific Land of Israel.

This is explained in the continuation of his exegesis in which Rabbi

Joshua tells Israel how to respond to its challengers. Israel must respond, "And do ye not hold [your lands] as spoil [i.e., the occupation by other nations of lands not originally within their sphere of possession]." In so stating, he establishes that other nations have claimed as their own land that was not necessarily theirs to begin. To illustrate his point, he then recounts the history of the ancient nation of Caphtor: "For surely the Caphtorim [another people] that came forth out of Caphtor, destroyed [the original people on what is now the Land of the Caphtorim], and dwelt in their stead [in the same way that Israel occupies what is now the Land of Israel] (Deuteronomy 2:23)!" In this statement, Rabbi Joshua quotes biblical Deuteronomy, in which God tells Israel which lands he will give and not give it for its possession. The quote substantiates and validates his response to other nations or faiths challenging Israel regarding its possession of the Land of Israel.

Rabbi Joshua concludes his interpretation of "In the beginning God created the heaven and the earth" as follows: "The world and the fullness thereof belong to God. When He wished, He gave it to you; and when He wished, He took it from you and gave it to us." Thus, what began as a simple statement concludes as an elaborate justification for Israel's possession of its homeland. This *midrash*, like the one on Israel's collective identity, is a declaration of an ancient ethnocentric nationalism. In other *midrashim* in *Genesis Rabbah*, this theme is reiterated, using other biblical sources as validation of the claim.

Therefore, in his interpretation, Rabbi Joshua of Siknin reinforces the belief that Israel is unique among the nations of the world, and that status is not undermined by the Roman occupation and its loss of sovereignty. To the contrary, it is God's will that Israel has lost the Land, and it is God's will that the Land will be restored to Israel. This reflects a fundamental concept within fourth-century rabbinic thought on the Jewish homeland: maintain the Land as a central focus for world Jewry, but do not inspire further Palestinian Jewish revolt. Thus, in general, the *midrashim* on the subject of possession of the Land are irredentist, aimed at preserving what had been conquered and was once theirs, and staking a future claim on what has been promised in biblical Genesis.

Genesis Rabbah's midrashim on territory suggest that the rabbis went to great lengths to link Israel's collective identity and cohesion with past, present, and future possession of the Land. In rabbinic thought, Israel was to be a holy people whose very presence in the Land sanctified it. This is a theme that pervades several of the *midrashim* in *Genesis Rabbah*.

CONCLUSION

Was there an ethnocentric rhetoric in other ancient groups? Ancient Egyptian and Mesopotamian inscriptions and texts have a paucity of references to peoples or nations as such. In some cases, however, groups identified themselves and others by referring to their cultural distinctiveness and territorial contiguity, rhetorically creating the mixture of cultural-regional criteria that characterizes an ethnic group. They expressed sentiments for the preservation of collective solidarity and cultural and political autarchy. They, as did Israel, asserted a nation that was assumed to be the center of the world. Yet, most of those nations were extinct by late antiquity.

This study argues that the Jews were different from other ancient nations because of the vitality *midrash* brought to the interpretation of scripture. Verses of biblical Genesis could be interpreted and reinterpreted to address contemporary situations, whatever they were. *Midrash* was therefore a perfect medium with which to transmit the theological and political thought of rabbinic elites to their constituents. Scriptural interpretation provided exegetical opportunities for rabbis to espouse an ancient nationalism that gave a sense of cohesion and homeland to Jews in both Palestine and the Diaspora. It provided authoritative and timeless concepts of collective identity and territorial attachment to the Jewish homeland because Jewish tradition held that the practice of *midrash*, validated and affirmed by references to other older scriptural passages, constituted Divine revelation and therefore was authentic.

The rhetoric of Jewish collective identity and territorial attachment as found in *Genesis Rabbah's midrashim* is significant because it provides a glimpse of texts that were studied, debated, and memorized by generations of observant Jews, including those of the present day. The political messages within these selected texts are manifest. Because articulations of a territorially based ethnocentrism exists within these texts, they are important indicators of ancient Jewish political thought.

Further research on rabbinic rhetoric as it pertains to Jewish collective identity should examine *midrashim* that were written and compiled in later centuries. Also, the rhetoric within the sacred texts of other traditions might be examined in this light, as in Lewis's study (1988), wherein he argues that understanding the politics of Islam and of movements and changes that are perceived in Islamic terms requires an understanding of the origins of Islamic political language as found in the *Qu'ran*, the Traditions of the Prophet, and the practice of early Muslims.

Sacred texts offer rhetorical sources for a better understanding the endurance of distinctive concepts of collective identity and homelands. The Jewish tradition offers a wealth of texts that can assist scholars who seek the foundations of Jewish political thought in various subjects over time.

REFERENCES

Lewis, B. (1988). *The political language of Islam.* Chicago: University of Chicago Press.

Strack, H. L., & Stemberger, G. (1992). *Introduction to the Talmud and Midrash.* Markus Bockmuehl, trans. Minneapolis, Minn.: Fortress Press.

CHAPTER 6

Pragmatic Ambiguity and Partisanship in Russia's Emerging Democracy

RICHARD D. ANDERSON, JR.

INTRODUCTION

How does change in the language of politics promote a transition from undemocratic rule to a democratic polity such as the one that has been forming in Russia since 1991? Undemocratic rulers and electoral politicians use their public speech to pursue contrasting strategic objectives. In either of the two types of undemocratic polity, dynastic or dictatorial, the rulers seek to exclude the general population from joining in the choice of leaders and policies—to suppress democratic participation. In a democracy, each politician competing for office seeks to stimulate participation by those voters likely to support the politician's candidacy. When each of several politicians tries to stimulate participation by that politician's likely voters, the politicians' separate efforts combine to stimulate participation by the populace as a whole. Electoral campaigns stimulate participation, even though some politicians' concurrent efforts to discourage participation by voters supporting their rivals can limit overall participation.

Dynasts and dictators achieve their objectives of discouraging people from taking sides in the political contest, in part, by restricting their public speech. Utterances, Chafe (1994: 57–65; cf. Pinker, 1994: 15–16) observes, shape the current contents of a hearer's or reader's attention. In turn, the contents of attention decide a person's behavior. To depress participation, undemocratic rulers need to avoid utterances that might draw popular attention to their internecine political contest, in which members of the populace might otherwise try to take sides. Dynasts and dictators therefore prefer to talk about the community as a unified whole. Dynastic rulers talk about the military threat posed by their foreign rivals to all members of the community and about the threats posed by domestic disorder to the community's unity, with the result that in a world dominated by dynasties the image of the "night watchman state" prevails. Transformational dictatorships of the Soviet type add talk about social progress, again by society as a whole. Although electoral politicians also address issues of external security, domestic order, and social progress that face the whole community, their need to stimulate participation adds a distinctive feature to their language. In addition to problems facing the whole community, electoral politicians seek to focus citizens' attention on the politicians themselves and on the citizens' relationship with the politicians.

Language offers a variety of resources for directing attention to the external world, to the self, or to the relationship between speaker and audience. Among these resources are modal constructions (e.g., in English, must, ought, need, should, can) that inject possibility, necessity, or obligation into unmodified utterances. In both English and Russian, some modal constructions can vary the focus of attention among the external world, the self, or the relationship of speaker to audience. It is possible to test the hypothesis that electoral politicians are more likely than authoritarian rulers to direct attention to the self and to relationships by examining the frequency of each kind of modality in Russian texts drawn from the authoritarian Soviet past or the electoral Russian present.

PARTISANSHIP AND PARTICIPATION

Electoral politicians need to draw citizens' attention to questions of self and relationship because participation depends on partisanship, or citizens' identification with the beliefs espoused by candidates for office. Striving to preclude participation, dynastic or dictatorial rulers block the development of partisanship by banning political parties outright or by subjecting parties to close control. In the Soviet Union, only one organization, the Communist Party, could legally call itself a political party, and that organization functioned not as a party but as a combination of personnel office and territorial administration for the Soviet state. The very concept of partisanship had a different meaning. The term *partisans (partiinye)* was applied to party members, and everyone else was classified as a *nonpartisan (bespartiinyi)*. In an established democracy, such as the United States, partisans are much more likely than nonpartisans to engage in voting and other forms of participation. Persons who consider themselves strong Democrats or strong Republicans in the United States vote at a rate thirty percentage points higher than the rate for persons who consider themselves Independents (sum of increments from various measures of partisanship reported by Rosenstone and Hansen, 1993: 273).

In an established democracy with strong partisanship, political speech can stimulate participation simply by reminding voters of their political identity (Ansolabehere and Iyengar, 1995: 75). *Republican* and *Democrat* are condensation symbols that abbreviate far more elaborate (even if still quite simple) propositions about the political world. Being a Republican or Democrat means having learned a list (perhaps relatively short) of dislikes associated with one party and likes associated with the other party. The self-identification, "I am a strong Democrat," abbreviates a pair of propositions: "I reject some beliefs stereotypically associated with Republicans" and "I affirm some beliefs stereotypically associated with Democrats." These propositions, in turn, abbreviate lists of beliefs (e.g., abortion is right or wrong, tax cuts are right or wrong, federal intervention is good or bad, the death penalty is just or unjust). Espousal by the candidate of a variety of issue beliefs suffices to cue the voter to identify (or not to identify) with the candidate who shares (or rejects) the voter's political identity, which typically has been learned in childhood from the voter's parents (Beck and Jennings, 1991).

In a new democracy such as Russia, the electoral politician's task of stimulating participation is more difficult. Potential voters in Russia cannot have learned political identities from their parents during childhood because there were no political parties from which to choose identities (White, Rose, and McAllister, 1997: 43–44). Today's Communist Party of the Russian Federation, which claims organizational continuity with the Soviet Communist Party, might offer one exception to this generalization, but the circumstance that the old Communist Party did not compete in elections might also imply that today's communist voters must associate political identification with a new kind of behavior. Electoral politicians in Russia, therefore, need to tell voters about more than their beliefs relating to the issues of the day. If people are more likely to share beliefs that they regard as reasonable, a politician can pave the way for voters to share his or her beliefs by making them think about the reasonableness of the politician's thought process. Similarly, if people are more likely to form new relationships when they think about themselves in relation to another, a politician can build relationships by stimulating voters to think about their relationship to the politician.

THE PRAGMATIC AMBIGUITY OF MODAL CONSTRUCTIONS

Language offers resources to a speaker, whether ruler or politician, for directing audience attention to the state of the world facing both speaker and audience, to the reasonableness of the speaker, or to the relationship between speaker and audience. One category of utterance combining all three of these capabilities is the class of modal constructions. Sweetser (1990) uses the term *pragmatic ambiguity* for the capacity of modals to vary the direction of audience attention. In contrast to semantic ambiguity, which exists when a single lexical item can express different meanings in one context, pragmatic ambiguity exists when a lexical item retains a single semantic meaning across contexts but speakers use that meaning for different purposes in different contexts. A pragmatically ambiguous utterance can express (1) a content meaning about the situation facing both speaker and audience, (2) an epistemic meaning concerning the reasonableness of the speaker's inferences about the situation, or (3) a speech-act meaning that defines the relationship between speaker and audience. An example of pragmatic ambiguity is sentence (1), which depending on context could express any of these three meanings:

(1) We ought to be there.

English "ought," Sweetser argues, always bears the same semantic meaning of a "not wholly binding" obligation but conveys a pragmatic meaning that can vary depending on what the speaker intends to assert. First, a speaker uttering sentence (1) can be asserting that the speaker recognizes a not wholly binding obligation to be present somewhere. For example, if the speaker and his or her spouse have accepted an invitation to a dinner, the speaker might remind the spouse that both are obligated to attend. In this context, "ought" conveys the real-world content of a social obligation.

Second, suppose that the speaker and spouse have become lost en route to the dinner. Then the speaker might utter sentence (1) while looking around in dismay. In this case, the speaker says nothing about social obligation; instead, the speaker expresses the not wholly binding obligation to believe that the couple's location corresponds to the destination. This epistemic usage of "ought" defines the speaker's state of mind: the speaker has an opinion about, but is not certain of, the couple's location.

Third, suppose yet again that the speaker is addressing not the spouse but the friend who has invited them to dinner. A speaker uttering sentence (1) is not asserting that the speaker and the friend are obligated to some third party, as in the first reading; instead, the speaker is performing the speech act, on behalf of the speaker and spouse, of establishing a not wholly binding promissory relationship with the friend, in which the promise concerns attendance at the dinner.

In sentence (1) "ought" consistently retains the stable semantic reference to an obligation, an inference, or a promise that is not wholly binding on the speaker. At the same time, context enables the listener to disambiguate (perhaps not with high reliability) among the possible pragmatic intents of the speaker.

Because some modals are pragmatically ambiguous, an audience encountering these parts of speech must think about, however momentarily, whether the speaker is communicating about the content of the message, the reasonableness of the speaker, or the relationship with the audience established by the utterance. Of course, resolution of the ambiguity goes unnoticed; the decision is overlearned and automatic. It is quite fleeting, and notice of it is suppressed as the audience continues to the next element of the utterance. Nevertheless, this unnoticed decision controls the interpretation of the whole utterance. Control of the interpretation determines whether the audience attends to the event reported by the speaker, to the warrant for the speaker's belief about the event, or to the linguistic interaction between the speaker and the audience.

HYPOTHESIS AND PROCEDURE

By directing attention to the situation facing the speaker and the audience, content modality serves the purpose necessary to political leadership in both undemocratic and democratic polities of mobilizing popular effort to address needs of the community. But by directing audience attention to the speaker or to the speaker's relationship with the audience, epistemic and speech-act modality achieve an effect disadvantageous to dynasts and dictators but necessary for electoral competitors. This effect is to pave the way for the citizens to decide whether to accept the beliefs of the speaker and whether to enter into a relationship of political support. Although political candidates in an established democracy, who are able to exploit partisanship acquired in childhood by many voters, might be less dependent on linguistic cues to motivate partisanship than their counterparts in a new democracy such as Russia, politicians even in established democracies seek to convert some voters from the opposing party and to attract nonpartisans. Thus, it should be expected that the use of epistemic and speech-act modality will distinguish electoral speech in general from the language of undemocratic rule.

To test this hypothesis, I collected 50 texts from the authoritarian era in the Soviet Union and 50 texts from the first two years of electoral politics in Russia. The texts in the first group were originally spoken between 1964 and 1985 by members of the Soviet Politburo, a team of ten to fifteen elderly men (one woman was once a member) who held the formal power to decide any question concerning the lives of the Soviet population. Like all authoritarians, they were chosen by someone other than the voting population, in the Soviet case, by the Central Committee, a group of as many as 300 persons whom the Politburo had previously appointed. Since the fall of the Soviet Union in 1991, Russian politicians have qualified for office by winning elections in which all adult citizens are entitled to vote. In each corpus of texts, I identified all instances of the three Russian modals capable of expressing pragmatic ambiguity: the verb pair *moch'/smoch'* (can/may) and the predicatives *mozhno* (also can/may) and *dolzhna* (ought/should/must) (Beliaeva, 1985: 126–53; Choi, 1994: 157–60, 187).

I then reviewed the context of each instance to classify the modality as

Table 6.1
Modality in Authoritarian and Electoral Speech

	Content	**Epistemic**	**Speech-Act**	**Total**
Authoritarian	658	0	1	659
Electoral	470	60	23	553
Total	1,128	60	24	1,212

Pearson chi^2 = 103.0; p < 0.0005.

a content, epistemic, or speech-act usage. In classifying the modal or causal conjunction, I followed the rules for interpretation stated by Sweetser. Of modals, she writes (1990: 72–73): "A modal verb may be interpreted as applying the relevant modality to: 1. the content of the sentence: the real world event must or may take place; 2. the epistemic entity represented by the sentence: the speaker is forced to, or (not) barred from, concluding the truth of the sentence; 3. the speech act represented by the sentence: the speaker (or people in general) is forced to, or (not) barred from, saying what the sentence says."

RESULTS: REASONABLENESS AND RELATIONSHIP IN AUTHORITARIAN AND ELECTORAL RUSSIAN

The hypothesis predicts that undemocratic rulers avoid epistemic and speech-act modality in favor of content modality, whereas electoral politicians combine all three types. The authoritarian texts display no clear cases of epistemic modality and only one clear case of speech-act modality. By contrast, at least 11 percent of the modals in the electoral texts are used in the epistemic sense, and 4 percent are speech-act usages.

Table 6.1 displays the distribution of content, epistemic, and speech-act usages of the pragmatically ambiguous Russian modals in the authoritarian and electoral texts. Because the 50 authoritarian texts contain 2.2 times as many words as the 50 electoral texts, electoral speakers not only increase the proportion of epistemic and speech-act usages among all modals, but they use the pragmatically ambiguous modals significantly more often in proportion to all parts of speech.

The authoritarian texts contain many instances of the three modals used in sentences like (2), in which *mozhno* (can) communicates typical content modality:

(2) I, tol'ko opiraias' na noveishie dostizheniia nauki o prirode i obshchestve, mozhno uspeshno stroit' sotsializm i kommunizm.
(And only relying on the latest achievements of the science of nature and society can socialism and communism be successfully built.)

Sentence (2) comes from a speech delivered in 1975 by the former top official of the Communist Party, General Secretary Leonid Brezhnev, to a gathering of senior officials and prominent researchers on the occasion of the 250th anniversary of the Academy of Sciences. In the paragraph in which it appears, Brezhnev explains the connection between state support for science and the problem facing the whole regime of the conflict between state socialism and world capitalism.

The communist texts contain, of course, a number of modals whose classification is very open to question, for instance sentences (3) and (4):

(3) S samogo nachala bylo iasno, chto nadezhno obespechit' mir i razriadku mozhno budet lish' v upornoi politicheskoi bor'be.
(From the very beginning, it was clear that we could reliably assure peace and detente only in a stubborn political struggle.)

(4) Dumaetsia, chto osoboe mesto v ikh deiatel'nosti seichas dolzhna zaniat' rabota po rukovodstvu Sovetami vsekh stupenei. . . .
(It is thought that in their activity, work on leadership of Soviets of all levels ought to take a special place. . . .)

Epistemic readings of *mozhno* (could) and *dolzhna* (should) might be warranted in these cases by the explicit references—"it was clear" or "it is thought"—to the speaker's thinking. The question, however, is how to understand these utterances. Is the speaker uttering (3) saying that from the very start a stubborn political struggle was logically foreseeable during the pursuit of peace and detente (the epistemic reading), or that from the very beginning achievement of peace and detente was possible only through stubborn political struggle (the content reading)? The speaker of (3) is Brezhnev again, now addressing a gathering of Moscow officials and selected citizens at the culmination of meetings between voters and nominees in the uncontested elections of deputies to the national Supreme Soviet, a nominal legislature with some executive functions that uniformly approved decisions prepared by Communist Party staffers under the ultimate direction of the general secretary. Brezhnev and other Politburo members used these occasions to voice their public stands on domestic and international issues facing the Soviet Union. The choice between epistemic and content readings of (3) is easier if one also knows, as attentive Soviet publics could, that Brezhnev was repeating his routine assertion that only "stubborn political struggle" could make "peace and detente" possible in a world dominated by the class conflict with capitalism (Anderson, 1993: 2, 132, 135, 157, 192–210).

The classification is clearer in the case of (4). Here the speaker is Konstantin Chernenko, general secretary from 1984 to 1985, addressing the Supreme Soviet. Despite the epistemic "it is thought," when Chernenko tells the Supreme Soviet that it and its collective presidency (the Presidium, the referent of "their") have an obligation to exercise control over regional and local Soviets nominally under their authority, he is mentioning a real-world obligation binding on deputies subordinate to him. The "it is thought" is inserted as a courtesy designed to maintain the fiction of the Supreme Soviet's formal superiority to Chernenko who addresses it in his capacity as an ordinary deputy.

Although also presenting many ambiguous cases, the electoral texts, unlike the authoritarian texts, present numerous cases in which the epistemic reading seems unavoidable. Consider sentence (5):

(5) Vrode po vsem makroekonomicheskim pokazateliam dolzhen proizoiti kollaps, no ne proiskhodit.
(Seemingly by all macroeconomic indicators, [the economy] ought to fall into a faint, but it doesn't.)

This sentence comes from a 1993 interview with Grigorii Yavlinskii, who led the social-democratic party *Yabloko* (Apple) in the 1993 and 1995 elections to the *Duma* and ran for president as its candidate in 1996. Arguing that the Russian economy can flourish, despite its economic problems, without aid from the West, Yavlinskii obviously is not asserting the Russian economy's actual obligation to collapse (the content reading). Instead, he is mentioning a logically foreseeable contingency (the epistemic reading) only to deny that it has actually occurred.

The difference between contemplation of logical alternatives and assertion of real possibilities frequently emerges in seemingly more ambiguous cases that occur in the electoral texts. Consider passages (6) and (7):

(6) Mozhno, konechno, razdelit' vse naselenie strany mekhanicheski na kolichestvo izbiratel'nykh okrugov. No togda vy neizbezhno poluchite narushenie granits sub"ektov Federatsii.
(The whole population of the country could, of course, be divided mechanically by the number of electoral districts. But then you would inevitably get a violation of the boundaries of the Federation's constituent parts.)

(7) Konechno, namerenie Khasbulatova, Rutskogo i Il'i Konstantinova razviazat' v Rossii iadernuiu grazhdanskuiu voinu mozhno schitat' smeshnym i dazhe posmeiat'cia. Odnako delu—vremia, a potekhe—chas. Nado obespechit' sebe vozmozhnost' smeiat'sia poslednimi.
(Of course, the intention of Khasbulatov, Rutskoi, and Il'ya Konstantinov to unleash a nuclear civil war in Russia may be thought ridiculous and even ridiculed. However, work deserves your time and fun, only an hour. One needs to assure oneself the chance to laugh last.)

In (6) Viktor Sheinis, the deputy who designed Russia's elaborate electoral rules, denies real-world possibility while asserting logical foreseeability. The sentence comes from an interview in which Sheinis tries to win public support for new election rules that he has proposed. The positive *mozhno* (could) introduces a logical alternative rejected by the speaker as impossible in practice. Similarly, in (7) the radical democrat Valeriia Novodvorskaia (Russia's Tom Paine) writes in the heat of the 1993 constitutional crisis occasioned by President Boris Yeltsin's unconstitutional dismissal of parliament and the threat of his parliamentary opponents (Speaker Ruslan Khasbulatov, Vice President Aleksandr Rutskoi, and the extreme nationalist Il'ya Konstantinov) to begin a civil war. Trying to win adherents to her opposition to parliament, a stand which leads her to back Yeltsin in the crisis, Novodvorskaia raises the logical contingency of someone ridiculing the intention to start a civil war fought with nuclear weapons, only to warn against taking the threat lightly. In other words, each case raises a logical consideration for the purpose of contrasting it with reality. If a politician wants others to attend to his or her state of mind as a preliminary to accepting his or her assertions about the world, then appearing to consider alternatives aloud calls attention to the politician's process of reasoning.

The sole case of speech-act modality in the authoritarian texts deserves to be quoted, if only for its uniqueness:

(8) Tak mozhet li nam, sovetskim kommunistam i vsem sovetskim liudiam, byt' chto-libo blizhe v okruzhaiushchem mire, chem eta sotsialisticheskaia sem'ia?
(So could anything in the surrounding world be closer to us, Soviet Communists and all Soviet people, than this socialist family?)

By Sweetser's argument, a modal is being used as a speech act when it makes an assertion about what is admissible or obligatory in the linguistic interaction between speaker and audience. The test of a speech-act usage is the possiblity of paraphrasing the utterance by replacing the modal with a speech-act verb. In (8), drawn from the 1977 speech commemorating the sixtieth anniversary of the October Revolution, Brezhnev uses *mozhet* (could) to do an act of inviting, in this case agreement with the proposition that other socialist states ("this socialist family") have the highest priority for "us." The utterance cannot be read as an inquiry concerning the real possibility of something lying closer to the hearts of Soviet communists and people, nor as a conclusion from some unstated premise that the socialist countries are closer than any others. Brezhnev's utterance can be paraphrased (with the speech-act verb italicized): "Into our conversation, do I *admit* reference to any part of the world as closer to us than the socialist countries?" This usage does draw attention to a relationship between Brezhnev and "all Soviet people"—their joint membership in "us"—but in the context the relationship is national rather than partisan. Although the authoritarian texts contain many instances of modals modifying speech-act verbs, particularly *mozhno skazat'* (I may say) and *dolzhen skazat'* (I must say), Sweetser observes that in such cases content modality is being applied to the speech-act verb, rather than speech-act modality to the clause.

Represented by a sole instance in the 50 authoritarian texts, speech-act usages also appear rarely in electoral texts but more than uniquely:

(9) Stroit' mozhno doma, dorogi, a v obshchestve mozhno lish' postepenno, no postoianno provodit' malye reformy.
(Houses can be built, roads, but in society one can only gradually but continually conduct small reforms.)

The speaker in (9) is Vladimir Zhirinovskii, whose Liberal Democratic Party (despite its name, an extreme nationalist group) won the most votes in the 1993 parliamentary election. Sentence (9) comes from an article in a party flyer signed by Zhirinovskii, who contrasts his conception for Russian democracy with the familiar order of the communist past. The sentence needs to be read against the backdrop of a sentence such as (2) as countertext, with its discussion of the contribution of science to "building socialism." Zhirinovskii contrasts the appropriateness of *stroit'* (build) to discussion of physical objects with its inappropriateness to discussion of society. To emphasize that he is commenting on the action of building rather than on the possibility of building, the speaker inverts the normal order of *stroit'* (build) and *mozhno* (one can). The speaker is doing a speech act of excluding, using the exclusion of "build" from discussion of society to symbolize separation of himself and his adherents from the society built by Soviet communism. *Mozhno* (can) comments on a metaphor, an act of communication, rather than on a real possibility. Such an utterance defines the relationship among speaker and audience: it is equivalent to an assertion that the "we" of the relationship excludes any communists (i.e., those who would use *stroit'* to talk about society).

A special class of speech-act modality regularly encountered in the electoral texts, but absent from the authoritarian ones, is the emphatic use of *moch'* (can/may), as in (10):

(10) Rossiia ne mozhet byt' krokhotnoi, a tol'ko ogromnoi, velikoi.
(Russia cannot be fragmentary, but only enormous and great.)

Here the speaker is Aleksandr Prokhanov, a leader of the so-called "irreconcilable opposition" to Yeltsin, speaking at the founding congress of a unified opposition and summoning Russians to support his new movement. In contrast to a content reading that would interpret (10) to deny the possibility that Russia could break apart, Prokhanov is engaged in a verdictive speech-act, condemning Yeltsin for having accepted the dissolution of the Soviet Union. The sentence may be paraphrased: "I disallow the appellation 'Russia' to our country if it should fragment and cease to be enormous and great." By implication, if a divided country does not warrant the name

"Russia," the man associated with its dissolution, whom Prokhanov calls a *zlodei* (evildoer), cannot deserve the title "President of Russia." The utterance serves to associate Prokhanov with other Russians resentful of the loss of the Soviet periphery.

CONCLUSION

Utterances by electoral speakers in Russia are significantly more likely to draw attention to the reasonableness of the speaker than are utterances by their authoritarian communist predecessors in the Soviet Union. The texts of authoritarian Russian reported in this chapter strictly avoid epistemic usages of the frequently occurring, pragmatically ambiguous modals (*moch'/smoch'*, *mozhno*, and *dolzhen*). Speech-act usages of these modals are also quite rare. By contrast, epistemic and speech-act uses become reasonably frequent in public statements by electoral politicians. These observations disconfirm the null hypotheses that authoritarians are more, or equally, likely to draw public attention to the reasonableness of their beliefs and also that authoritarians are more, or equally, likely to define the relationship between speaker and audience.

The claims of linguists, such as Sweetser, Chafe, and Pinker, that linguistic performances direct the attention of audiences are easily reinforced by one's own introspection and by the regular experimental result that responses vary with change in cues. If we take these claims seriously, then we must conclude that anyone knowing Russian who encounters electoral speech cannot avoid thinking about the reasonableness of the speaker's beliefs and the citizen's relationship to the speaker. In a society with established political parties where people use their own partisan identity to evaluate the match between a candidate's avowed beliefs and their own beliefs and where the evaluation is biased by people's prior acceptance of some political party as the group to which they belong, efforts by political candidates to draw attention to their reasonableness or their relationship with citizens might influence only those few potential voters who lack partisanship or who are in the process of changing their partisan identity. In a society where adults are acquiring partisan identities for the first time because no political parties have yet established themselves and parents have had no opportunities to supply partisan cues, linguistic cues that direct the attention of potential political participants to the questions of whether the beliefs of politicians are reasonable and whether the citizen belongs to the politician's group could encourage formation of the partisan identifications that promote participation.

NOTES

I thank Professors Henning Andersen, Eve Sweetser, and Olga Yokoyama for helpful comments, and the Academic Senate at the University of California, Los

REFERENCES

Anderson, R. D., Jr. (1993). *Public politics in an authoritarian state: Making foreign policy during the Brezhnev years.* Ithaca: Cornell University Press.

Ansolabehere, S., & Iyengar, S. (1995). *Going negative: How attack ads shrink and polarize the electorate.* New York: Free Press.

Beck, P. A. & Jennings, M. Kent (1991). Family traditions, political periods, and the development of partisan orientations. *Journal of Politics, 53,* 742–63.

Beliaeva, E. I. (1985). *Funktsional'no-semanticheskie polia modal'nosti v angliiskom i russkom iazykakh* [Functional-semantic fields of modality in the English and Russian languages]. Voronezh, U.S.S.R.: Izdatel'stvo Voronezhskogo Universiteta.

Chafe, W. L. (1994). *Discourse, consciousness, and time: The flow and displacement of conscious experience in speaking and writing.* Chicago: University of Chicago Press.

Choi, S. (1994). *Modal predicates in Russian: Semantics and syntax.* Unpublished doctoral dissertation. University of California, Los Angeles.

Pinker, S. (1994). *The language instinct: How the mind creates language.* New York: William Morrow.

Rosenstone, S. J., & Hansen, J. M. (1993). *Mobilization, participation, and democracy in America.* New York: Macmillan.

Sweetser, E. (1990). *From etymology to pragmatics: Metaphorical and cultural aspects of semantic structure.* New York: Cambridge University Press.

White, S., Rose, R., & McAllister, I. (1997). *How Russia votes.* Chatham, N.J.: Chatham House.

PART II

The Discourse of the Political Elite

CHAPTER 7

The Crisis Tool in American Political Discourse

AMOS KIEWE

THE CASE FOR CRISIS RHETORIC

The importance of discourse in American culture is prevalent in social and political life, and it is most profound in the office of the presidency. The twentieth-century presidency, in particular, has been labeled the *rhetorical presidency* to denote a style of governing and leadership that relies heavily on public discourse and whose rhetoric equals action (Tulis, 1987). Beginning with Theodore Roosevelt and Woodrow Wilson, the presidency as a symbolic and bully pulpit has set a standard for future presidents (Denton & Woodward, 1990: 55). In turn, the nation began to consider the rhetorical and the oratorical as the primary features of the executive branch (Hart, 1987).

Indeed, the more successful presidents have been those known for their strong rhetorical abilities: Theodore Roosevelt, Woodrow Wilson, Franklin D. Roosevelt, John F. Kennedy, Ronald Reagan, and perhaps even William J. Clinton. The presidents whose terms in the White House have been described as less than inspiring are those also considered the least rhetorically gifted: Calvin Coolidge, Herbert Hoover, Gerald Ford, Jimmy Carter, and George Bush. This quick survey is not meant to prove a causal link between rhetorical skills and a successful presidency but to suggest that successful presidents, especially twentieth century presidents, in addition to their leadership qualities, negotiation skills, and good working relationships with Congress, also enjoyed strong rhetorical inclinations that allowed them the ability to communicate effectively.

Numerous studies point to the presidency as a talking institution wherein the American president presides by discourse (Hart, 1987; Tulis, 1987).

The president is the symbolic embodiment of the nation, and his role is that of chief communicator. In the age of image-executive, the president is seen continuously addressing constituencies at locations where the scene has become an integral part of the governing process. Because the visual and the visceral have become the main vehicles for political action, the political process has become an unfolding drama whose primary features are persona and narrative (Jamieson, 1992: 15–22).

One area that significantly illustrates the acute function of discourse in presidential politics is crisis situations. In crisis situations, the discursive in presidential politics is magnified, both in its presence and absence. Crises are sociorhetorical constructs that call for extraordinary action and resources. A crisis situation frames an issue, an event, or an occurrence as urgent, unusual, and in need of a quick solution for the resumption of normality. Crises are communicative entities because they require adherents for a given perception to prevail and to legitimate action.

Crises can be real or manufactured, believable or not, serious for some and not-so-serious for others. The presidency might need to confront political crises of various sorts, including social, religious, economic, constitutional, and international. Crises have no limitation on subject matter, nor do they fall neatly into categories. An international crisis is not necessarily the opposite of a domestic crisis, as one can aid or obviate the other. An economic crisis can turn into a leadership crisis, and an insoluble or difficult process can reach a quicker solution if a situation is defined as critical, whereby routine processes are replaced by the expedient and the decisive.

A survey of presidential crisis rhetoric since World War II reveals a preference for crises defined by the president and an aversion to crises defined by others (Kiewe, 1994). Presidents do well when they are in control of the crisis definition. They do not like to react to crisis definitions constructed by others, such as the opposition, the media, or the public. Presidents have been known to construe crises as political tools used manipulatively as the means for other ends (e.g., Lyndon B. Johnson and the Gulf of Tonkin Resolution, Richard Nixon and his many crises). When crises are defined by others than the president (President Bush and the recession of 1990–1992), presidents often confront legitimate issues and warranted concerns. Yet, reacting to crises is a position that takes the initiative and the active role away from the president.

Different categories of crisis rhetoric do not necessarily translate into specific types of presidential behavior. Indeed, attempts to categorize crisis rhetoric into international or domestic, ceremonial or deliberative, consummatory or justificatory (Cherwitz and Zagacki, 1980 Dow, 1989; Windt, 1973), suffer from strict adherence to generic orthodoxy that leaves no room for the more varied, flexible, and fluid nature of crisis rhetoric. I go so far as to claim that crisis rhetoric is not altogether different from routine rhetoric except for the element of urgency inserted into the situation.

CRISES AS RHETORICAL CONSTRUCTS

Crises, then, are discursive constructs that communicate an urgency and call for out-of-the-ordinary decisions and actions. A crisis is a selection of a situation as critical (and a deflection of a competing definition), calling for perceiving the situation as urgent and suggesting the willingness to suspend normal and routine processes for the immediate and the decisive. The term *crisis* also suggests unique leadership qualities not found during noncritical situations.

A pragmatic and flexible approach is that of crisis rhetoric as a terministic/dramatistic screen. A terministic screen is a lens that directs our attention and through which one sees reality. Burke (1966: 44–55) identifies two kinds of terms: terms that put things together, and terms that take things apart. That the terministic screen is to be viewed "as a paradoxical way of 'uniting' us with things on a 'higher level of awareness,' " or encountering the principle of continuity and discontinuity (cited in Gusfield, 1989: 123). The very selection of a term frames a given reality to be experienced one way and not another way. The use of a specific term puts invisible boundaries for human perception and suggests attitudes for its evaluation. A terministic screen is thus a dramatistic lens whereby one selects a word for action (Gusfield, 1989: 124). The dramatism in crisis situations is most acute. A crisis, then, is a term that is ostensibly dramatic and that, by its very definition, is used to unite people around a plot and a narrative.

The reason for the growing use of crisis rhetoric lies in the very perception of a crisis as a unique, dynamic, and dramatic situation, and the communal need for strong leadership and special discourse that can restore normality. Although the founding conception of the presidency was for normal times, the "fit" between the presidential office and its modern occupant is most pronounced during crises, claims Tulis (1987: 176). Nichols (1994: 143) goes so far as to claim, "Presidents must often exaggerate the emergency character of situations in order to justify a departure from strict rule of law" in order not to be too constrained in their ability to act.

Crises have become routine and are thus symptomatic of the growing difficulty of the modern presidency to act unencumbered, efficiently, and promptly. The modern presidency's increased use of the crisis tool to aid a wide and varied range of political objectives should caution scholars to be tuned more to the practical use of crisis rhetoric than to theoretical conceptualization. The need for a theoretical grounding that has an explanatory power is not discounted here, but such a need has to be mitigated against more pragmatic considerations. The following discussion presents four case studies that illustrate the "fit" among crisis, discourse, and the presidency.[1]

TAKING ADVANTAGE OF A CRISIS SITUATION

Franklin D. Roosevelt came to the White House after campaigning as the rescuer of the nation from one of the most severe crises it had faced (Biles, 1991: 9–11; Freidel, 1973: 11). As a presidential candidate, Roosevelt had projected optimism in his ability to restore confidence to a nation that needed hope more than anything else. His successful candidacy and his growing reliance on rhetorical and symbolic appeals became staples of his presidential stature. Roosevelt broke with tradition when he asked the 1932 Democratic Convention in Chicago to wait for his arrival to accept the party nomination. He flew to Chicago, an unprecedented symbolic move, and addressed the convention directly. Roosevelt understood the importance that his maverick gesture would have on a sick nation, notwithstanding his own severe physical limitations (Houck, 1995).

In his campaign, Roosevelt promised a New Deal between the nation and its government—his metaphorical policy frame. He conceived a new relationship between the government and its people whereby the government's function was to help the people, especially in times of distress. Yet, the financial crisis worsened during the winter of 1932–1933, when U.S. gold reserves were quickly depleted and a run on the banks sent many to the brink of panic. Although president Hoover repeatedly requested Roosevelt's help in speaking to the nation and restoring confidence to the market, Roosevelt declined (Freidel, 1973: 30–32). By his very appeals for Roosevelt's help, Hoover suggested that Roosevelt had made irresponsible statements about getting the United States off the gold standard and thus had caused the latest crisis. Doing nothing, Roosevelt allowed the situation to worsen, only to be hailed as the nation's rescuer once he became president. Roosevelt's acute sense of timing was paramount to his crisis rhetoric—specifically, his silence. Indeed, hours after his inauguration, Roosevelt shut the banks and, with a series of speeches, stopped the run on them.

Roosevelt's inaugural address, his appealing radio talks, and the subsequent impressive legislative agenda that he set forth during his first 100 days in office were all designed to project confidence in the new administration's recovery plan. In his inaugural address, Roosevelt provided the nation with both the culprit for the crisis, namely unscrupulous bankers, and a new vision for a better tomorrow (Rosenman, 1938: 12–13). The inaugural address was foremost about "action now," about enlisting the people in a "great army" that would "go forward" (Rosenman, 1938: 14). The outline of several measures and the decisive move of closing the banks were sufficient to convince the nation that the new president meant business.

The active, even rapid sequence of legislation did not bring recovery per se, but it instilled the confidence necessary for the nation to resume economic activities. During his first 100 days, Roosevelt understood what Hoover also had understood but failed to implement—the economic crisis could be modified and the course of events could be reversed if confidence and optimism were used to convince the nation that the government was doing all it could to avert the crisis, that the banks were safe, and that the currency was stable. The first 100 days represented the prerequisite symbolic and rhetorical phase that preceded actual recovery. Roosevelt pushed through one piece of legislation after another: the Banking Act, the Farm Relief Bill, the Employment Bill, the Railroad Coordination Act, the Tennessee Valley Authority Act, and the National Industrial Recovery Act. Roosevelt also took the United States off the gold standard, which devalued the dollar. The subsequent inflationary measures increased produce prices, and the economic engines began to move again. The nation approved of this active and vibrant president. By mid-1933, the terrible crisis began to dissipate.

With hindsight, Roosevelt would reflect in his second fireside chat on his first 100 days: "I have no sympathy with the professional economists who insist that things must run their course and that human agencies can have no influence on economic ills" (quoted in Rosenman, 1938: 302). Indeed, rhetorical forces would bring the recovery. Roosevelt realized that his active first 100 would impress the nation and thus build the confidence necessary to avert the crisis. His task was rhetorical—to articulate confidence, to project trust, to impress, to ingratiate, to be bold, and to charm. "When all is said," reflected his close advisor, Rexford Tugwell, "there must have been some magic in mere words" (Tugwell, 1972: 233).

MISMANAGING A CRISIS SITUATION

After the success of the 1991 Gulf War and the 90 percent approval rating given to President George Bush, the economy soured. Unemployment, recession, downsizing, and the administration's inability to reverse the economic downturn all resulted in Bush's losing his high public approval, which hovered around the 45 percent mark.[2] The upcoming 1992 election would prove more difficult than anticipated. Seeking to regain control over the political and economic agenda, Bush began to forecast a major economic plan to be unveiled in his State of the Union address in late January 1992. Repeatedly, Bush made public statements regarding his "very strong State of the Union message" (*Public Papers*, November 6 to December 17, 1991: 1592–1844).

The frequency with which Bush talked about his upcoming State of the

Union address and the economic plan therein resulted in some of Bush's aides declaring that the State of the Union address would be Bush's most important address of his term. With his constant "stay tuned," the president built expectations and raised the stakes for a major address that left no room for anything less than an impressive economic recovery plan. On the eve of his address, the *New York Times*, describing the nation as the gloomiest in thirteen years, referred to the president's upcoming speech as "the most important of his presidency" ("Bad News for Bush," 1991: A1).

For roughly two months, Bush built expectations for a significant policy initiative that could cure the nation's economy. The president, and consequently the media and the public, turned an annual State of the Union address into a critical event. Yet, the State of the Union address that Bush delivered on January 28, 1992, was anything but impressive. The address was partially a rendition of the success of the United States in the Gulf War and other foreign policy successes. Only after praising America for achievements of "Biblical proportions," and buried in the middle of the speech, did Bush address the economy (Bush, 1992: 170). The very arrangement of main points signaled the lack of any real plan. Indeed, no plan for ending the recession was offered. What Bush outlined were small measures, such as proposing a change in tax withholding requirements, a $5,000 tax credit for first-time home buyers, and a proposal to cut the capital gains tax. Bush also presented general guidelines for reducing government red tape, breaking down tariffs, and calling for a more competitive America.

Not only did President Bush fail to deliver on his promise for an impressive economic plan, he also failed to appreciate his role in creating a disadvantageous context for his rhetoric. While seeking to avert an economic crisis, Bush further exacerbated the situation by signaling his inability to offer a solution to a gloomy nation. The reaction to the president's speech was critical. *Newsweek* described the president's proposal to stimulate the economy as "a gigantic accounting gimmick" ("Decoding Bush," 1992). The *New York Times*, in an article titled "The Tinkerer," called the address "a laundry list with no main text" (1992). The *Washington Post* stated, "Virtually all of Bush's political aides, watching in horror and gloom, acknowledge now that the strategy of the past 10 weeks of waiting until last night to offer a program to combat the recession was a mistake" ("A Declaration," 1992).

By conceiving the State of the Union address as crucial but not delivering a speech commensurate with the critical definition of the situation, Bush not only did little to avert a crisis, he further weakened his credibility at the outset of the 1992 presidential election. Perhaps the strategy conceived in early November 1991 was never a serious one and the administration simply hoped that, by January 1992, the economy would recover naturally without any government-sponsored stimulus. Such a policy would be consistent with Republican and conservative economic thinking. If this indeed was the thinking, however, the frequent promotion of an economic plan to be unveiled in the State of the Union address was cynical at best and manipulative at worst.

CONSTRUCTING A CRISIS AS A MEANS

John F. Kennedy's entry to the White House had been a difficult one. In his inaugural address, Kennedy exhibited an inordinate concern for foreign issues, specifically his concern over the Soviet perception of his strength and determination. The Soviets had tested every new American president since Harry Truman, and it was now Kennedy's turn. His first six months in office were marred with failures: the Bay of Pigs fiasco and the failure of American foreign policy in Laos. The communist threat clearly occupied Kennedy as he repeatedly made references to the "hour of maximum danger" (Inaugural Address, *Public Papers*, January 20, 1961: 2–3). In his first State of the Union address, he said, "Each day the crises multiply. . . . Each day we draw nearer to the hour of maximum danger . . . the tide of events has been running out and time has not been our friend" (State of the Union Address, *Public Papers*, January 30, 1961: 22–23). After the Bay of Pigs (April 17, 1961), Kennedy stated that "we face a relentless struggle in every corner of the globe" (address before the American Society of Newspaper Editors, *Public Papers*, April 20, 1961: 305–6), and "the danger has never been more clear and its presence has never been more imminent" (address before the American Society of Newspaper Editors, *Public Papers*, April 27, 1961: 336). With such ominous threats, Kennedy requested, in a May 1961 speech before a joint session of Congress, that the military be strengthened and that a "flexible response" be adopted as the new nuclear strategy (cited in Kiewe, 1994: 55–56).

The Soviets had tested each new U.S. president during the previous sixteen years with Berlin. The city's unique status, an Allied trusteeship in a communist country, was never to the Soviets' liking. On several occasions, Soviet leaders demanded that West Berlin be demilitarized and handed over to East Germany (Kiewe, 1994:57). Berlin was on the agenda for the Vienna summit of June 3–4, 1961, between Kennedy and Soviet Premier Nikita Khrushchev. The Soviet leader demanded that Kennedy negotiate on Berlin. He threatened that a refusal to negotiate would result in the Soviets' signing a peace treaty with East Germany and that any violation of East Germany sovereignty—namely, the presence of the United States in the city—would be considered a threat to peace (Kiewe, 1994: 58). Kennedy rejected the ultimatum. Although Khrushchev went so far as to state that "if you [Kennedy] want war, that is your problem" (cited in Kiewe, 1994: 59), Kennedy, in an address to the nation on June 6, 1961, stated that the

United States was determined to maintain its rights in Berlin "at any risk" (*Public Papers*, June 6, 1961: 444).

In the meantime, some 60,000 East German refugees had fled to West Berlin (Kiewe, 1994: 62). In a June 28, 1961, press conference, Kennedy accused the Soviets of manufacturing the Berlin crisis. On July 25, 1961, Kennedy addressed the nation specifically on the Berlin crisis. He linked the events in Berlin to the aggressive spread of communism around the world. Berlin had thus became "a showcase of liberty" and "a beacon of hope behind the Iron curtain" (*Public Papers*, 1961: 534). Kennedy's most ominous show of determination was in the following statement: "We do not want to fight—but we have fought before" (*Public Papers*, 1961: 534). Public response was very supportive of the president, and Congress enthusiastically supported his proposed new military spending. The ultimate Soviet response came as a complete shock to the Kennedy administration—the construction of a wall that completely sealed off East Berlin from West Berlin.

Enrico Pucci noted the lack of material cause in this crisis, and stated that the Berlin crisis, from beginning to end, was purely rhetorical (in Kiewe, 1994: 67). Only words created the crisis. But the crisis was real and the danger of nuclear war tangible. The only material aspect in this crisis came at its conclusion in the form of a physical wall. By ending the crisis on their own terms, the Soviets had left Kennedy with no act to follow theirs. Kennedy did achieve his defense program and reasserted his leadership in Western Europe after earlier failures. But the Berlin crisis ought to be considered a failure as well. The construction of the wall ended the crisis abruptly and without fanfare (Kiewe, 1994: 67). The Berlin Wall was a permanent fixture for decades and became symbolic of the cold war. More immediately, however, the Berlin crisis served as a prelude to the Cuban missile crisis a year later (Kiewe, 1994: 47).

MANAGING A POTENTIALLY RISKY CRISIS

After six years in office, President Ronald Reagan established his credentials as a master communicator. The affable Reagan, who gained the reputation of a "Teflon president," managed to get out of sticky situations with a rhetorical ease that few could match. Yet, when he faced the Iran-Contra crisis, Greg Dickinson notes, Reagan's rhetorical magic almost failed to produce the effect that he had previously relied on (in Kiewe, 1994: 155–77).

The inception of the crisis occurred on November 4, 1986, when the *Washington Post* reported on a Beirut magazine story about National Security Advisor Robert McFarlane's secret visit to Iran. The visit was connected with the shipment of arms to Iran and the later release of American hostage Donald Jacobsen. The following day, the *Washington Post* and the

New York Times gave front page coverage to the story. They both charged the Reagan administration with trading arms for hostages and thereby breaking a cherished American principle (Kiewe, 1994: 158–59).

A crisis had thus been constructed, and it required the president to address the issues. The sequence of rhetorical acts that Reagan employed are revealing of his crisis discourse. Reagan's initial response was to deny wrongdoing. In an address to the nation on November 13, 1986, Reagan denied the allegation of wrongdoing but not the facts of the crisis. His address was defensive and lacked the rhetorical features that usually characterized his speeches (Kiewe, 1994: 160–63). He ridiculed the many rumors surrounding McFarlane's visit to Iran and defensively countered, "Well, now you're going to hear the facts from a White House Source, and you know my name" (*Public Papers*, 1986: 1546). Reagan's sought to restore his seriously questioned credibility. He denied the arms-for-hostages deal and called it "false," but he rationalized the shipment of arms to Iran as an important and secret diplomatic initiative aimed at restoring stability to the Persian Gulf and peace to the Middle East. This covert initiative was now in jeopardy given its irresponsible exposure by the press. Releasing hostages, Reagan stated, was the least important objective of this initiative. But the address failed to allay public concerns about inappropriate, even illegal activities.

Realizing that the initial rhetorical strategy did not produce the sought results, Reagan addressed the nation again. On December 2, 1986, he promised to investigate the facts behind the allegations. Reagan acknowledged that certain unauthorized actions that disregarded his strong antiterrorism policy might have taken place (Kiewe, 1994: 164–65). The main feature of this action-oriented address was the appointment of the Tower Commission to probe into the allegations. In a radio address on December 6, Reagan admitted "that mistakes were made" (Reagan, *Public Papers*, 1986: 168). After the initial denial, a major rhetorical shift took place. Reagan now admitted the potential of mistakes and the need to probe into the allegations.

The Tower Commission report (February 1987), critical of Reagan's overall management style, detailed his lack of attention and his out-of-touch approach. The damaging report intensified the crisis. Polls indicated that many called on Reagan to resign, and others doubted the president's ability to do his job (Kiewe, 1994: 166). In a short but pointed address to the nation on March 4, 1987, Reagan resumed his old rhetorical features. He began by stating that after three months of silence while the commission had been investigating various allegations, it was now time to address the issue. He talked about the importance of the nation's trust in its president and the possibility that the trust had been damaged because of the length of his silence. Yet, he explained, he could not talk about the matter until the commission had presented its findings. With this short introduction,

"Reagan transformed the political crisis into a crisis of a nation's trust in him" (cited in Kiewe, 1994: 168). He declared his complete responsibility over actions taken in his behalf, including those actions taken without his knowledge. Responsibility but distance was the rhetorical strategy. Reagan expressed his "anger," "disappointment," and "distaste" over such actions. With words and phrases that included "responsibility," "accountable," "I am . . . the one who must answer to the American people," and "this happened on my watch," Reagan found the rhetorical formula to restore trust in him (*Public Papers*, 1987: 209). Reagan also presented a series of moves meant to ensure "compliance with American values" and that such actions would not be repeated (*Public Papers*, 1987: 210). Finally, in his familiar jovial style, Reagan acknowledged that "by the time you reach my age, you've made plenty of mistakes. And if you've lived your life properly—so, you learn. . . . You change. You go forward" (*Public Papers*, 1987: 210–11).

The last rhetorical phase was a success. The Reagan of old resumed his familiar rhetorical style. The strategy of admitting mistakes and restoring trust diffused a potentially risky crisis. The public reaction was approving and strong. Reagan's initial denial was most likely intuitive and commonplace. Once his denial carried no credibility, he was quick to understand that further denials could backfire. Unlike Nixon during Watergate, Reagan realized that once the denial was rejected, some measure of responsibility was the better rhetorical route, notwithstanding its ethical implications.

IMPLICATIONS

Crises are not alike. The inception of crises varies, their topicality is diverse, and their management attests to the rhetorical and political skills of a given president. For presidential scholars, the important consideration is the rhetorical nature of crises. A crisis come to life discursively by the participants in a public drama, whether they include the president, the public, and/or the press. Crises are communicative entities because the very term implies a perception of extraordinary events. The definitions of crises are rhetorical screens or lenses through which certain events are articulated. Crises are special events, distinct from the routine. The modern presidency, save for few exceptions, has transported the crisis tool into a convenient means instead of an end to be confronted. As illustrated in this chapter, some presidents take advantage of a crisis situation and exemplify superb leadership qualities, whereas others fail to respond properly to a critical situation. Some can find an opportunity in a crisis situation, and others manufacture a crisis. All situations and issues that presidents confront are conceivably prone to crisis manipulation.

Because crisis rhetoric is not altogether different from routine rhetoric, a generic configuration that divides crises into categories would do little in comprehending crisis situations. The distinction to be made, and thus the more proper test for assessing the viability and strategic use of presidential crisis rhetoric, is the ethical one. Regardless of the varied nature of the many crises that presidents confront, the essential question to ask is whether or not the crisis in question is ethical. In an ethical crisis, the nation's viability is clearly threatened, the consequences are detrimental, immediate actions are called for, urgency is clearly needed, the situations gain quick public legitimacy, and presidential leadership is acute. A manufactured crisis lacks these qualities because it smacks of opportunism of various sorts. Precisely for this reason—the perception of urgency and drama and the growing reliance on rhetorical means—the modern presidency has found crisis rhetoric an attractive formula for leadership. Like the analogy of the boy who cried wolf, too many wolf crises will blunt the nation's ability to recognize a real crisis when it arrives.

NOTES

1. Two of the four case studies are excerpted from my edited book, *The Modern Presidency and Crisis Rhetoric*: Enrico Pucci's chapter, "Crisis as Pretext: John F. Kennedy and the Rhetorical Construction of the Berlin Crisis," and Greg Dickinson's chapter, "Creating His Own Constraint: Ronald Reagan and the Iran-Contra Crisis."

2. The budget deficit was forecast to reach $350 billion, unemployment was at 7 percent, and about 10 percent of the population was on food stamps. See Andrew Tobias, "What George—and You—Should Do Next," *Time* (November 25, 1991), 67; *Washington Post* (January 31, 1992), A1.

REFERENCES

Bad news for Bush as poll shows national gloom. (1991, January 28). *New York Times*, p. A1.

Biles, R. (1991). *A new deal for the American people*. De Kalb: Northern Illinois University Press.

Burke, K. (1966). *Language as symbolic action: Essays on life, literature, and method*. Berkeley: University of California Press.

Bush, G. W. (1991, 1992). *Weekly compilation of presidential documents*. Washington, D.C.: U.S. Government Printing Office.

Bush, G. W. (1991). *Public Papers of the presidents of the United States*. Washington, D.C.: U.S. Government Printing Office.

Cherwitz, R. A., & Zagacki, K. (1986). Consummatory versus justificatory crisis rhetoric. *Western Journal of Speech Communication*, 50, 307–24.

A declaration of political war on the Democrats. (1992, January 29). *Washington Post*, p. A15.

Decoding Bush. (1992, February 10). *Newsweek*, p. 23.

Denton, R. E., Jr., and Woodward, G. C. (1990). *Political communication in America*. New York: Praeger.
Dow, B. J. (1989). The function of epideictic and deliberative strategies in presidential crisis rhetoric. *Western Journal of Speech Communication*, 53, 294–310.
Freidel, F. (1973). *Franklin D. Roosevelt: Launching the New Deal*. Boston: Little, Brown and Co.
Gusfield, J. D. (Ed.) (1989). *Kenneth Burke on symbols and society*. Chicago: University of Chicago Press.
Hart, R. P. (1987). *The sound of leadership: Presidential communication in the modern age*. Chicago: University of Chicago Press.
Houck, D. W. (1995). *Disability, deception and democracy: FDR's 1932 presidential campaign*. Unpublished dissertation, Pennsylvania State University, University Park.
Jamieson, K. H. (1992). *Dirty politics: Deception, distraction and democracy*. New York: Oxford University Press.
Kennedy, J. F. (1961). *Public papers of the presidents of the United States*. Washington, D.C.: U.S. Government Printing Office.
Kiewe, A. (1994). *The modern presidency and crisis rhetoric*. Westport, Conn.: Praeger.
Nichols, D. K. (1994). *The Myth of the modern presidency*. University Park: Pennsylvania State University Press.
Reagan, R. (1986, 1987). *Public papers of the presidents of the United States*. Washington, D.C.: U.S. Government Printing Office.
Rosenman, S. I. (Ed.) (1938). *The public papers and addresses of Franklin D. Roosevelt* (Vol. 2). New York: Random House.
The tinkerer. (1992, January 30). *New York Times*, A20.
Tugwell, R. G. (1972). *In search of Roosevelt*. Cambridge, Mass.: Harvard University Press.
Tulis, J. K. (1987). *The rhetorical presidency*. Princeton, N.J.: Princeton University Press.
Washington Post (1992, January 31), p. A1.
What George—and you—should do next. (1991, November 25). *Time*, p. 67.
Windt, O. T., Jr. (1973). The presidency and speeches on international crises: Repeating the rhetorical past. *Speaker and Gavel*, 2, 6–14.

CHAPTER 8

Discourse as a Stage for Political Actors: An Analysis of Presidential Addresses in Argentina, Brazil, and Venezuela

MARITZA MONTERO AND
ISABEL RODRIGUEZ-MORA

INTRODUCTION

This chapter analyzes the discourse of three Latin American presidents: Rafael Caldera (Venezuela, a Social-Christian), Fernando Henrique Cardoso (Brazil, a Social-Democrat), and Carlos Saul Menem (Argentina, supported by the Peronists), who were democratically elected in 1993, 1994, and 1989 with reelection in 1994, respectively. It examines the extent to which political discourse sets up a stage where certain actions and actors have the lead and others remain behind. This stage contains the limits of a reality presented in the discourse as the *truth*. Presidential addresses are the most suitable stage for displaying those features because they aim to present and justify certain policies, as well as to convince a national audience of their appropriateness and benefits.

METHOD

The corpus that is analyzed deals with the language used by social actors invested with social power by a significant position held within the state. The texts were chosen for their relevance, their mass media coverage in the respective countries considered, and their official character concerning each president's political line. The corpus contains discourses pronounced between 1990 and 1996 by the presidents of Argentina, Brazil, and Venezuela.

Discourses of Venezuelan president Rafael Caldera:

- Inaugural address. Published by the Presidential Office, Caracas, 1994. (IA)
- Address in the Presentation of the Social Development Programs. Central Bureau of Information, Caracas, July 11, 1994. (PSDP)

Discourses of Brazilian president Fernando Henrique Cardoso (FHC):

- "O Brasil está com rumo" [Brazil has direction]. Appeared in *Veja*, Vol. 1427, (3), January 17, 1996, pp. 20–27 (interview with FHC, conducted by Paulo Moreira Leite and Tales Alvarenga) (V).
- "FHC discute as consequencias da globalizacao" [FHC discusses the consequences of globalization]. Appeared in *Folha de Sao Paulo*, January 28, 1996, pp. 1–8 (address given in India) (FSP).
- Collective interview (complete transcription). Appeared in *O Estado de Sao Paulo*, January 18, 1996, pp. B-16–17 (OESP).

Discourses of Argentinean president Carlos Saul Menem:

- "Presidential Message to the Honorable Legislative Assembly at the beginning of its 108th period of ordinary sessions." Document of the Argentine Presidency, May 1, 1993 (DAP).
- "Address of President Carlos Saul Menem to the United Nations Conference on Environment." Rio de Janeiro, Brazil, June 12, 1992 (UNCE).
- "Argentina Protagonist of a New World." Buenos Aires, Argentina, Direccion General de Difusion. Secretaria de Medios de Comunicación. Presidencia de la Nacion, no date (NW).

A qualitative methodological procedure was followed, according to an hermeneutical approach (Gadamer, 1973), consisting of:

1. Selecting the texts according to their relevant character, to important moments of the presidencies, or to their repercussion in the media, and the diffusion given by the presidential offices.
2. Reading them several times and revising our "anticipatory project," that is, what we thought we might find, what we expected, and what the literature advised to expect.
3. Registering those aspects of the discourses that we thought made specific senses.
4. Registering and discussing rival projects elicited by the reading of the texts.
5. Agreeing in the sense ("unity of sense") of the discourse.
6. Constructing the dimensions for the interpretive analysis. Those dimensions were argumentative strategies used in the discourses; political actors referred to, distinguishing interlocutors and competitors, and allies and enemies; role of the political actors in terms of the activity or passivity attributed to them by the speaker.

7. Revising dimensions and concepts, as the research advanced. In this way the "hermeneutical circle" was closed.

The argumentative strategies were produced as analytical categories, through the deconstruction of the texts carried out during their reading. They consist of verbal social practices in which ways of imposing and/or instilling particular conceptions are presented in a favorable and convincing manner, in order to sustain a certain argumentation as if it were not subject to controversy or discussion (Montero, 1994).

BRIEF DESCRIPTION OF CONTENT OF THE TEXTS

Rafael Caldera: His inaugural address presents what he called his commitment with solidarity and points out the main lines that he planned to develop during his presidency. Those lines, defined in economic terms, consist of: an alternative to "neoliberal measures of economic adjustment," with a "social accent"; "national reconstruction"; stimulation of private investments, both national and foreign; ensuring institutional stability; promoting reactivation of productive sectors; and changing the "old system." The address about social development programs presents the main trends of the social development strategies of his government.

Fernando Henrique Cardoso (FHC): The analyzed interviews explain, defend, and justify his political line of action, mainly regarding economic and social measures, including the privatization process and the role played by some national and international organizations (commercial) linked to that process. In each interview, questions are presented by the journalists (a large group of them for the interview transcribed by O *Estado de Sao Paulo*, two in the case of *Veja*). The January 1996 address given in India presents his conception of the globalization process. In it, FHC discusses the different meanings of the term; its consequences, mainly the changes it has introduced in the role played by the state; political considerations about globalization, specifically referring to economic aspects (revising his previous theory about dependency); the problem of the exclusion and inclusion of certain nations, considering the positive and negative effects of globalization; and his conclusions that point out how globalization can be a field for international action and that present his idea of how that could be done through what he calls "the ethics of solidarity," briefly explained.

President Carlos Saul Menem: Menem's presidential address to Congress in 1990 (at the beginning of his first presidency) presents a balance of his actions and points out the main goals to be achieved: transforming Argentine from a populist system to a system of social and economic growth within the context of "humanized capitalism." He defines his conception of the people, defends what he calls his revolution, and exhorts Argentine to "stand up and walk." In the address to the United Nations Conference on the Environment in Rio de Janeiro, he speaks about the need to reconcile ecology and sustainable development, regulated by the market economy, which must be promoted in order to preserve the environment. The official presentation of Menem's presidency, published by the Communication Media secretariat of the Argentine Presidency, presents the "Argentine miracle," along with a balance of the productive revolution he claims to have carried out (the "Menem phenomenon"), expressed as: change of the people's mentality, based on a culture of speculation, for a new attitude based on investment; and building a new country with an efficient and modern government.

RESULTS

All quotations from the presidents' discourses are identified by the letters included at the presentation of each text as they appear in the Method section.

Argumentative Strategies

1. *Labeling.* As in the use given by the presidents to the adjective *democratic*, which becomes a means to turn democracy into an instrument or into a qualification.

Menem: Democratic society (DAP); democratic experiences that lead to economic growth (UNCE); democratic institutions (DAP, NW).
Caldera: Democratic Venezuela [meaning a historical period] (IA).
Cardoso: Democratic country (FSP, OESP).

2. *De-personalizing the Referent.* This strategy creates parameters defined by the speaker, where the other is present, but deprived of a specific identity. This type of reference to the other allows the speaker to position himself by contrast with what that other is saying, without assuming the political cost of confronting some specific actors and displacing the responsibility for the statement to them. This can be seen in the three presidents' discourses when they use the expression "those who . . . ," "some people . . . ," or "folks" (*la gente*), as can be seen in the following phrases:

Cardoso: People ought to be very objective about those things. [They should] not deny reality (OESP). Those people are not opposing the government; at the base it is [opposition] to themselves. They are losing their course. Probably those who defined it [his welfare policy] as a blunder never read a [government] proposal (OESP). Here in Brazil folks get nervous. They want you to run over the law in order to make a decision . . . (V).

Here Cardoso constructs and attributes an intention and, implicitly, associates the idea that while "folks" get nervous, he does not. This strategy is used to present consensus, or pressure groups, constructed by the speaker and subsequently criticized by him.

Caldera: There are those who think that in order to overcome the crisis we ought to declare a state of emergency and to implement a war economy, . . . (IA). There are those who have proposed, almost in a daring tone, that there is no alternative but to impose a rigid neoliberal orthodoxy besides dramatic adjustments . . . (IA).

Menem: Those who remain clinging to outdated dogmas (NW). Those who excluded themselves . . . (NW).

3. *Juxtaposition*. This strategy associates certain ideas in the discourse and places them together, one beside the other, in such a way that by transitivity, a statement acquires the attributes of the other, without the need for the speaker to establish directly the relationship.

Caldera: The country is needing a governing government. It needs an authority that orders the house within the State of Law. I am willing to provide for that (IA).

Cardoso: It is necessary that people be humble. I am (OESP).

Menem: A people's courage is also proved by the amount of truth they are capable of bearing. Because of that, today more than ever, I come to speak to all the Argentinean people with truth in my hand (DAP).

Menem's text juxtaposes two ideas: The first is courage by accepting truth. And the second is Menem as a source of truth; therefore, Menem is able to validate the people's courage. It also conveys the idea that if what Menem says is not accepted by the people, that shows a lack in them and displaces the fault toward them.

Juxtaposition also employs implicits, that is, the meaning of a phrase transcends certain explicit information, deriving from associations made by the addressees.

Cardoso: The leader of a democratic country has to listen. [He] cannot decide impulsively, in order only to please (OESP).

Cardoso is pointing out one of the characteristics of a good leader. Because he is the one stating it, implicitly, he introduces the idea that he possesses that asset. Moreover, he is giving a collective interview to the press; therefore, he is listening.

4. *Attribution of Passivity to the Other*. This is achieved by use of the passive voice and use of verbs expressing actions in which the subject is the object of the deeds of someone invested with the activity the object lacks. Also, metaphors of passivity, immobilization, and paralysis are used in this strategy.

For example, when referring to Argentina in his 1990 address, President Menem uses these metaphors:

We still suffer an Argentina with many cinders, with many painful wounds, with much smoldering debris.
A country enclosed in the vicious circle of speculation, institutional swindling and, decline.... Argentina has been infected by sick behaviors.... This dying country could not tolerate more adventurism of any persuasion.... This sick country is not cured with old medicines.... When I assumed the responsibility of ruling the destiny of my country, I made an invocation and a plea. I said: ARGENTINA, RAISE UP AND WALK (DAP).

Although he recognizes once (against eight references to stillness and decay), that Argentina is standing up, nothing in his discourse refers to mobility or activity in relation to the country.

Caldera also uses this type of image:

We want the survival of the small and medium enterprises (PSDP).

5. *Self-references in the Discourse.* These references are expressed in statements in which the presidents refer to themselves in the third person singular and to recognize their own figures as personages, celebrities, or main characters in a play.

Menem: The president of the Nation is ready to continue paying for all the political costs of the Argentinean ... [here there is not only a self-reference, but also Menem presents himself as the scapegoat for the Argentinean people, someone sacrificing himself]. Once more I must reiterate the nonrenounceable and nonmodifiable decision of the president of the Nation in this matter (DAP).

In Cardoso's discourse, there is another form of self-reference: use of the pronoun "you" as a hypothetical actor who expresses actions corresponding to the speaker's own way of doing:

You pilot day to day (V). You did the basic very well. Then you say: That must have a very positive effect (V). You have, then, to build an authority that is not a manager of the sector, but that only regulates and inspects (OESP).

This strategy allows the speaker to use that imaginary other as a mirror for his own ideas and actions and lets that hypothetical subject to enter the discourse, thus creating a not less imaginary possibility for actions while keeping the power and direction.

6. *Use of De-politicizing Terms and Choosing a Discursive Option That*

Evades Conflict. This can be seen in the care taken not to speak about social classes but, instead, to use words such as sectors or layers.

Menem: The humble; the more dispossessed; those who are simply hungry (DAP).

Caldera: We are suffering the effects of a deep crisis, that paradoxically, started twenty years ago, when reaching fairer prices for our main product, petroleum, brought an avalanche of money, that made us fall into the mistake of believing that we were very rich. That illusion of richness made us to commit infinite mistakes. Since then we have lived a process of confusion and disorientation, which produced extended moral corruption, and finally, created a state which in order to be overcome will need an intense and binding, national effort (IA).

In this paragraph, several strategies contribute to de-politicization: displacing responsibility from government to citizens, which are equally blamed for the crisis. In such a way, the state appears as one among the many sharing the blame. There is also a disempowered view of social actors, who suffer delusions, are deceived, and make mistakes. And at the same time, moral responsibility is affecting their behavior: confusion and disorientation reign. Thus, Venezuela's main product is pointed out as the culprit. So the source of wealth is actually the source of sorrow and misery. In such a way, corrupt administration by past governments vanishes. Moreover, the government is not leading the course of political events; they are the consequences of fateful forces linked to oil-produced riches.

7. *Presence of Deixis and Referentializations.* Deixis is present in phrases in which the speakers directly assume the responsibility for the statements. Referentialization is the strategy of displacing that responsibility to other agents or leaving it undetermined (i.e., "it is said," or "people say").

Deixis:

Menem: I, Carlos Saul Menem, President by the will and election of those who voted for me, and by the generous support of those who did not, affirm before the presence of this Honorable Congress and before the testimony of my people, that the Argentinean democracy has a social debt. What did I do, as president of the republic, to fulfill my duty, to defend the national interest, to interpret the clamor of my folks? (DAP)

Cardoso: But, with reserves going down and imports increasing, I had to restrain growth (V). I am going to fight.... I do not accept that (V). I do not want any more of the inflationary mentality (OESP).

Caldera: I am determined to achieve that the idea of generic medication becomes a reality. Because of that, indeed, I received in these days the Ambassador and a representative group of a country where this has been a major activity (PSDP).

Referentialization:

Caldera: What might be necessary to guarantee the devolution of their funds to the savers will be done (IA).

Menem: The option chosen was the hardest, the more complex, the more painful. ... May no one be mistaken. May no one be confused (DAP).

In Menem's discourse, 55 percent of the statements are referentialized. And of the remaining 45 percent, 58.9 percent use the first person plural. Only 18.4 percent of the total are presented in the first person singular. In Caldera's case, deixis predominates over referentializations (65 percent versus 35 percent, respectively). Both presidents use the first person singular and plural to point out the power of the speaker, but neither uses it with regard to his responsibility, nor to his commitment to specific actions. In Cardoso's discourse, the use of deixis (80 percent) also predominates over referentializations. Sixty percent are in first person singular, but, in contrast to Caldera's discourse, this feature reveals Cardoso's active engagement with his policies:

I am not satisfied by intellectual games. I like to build things, I like the street, constructions, farm fields (V).

Also, the same speaker can be an important referent for himself. As Bolivar (1995: 141–43) shows in her linguistic analysis of two of Caldera's interviews, self-reference is a characteristic of his discourse. It is present in his use of the first pronominal person, both singular and plural (I, we), explicitly (I say, we say) and implicitly. And it is also present in the use of a hypothetical speaker expressed by the pronoun "you" (Bolivar, 1995: 133) in relation to his possible or actual actions, a strategy equally used by president Cardoso in his discourse.

Declarative verbs predominate in Menem's discourse. In Caldera's discourse, state and declarative verbs have the same frequency (sixteen state verbs, fifteen declarative verbs), whereas action verbs have an insignificant presence (only five). In Cardoso's discourse, there is a prevalence of action and declarative verbs.

8. *De-population of Discourses*. This strategy consists of presenting actions without actors, as if the circumstances being described happen by themselves, without the intervention of a human agency. The statements present disembodied actions, thus constructing a deserted discourse. Politically, this strategy allows the speaker to maintain distance from the facts and from the decisions and their consequences; in this way, he or she is distant, passive, and detached from "reality," with no resources to intervene directly in its course. This strategy is very prominent in Caldera's discourse, as can be seen in the following example:

The announcements presented five years ago concerning the reconversion of the productive system in order to turn it into a competitive one, did not result as promised (IA).

9. *Circumscription of Actions to Their Perceptual Levels*. The discourse refers to changes at the perceptive and cognitive levels (intentions, wishes, beliefs) and substitutes "concrete" doings. Again, this strategy allows the speaker to talk about certain phenomena without assuming any commitment, decision, or responsibility, although apparently addressing them. In fact, this impedes the establishment of specific standards of achievement that could be used to contrast the speaker's action. Once more, this is present in Caldera's discourse:

We will do whatever is possible and impossible to evidence the government concern about this (IA).

In this statement, what is offered is the possibility of perceiving a state of mind, not concrete actions. Caldera's discourse is abundant in verbs, such as to see, to aspire, to feel, to intend, and to expect, conjugated in conditional future tense:

This requires a great effort, and we could be in the disposition to make it (PSDP).

Political Actors

The number of actors or protagonists that seem to be present in a text is limited. Political actors mentioned in the discourses are those who carry on an action or are affected by it. They may be executing or receiving it. In Caldera's discourse, there are 27 actors and in Menem's, 17. Cardoso's discourse is far richer; he refers to 39 categories of actors. He also mentions by name many ministries, governors, and consultants in his government, as well as many groups within civil society (e.g., families, mothers, the Left, workers, bankers).

We also identified in the discourses the active or passive character of the actors. The criterion for such a differentiation was the above-mentioned consideration about their relation with actions. The three presidents include themselves as actors in an active way. Caldera refers to 14 passive actors (country, everyone, masses, slum dwellers, civil society, the Pope, and almost anyone who is not in the government); he acknowledges the active character of Congress, communities, Army, neoliberals and, of course, himself and is ambivalent about youth, Venezuelans and ministries. For Menem, most actors are active, but passive actors include the people and those he criticizes. Cardoso sees the middle class, the poor, the elderly, the landless, the people, mothers, families, and children as passive.

Self-references expressed by the use of deixis, both in first person singular and in first person plural, or by directly alluding to themselves by name, as in the case of Menem (I, Carlos Saul Menem . . .), places the presidents as main actors and central protagonists of their discourses. As supporting actors appear, their countries, a variety of sectors of society, congressmen, the state, the government, and, in general, those clearly supporting the speakers or important for their political lines are not to be ignored or diminished. Finally, the stagehands or "extras" are those present who do not play a visible or fundamental role: the people, the poor, and some specific sectors of society.

Some political actors are mentioned by the speakers as interlocutors; others are presented as opponents or viewed as allies or enemies. Table 8.1 presents the actors considered as interlocutors by Presidents Caldera, Cardoso, and Menem and shows if their references to them are direct or indirect. Direct references are those statements in which the speaker explicitly directs his message to someone, placing that actor vis-à-vis with himself. Indirect references have to be inferred from the grammatical construction of the text. As can be seen from the table, the three presidents' discourses present almost the same amount of direct and indirect interlocutors.

Table 8.2 presents the allies, opponents, and enemies explicitly mentioned in the discourses. Allies and opponents represent the positive and negative others in a political project. The reference to enemies pre-supposes their exclusion from a political project. With opponents, a dialogue can be established and power shifts can be achieved, whereas enemies are not recognized as valid interlocutors but are considered a threat to the political system. In the discourses analyzed, there is scarce mention of enemies, which could mean that these presidents feel secure and able to establish dialogues with any recognized interlocutors.

An interesting aspect concerning President Menem's discourse is the possessive references he makes to the people and the country (my people, my country), thus enlarging his sphere of influence while separating from his people and his country those who oppose him or are out of his political reach.

Democracy

Democracy appears as an adjective, as an aggregate used to label a variety of features of society. In Caldera's and Cardoso's texts, direct references to the concept are absent. Cardoso refers to the Asian "tigers" as an economic success but adds immediately that they "are not democratic," whereas "Brazil has already a democratic society." Therefore, Brazil is a democratic country.

This use of *democratic* as a qualification does not fill the void, but it serves to cancel out any discussion about it. At the same time, it implicitly conveys the meaning that the speaker's society is a democracy. In Menem's discourse it is presented neither as an organizing frame for society nor as a governmental system. It is only an attribute, among others, characterizing the country, used to attract investments and induce trust.

Table 8.1
Interlocutors

RAFAEL CALDERA			F.H. CARDOSO			CARLOS MENEM		
INTERLOCUTOR	D[1]	I[2]	INTERLOCUTOR	D	I	INTERLOCUTOR	D	I
Rafael Caldera	■		Foreign countries and leaders			Argentina		■
Folks		■	Government, ministers, ministry	■		Government		■
Sectors of society	■		Brazilian state governments	■		The State		
Venezuelans	■		The landless leaders			Argentineans	■	
Neo-liberals	■		Brazil, the country			The opposition		■
National Armed Forces	■		Diverse sectors of society			Inhabitants	■	
God			Bankers			Congress		
Youth			Congressmen, legislators		■	Brothers and sisters of my homeland	■	
Judicial, legislative power & "other branches" of public powers	■		Folks, everyone, those who, the opposition			Everyone		
Religious authorities	■		Political parties		■	All of the Argentinean people	■	
Workers & entrepreneurs			The poor		■	Leadership of my homeland	■	
Physicians		■	Workers, employees		■			
			Industrial and financial sectors, business managers		■			
			The people, population	■				
			Citizenry, civil society					

[1]Direct.
[2]Indirect.

Source: Montero & Rodriguez, 1996.

Table 8.2
Allies, Opponents, and Enemies

	ALLIES	OPPONENTS	ENEMIES
CALDERA	Everyone Folks God All sectors of national life The youth The people The National Armed Forces	No opponents mentioned	No enemies mentioned
CARDOSO	Ministers National and international organizations Brazilian state governments Southern countries Brazilian enterprises and industries Trade unions Allies Foreign leaders	Those who..., some people, folks Some groups Certain sectors and social layers The private sector Folks Some political parties Some sectors of political parties The opposition Banks Bankers The landless Leaders of the landless Trade unions The press The Congress Destabilizing groups Brazilian elite	No enemies mentioned
MENEM	The great majority of the people The U.S.A.	Created interests Those still clinging to outdated dogma Opposition	Fidel Castro's regime Corruption

Source: Montero & Rodriguez, 1996.

[T]he most southern republic of the world is now a recipient of confidence and waves of investment, sheltered by a strong and independent democracy (DAP).

Menem's discourse separates his actions as president from the course followed by democracy, as if both were independent.

About Values

Two common characteristics of the corpus analyzed are (1) predominance of instrumental (e.g., order, security, health, fiscal order) over terminal values (e.g., freedom, social justice and harmony, peace), and (2) articulation of discourse around values related to economic processes. Examples of the latter are confidence for investment, economic reliability, and productivity (Caldera); participation in global economy, administrative reforms, service of public debt, and balance of payment (Cardoso); and integration through market, investment, monetary stability, production, fiscal order, and growth (Menem). These values appear as the axes of other values presented in the discourses.

CONCLUSIONS

As Ghiglione (1989: 9) says, in Western democratic societies, politics became a public spectacle. But even in those not so democratic and not so Western, it is the same. Politics are staged every day in multiple scenes provided by the media. Political discourses are carefully prepared to inform or to answer, directly or indirectly, certain interlocutors. Through their phrases and paragraphs, cross-political actors perform, according to the speaker, many deeds and misdeeds. In them, we find, as in the theater, main actors, supporting actors, and stagehands. We find monologues created to be heard by large audiences, occulting dialogues, and even conversations to be understood only after reading the multiplicity of discourses running in print and shown on audiovisual media, and determining the identity of the main addressees. Why does Argentinean President Carlos Menem, in an official brochure published by the Media Office of the Presidency (Secretaria de Medios de Comunicación, Presidencia de la Nacion), expressly state that Fidel Castro's regime is an enemy? To whom is directed that information? To the Argentinean people, among whom exists a multiplicity of opinions about the Cuban government or where no opinion at all might be found? To the tourists or the researchers interested in Argentina? Or, more likely, to the U.S. government imposing an embargo on Cuba? This, and the following conclusions, present what Antaki (1994: 187) calls the speaker's own practices, as shown through the argumentative strategies used by the current presidents of Argentina, Brazil, and Venezuela:

In brief, from our analysis we conclude:

1. The discourses analyzed show the three presidents' versions of politics and what they consider its main political actors, its supporting actors, and stagehands (political subjects in charge of preparing the stage for those who are considered protagonists). The three presidents place themselves as the heroes or positive protagonists. Caldera and Menem are the sole main actors in their discourses. Self-reference seems to be an important ingredient in presidential discourses, but it reaches its peak, as well as its poorest, expression in Caldera's discourses, where self-references and deixis dominate while, at the same time, that strategy de-populates his speeches and leaves him almost alone. God and the armed forces are recognized as his only explicit and active allies although he counts on "folks," "people," "youth," and a generic "everyone." But none of them has in his discourse as central a position as himself.

    Cardoso's discourse is the richest one in reference to political actors—not only different regions of Brazil, but local government, enterprises, a variety of social sectors, and public and private institutions (see Table 8.1). His discourse also reveals that, besides himself as main actor, he has a team (ministries, consultants) to whom he manifestly gives support and praise. At the same time, the discourses of all three presidents attribute activity and passivity according to the speakers' conceptions of society and their members. Thus, the people, the poor, the citizenry in all of the discourses analyzed are always presented as passive, recipients of the main actor's actions.

2. Democracy is predominantly presented as equivalent to the status quo, to the state of the societies where the discourses were produced. Democracy is assimilated with the qualities of those countries as they are perceived by the speakers, and it is constructed in the discourses as a means, with an instrumental value, qualifying certain social objects (i.e., institutions, countries).

3. There is no allusion in the discourses to a possible future defined in political terms (the death of Utopia). The idea of a perfect market is implicitly presented as a reality and as the condition for the display of freedom. Liberty is considered an individually acquired state, but it is absent as a concept or as a value in President Caldera's discourse.

4. Society is characterized in nonconflictive terms and integrated by a diversity of sectors that are supposed to have, or at least should have, the same access to the market but are more or less passive according to their wealth (more wealth, more activity). The condition of having free access to economic relations (market economy) is equivalent to freedom in the sense that it means the existence of a free society.

5. Instrumental values predominate in the discourses, and the discourses show coincidences among them regarding investment and the benefits of market economy. They also show the peculiarities of each president's relation with his country.

6. The discourses place the speakers in reference to their societies. Cardoso's discourse reveals the expert and the head of a team. Menem is the savior of his homeland, the physician curing an ailing country and reviving it. Caldera detaches himself from the people who elected him and places himself as the only—lonely and aloof—inhabitant of his discourse, above his country and all other possible political actors.
7. Discourse, as shown in the analysis, is constructed by the use of argumentative strategies: juxtaposition, labeling, self-reference, depersonalizing the other, attribution of passivity, de-politicization in terms used, deixis and referentialization, de-population, and predominance of the perceptual and cognitive levels of action.

REFERENCES

Antaki, C. (1994). *Explaining and arguing*. London: Sage.

Bolivar, A. (1995). La autorreferencia en la practica discursiva de Rafael Caldera [Self-reference in the discursive practice of Rafael Caldera]. In C. Kohn (Ed.), *Discurso politico y crisis de la democracia. Reflexiones desde la filosofia social, la etica y el analisis del lenguaje* [Political discourse and democracy crisis: Reflections from social philosophy, ethics, and language analysis]. Caracas: Cuadernos de Postgrado.

Gadamer, H. G. (1973). *Verite et method* [Truth and method]. Paris: Editions du Seuil.

Ghiglione, R. (1989). Preambule [Preface]. In R. Ghiglione (Ed.), *Je vous ai compris. Ou l'analyse des discours politiques* [I understood you. Or the analysis of political discourses] (pp. 9–16). Paris: Armand Colin.

Montero, M. (1994) Estrategias discursivas ideologicas [Ideological discursive strategies]. In M. Montero (Ed.), *Conocimiento, realidad e ideologia* [Knowledge, reality and ideology] (pp. 49–61). Caracas: Avepso.

CHAPTER 9

The Method of Argumentation of Jean-Marie Le Pen, Leader of the French Extreme Right Wing, in an Important Political Television Program

SIMONE BONNAFOUS

INTRODUCTION

The discourse of Jean-Marie Le Pen has been the subject of many studies. Some of the more interesting titles (translated from the French) are Jean-Paul Honore's (1986) "The Hierarchy of Sentiments: The Description and Presentation of the French and the Immigrant in the Discourse of the National Front," and several publications by P. A. Taguieff, including his article, "The Rhetoric of National-Populism: The Basic Rules of Xenophobic Propaganda" (1984); his contribution to the collection of essays "Discovering the Front National" (Mayer & Perrineau, 1996); and his edited volume (Taguieff, 1991), "Faced with Racism." During the course of this chapter, I refer to these and other, more general works on the ideology and themes of the extreme right wing, of which many have appeared.

My intention is to contribute to the works referred to above, all of which share a common cross-sectional approach to the Le Pen discourse, through the consideration of many texts and speeches that constitute a stratum for the analysis of identitarian ideology (Honore, 1985), demagogic rhetoric (Taguieff, 1984), or racist arguments. Even though these analyses are fruitful and pertinent, two essential factors of political discourse—the discursive chain of reasoning and processes of interaction—are left aside. I argue that the force of the Le Pen discourse is not only the result of his themes or rhetoric (i.e., in the sense of images and figures) or of accumulation of each and every argument, but rather of his ability to integrate all of these elements into an argumentative structure adapted to a specific context and a specific audience. I examine my thesis here through an analysis of Le Pen's presentation during the television program 7/7 aired on February 26, 1995.

The 7/7 program is one of the most-watched political discussion programs in France. It is, however (with the exception of Leroux, 1993), one of the least analyzed programs. The February 26, 1995, presentation perfectly illustrates Le Pen's ability to make all elements of his argument serve the most traditional extreme right wing themes and rhetoric. Similarly, it shows his talent in presenting an image of himself as a serious, poised, and reasonable presidential candidate.

More than any other party, the National Front faces two apparently contradictory imperatives: (1) to respond to the expectations of the most loyal factions of its electorate, particularly its militants; and (2) to expand its audience by attracting new voters. Because the presidential election is one of the most personalized elections in France, the image presented by a candidate is extremely important. Various opinion polls have shown, however, that for many years, National Front votes have been cast more on the basis of agreement with the program or values of the movement than on an account of Le Pen himself or his ability to make a good president of the republic (Soudais, 1996). In the context of this election period, the central issue for Le Pen was his personal image as a candidate.

The 7/7 program of February 26, 1995, consisted of two parts. During the first, preceding the commercial break, Le Pen is interviewed alone; during the second part, Le Pen and Brice Lalonde, president of the Generation Ecologie Party, are interviewed together. My analysis in this chapter relates only to the first part of the program. I demonstrate how (1) Le Pen initially tried to exonerate the accusations of racism and violence made against his movement through a specific, argumentative technique; (2) he made use of news events and common places in order to proceed in his usual denunciation of the political establishment; and (3) he eventually presented a dressed-up political program apparently based on common sense, facts, and the defense of the least privileged members of French society. I conclude with an analysis of the interactions between Le Pen and Gérard Carreyrou, which resulted in an advantageous image for the leader of the National Front.

REFUTING ACCUSATIONS OF VIOLENCE AND RACISM

"Whether one likes it or not, the extreme right wing is heretical," Le Pen himself noted in his book, *Les Français D'abord* (The French First), his political platform published in 1984 (cited in Soudais, 1996: 150). On this basis, he refused to be labeled "extreme right wing," as he wrote in a letter sent to various newspapers on January 31, 1995. Unlike "the leagues and Fascist movements of the pre-war period," he wrote, the National Front is not characterized by the refusal of democracy and elections, the call to violence, racism, and the desire to establish a single party in France (cited in Soudais, 1996: 150).

Le Pen probably was not surprised, therefore, to be asked about the image of violence associated with his movement during the first few minutes of 7/7. The comments by a Frenchman in the street were immediately taken up by Carreyrou, who referred to "the murder of Ibrahim Ali, a young, seventeen-year-old Comorian, who was shot in the back by two people putting up National Front posters, who have since been charged and imprisoned."

Faced with such a direct attack, the leader of the National Front now had to present counterarguments based on precise and established facts. These arguments should differ from his racist and xenophobic accusations and his usual strategies of refutation and counterrefutation (Honore, 1986). Because Le Pen could not choose the context, he practiced the strategy (Perelman, 1970) of disputing the interpretation. Le Pen sought to review the facts, which included a victim, the young Comorian, and two assailants, militant members of the National Front. He argued that the three young people were all "victims of the atmosphere which reigns in the suburbs and generates fear, anxiety, anguish, and sometimes actions of self-defence." Later he even specified:

I think they are all victims; it was an incident of self-defence. It was about people who were armed, wrongly, in a northern district at night, in their own area, I remind you, the billstickers' district in which, as we well know, there is a great deal of tension linked to the immigration phenomenon.

Thus, one comes full circle to the conclusion that the young Comorian is the victim of his own presence. This occurs before responsibility can be attributed for the crime:

In this instance I want to condemn those who call themselves lovers of justice, who have led the protest demonstrations and who are responsible for the policy which has brought ten million immigrants to our country in the space of twenty years.

Le Pen's strategy again reveals the central role of "argumentation of causality" in political rhetoric. In particular, he uses "the bias of complacency" (Gosselin, 1995). Le Pen exonerates himself by making his adversaries, in this case the traditional political establishment, responsible for "an unfortunate state of affairs."

Three conclusions can be drawn from his performance when one focuses on his redescription of the facts:

1. Le Pen is not innovative from the point of view of argumentative technique. His reinterpretation and redescription of facts, the dissociation of "reality" (three victims of the immigration policy) with "appearance" (a Comorian victim of two National Front militants) are old, well-known methods (Perelman, 1970).

2. Redescription of facts, including those concerned with racist violence, is a common method of the extreme right wing (Bonnafous, 1991). This technique, practiced in both speeches and the written press, is part of a series of *pret-a-porter* (a term from the French fashion world that means *practical*) arguments Le Pen and his lieutenants (the candidates themselves) advance, when necessary, for each violent incident committed against an immigrant (Birenbaum & François, 1987; Miller, 1992). This method of argumentation makes innocent those who act violently against immigrants. Because immigration, rather than immigrants, is denounced, it provides no opportunity for accusations of racism or xenophobia. Further, it allows the National Front to criticize traditional political parties.
3. The argumentative turnaround allows the accused to become the accuser. It is based on a number of presuppositions (the atmosphere of the suburbs) (Mouchon, 1995: 188) and received ideas (the environmental effects that deny all individual responsibility) (Amossy, 1994) that are not limited to the ranks of the National Front.

Le Pen's great skill is to support the brunt of his argument with an image of the suburbs that resembles the images found in mass media (Mouchon, 1995), in films (like *La Haine* by Kassovitz [1995] or *Hexagone* by Chibane [1994], or in the words of politicians (Jaques Chirac interview, *Liberation*, October 30, 1984; Birenbaum & François, 1987). Innumerable examples illustrate this claim, such as articles in *L'evenement du Jeudi* (1995) about the suburbs ("Hatred in Mureaux, in Noisy le Grand, or elsewhere... Autopsy of an Ordinary Riot," June 15–21, 1995). The headlines are often extreme: "The abandonment of the suburbs to unemployment, delinquency and ultimately to Islamism has opened the way to terrorism" (September 21–27, 1995) (Bonnafous, 1997). It was indeed to this old stigmatic notion of the cutthroat suburbs (the worker slums in big cities) that Le Pen referred. From an objective perspective, it is obvious that this vision reflects only part of reality and that there are also suburbs where the living is good.

CRITICIZING THE CORRUPTION OF THE FIFTH REPUBLIC

Later during the television program, Carreyrou asked Le Pen about the "news" of the last few weeks: telephone bugging at the Elysée, Central Intelligence Agency spies, and the Schuller-Marechal affair (a complex affair of political embezzlement). These events and their presentation by Carreyrou were a gift for Le Pen. There was no need for him to "re-frame" because the synopsis of the events concerned his political adversaries, both the Socialists and the Gaullists. This was a comfortable situation for the Front leader to exploit, not by discrediting any specific person but by including the whole political establishment in the disgrace. Le Pen, encouraged by Carreyrou to attack Minister of Interior Charles Pasqua, immediately qualified his argument. "But I should like to add that it is not only Monsieur Pasqua who is involved in this affair," Le Pen said. He added:

This scandal is just one amongst many millions of others. And if they are now being revealed at a rate of two or three a week, they only represent—the citizens should know this—the tip of the iceberg, there is in fact a huge part underneath that is left to be seen. The fifth Republic is profoundly and structurally corrupt.

In relation to the bugging in the Elysée, Le Pen stated:

This is a super-Watergate which could even set off a super-Chernobyl if there was a political opposition worthy of its name and not held tightly in check while . . . In other words, there is a kind of neutralization of the political establishment. Each of the parties has the same interest in letting some things be known, but not everything however, for fear that the country be disgusted by the widespread corruption.

The originality of Le Pen's method of argument is not the result of amalgamation and generalization (these are most common in political discourse, the press, and everyday conversation), but appropriation of this technique to criticize "corruption" of the political establishment. With an old populist tradition (Sternhell, 1978) as his leitmotiv ("the great spring cleaning of our institutions and our political body"), Le Pen justified his candidature as supreme magistrate on September 18, 1994 for a Sixth Republic.

According to a poll realized during the presidential elections of 1995 (Le Gall, 1996), 79 percent of the French believe that the law does not equitably punish ordinary people and those with connections; 64 percent believe that governments understand nothing about the problems of people "like us"; and two French people out of three think that most leaders are corrupt. It is unlikely that all of the French people who criticize the political establishment because of corruption would follow the conclusions drawn by Le Pen, which would mean a change of republic and the replacement of the traditional political members by those of the National Front. However, it may well be the strategy of the National Front to erode, little by little, the limits of what is thinkable and what can be said in the public realm.

THE ARGUMENT OF DEMAGOGY

A discussion of three aspects of the definition given for Le Pen's political program during the 7/7 television program follows.

A Euphemized Demagogic Program

Le Pen's political program is resumed in three measures: the expulsion of three million immigrants, the desengagement from the European Union, and the "suppression" of income taxes. No effort is asked of the French, in general or in particular, because responsibility for the problems of France lies with the immigrant, Europe, or the revenue service. Le Pen kept silent on all issues that are potentially problematic for some television viewers including the incitement for women to leave their jobs, easing of regulations concerning work hours, an increase in taxes on goods, the abeyance of direct inheritance rights, and limiting of social security to a minimum. The rejection of the immigrant, often justified in National Front texts in relation to the invasion of Islam, the incompatibility of cultures, or the degeneration of the French nation as a result of mixed marriages, appears to be motivated by economic concerns. This is the famous thesis of "national preference," one of the names of racism (Schnapper, 1995). It says: "Let's keep the privilege of jobs, housing and social security benefits for the French, and then everything will be all better."

A Manipulative Argument

The 7/7 program does not encourage political argument; the interviewed politician does not address a real opposition. Le Pen, therefore, indulged gleefully in a parody of arguments: pragmatic arguments, causal or reciprocal arguments, syllogisms, and reference to scientific authority relating to evidence and examples. He justified his political program with "obvious truths," which were, in fact, always debatable, uncertain, and partial at the best, or downright lies at the worst.

Here are a few examples:

(1) If we lower income taxes, this would progressively boost the economy and redistribute wealth. Since the lowering of income will enable people to invest or spend, money will hence either enter into the investment circuit or into the circuit of redistribution and economic stimulation.

Behind "since," two omissions are hidden: one relates to the increase in taxes on goods, which the National Front platform (*Trois cent mesures pour la renaissance de la France*, 1993) supports and which would hit the working classes the hardest by far—their income, incidentally, is not taxed heavily—and the other relates to the financing of public services that are so essential to this social group.

(2) Of course it was necessary to find a place for these immigrants in a country in which, in 1974, there were already a million immigrants. For it is entirely obvious

that when an immigrant comes to our country, in which there is unemployment, if he takes a job, he is taking the job of a French [worker]. If he does not find a job, he lives off French workers all the same, he and his family that is.

The tone of affirmation is a poor disguise for the fragility of the argument which, in the case of this particular point concerning the jobs held by immigrants on their arrival in France, has been disproved time and again (Taguieff, 1991).

(3) I would like to know how Monsieur Pasqua forces people out of national borders since they have been removed.

This is a pseudosyllogism, based on personal experience:

(4) Every month I travel to Brussels and Germany and I never see any customs officers or policemen.

Here, flagrant untruths are noticed because the press has talked about Pasqua's charter planes sufficiently for everyone to be aware that expulsions take place in the countries of origin, not at the French border.
All of these arguments are accompanied by statistical references to justify the policy of expelling immigrants. There is an enormous and unverifiable inflation of figures, (e.g., immigration costs 250 billion francs per year) that aim at the accumulation of the number of immigrants over several decades, the assimilation of unemployment and immigration figures, and so on.
As for illustrations, comparisons, and metaphors, they try to convince and seduce through their magic formulas rather than on the basis of accuracy. Thus, in a "factual" discourse, analogies between the nation and either the family or employment mix worlds of different orders. On the legal level, one belongs to constitutional laws, whereas the others belong to civil or labor laws. Although they are politically false, these analogies are used to justify, for example, the National Front proposal to expel immigrants ("Monsieur Carreyrou, if someone wants to come to your house and stay, you would accept that fact. Well, I, President of the French Republic...") or the slogan national preference ("as protector of the labor union of the French, the labor union of natives, I consider that they have a right to their home and to be given a priority at this home with their own money").

Exploiting "l'air du temps" (The Social Atmosphere)

In this sequence, Le Pen exploited the social atmosphere and emotional responses of his listeners. Since 1996, economic and social arguments have been emphasized in the National Front propaganda; unemployment becomes "the most serious and dangerous social problem for the future of our country." Thus is introduced the policy of expelling immigrants, instead of through the more metaphysical National Front rhetoric (i.e., mixed-blood (metissage) and de-culturation) (Taguieff, 1991). Although the word "worker" is used less and less frequently in political discourse, reference is made to "French workers," "two million heavily indebted families," and "the lack of public housing." These arguments probably convinced part of the working class electorate, particularly because at the same time, another candidate was campaigning on the theme of "social fracture."

Carreyrou is not an adversary of Le Pen. He served to offset the National Front leader, who depended on his aggressiveness and verbal excesses in order to construct an image of himself as a serene democrat.

CONSTRUCTING AN IMAGE OF DEMOCRATIC RESPECTABILITY

Le Pen contrasts two styles of public discourse: on the one hand, solemnly declaring democratic respectability, and, on the other hand, provoking the media, throwing scandalous propositions at the audience, and forcing political agents to react and journalists to comment (Taguieff, 1991). My hypothesis about the 7/7 program of February 26, 1995, says that Le Pen uses a well-polished strategy that consists of verbally bouncing off the journalist, who becomes the aggressive one, in bad faith and contrasting the journalist's image with the image of a calm and collected democrat.

Is Le Pen usually criticized for inciting violence and contesting the foundations of the republican order? He will give lessons in legality. The National Front leader adopted procedures similar to those used by politicians or company presidents who were—for some time—under investigation, and who have criticized the media for transforming the accused into guilty parties. He implicitly accused Carreyrou, along with the media and the political establishment, of judging the murder case of the young Comorian in advance. He then proceeded to do what he criticizes others for doing and thus concluded: "Concerning the event itself, there is not a person with a heart who would not be touched by the death of a young man and who would not share the suffering of his parents. That is one thing. The incurred responsibilities are of another nature and it is the legal investigation and the law which will decide. But I tell you, here and now, that the National Front is not implicated."

Is Le Pen usually accused of minimizing racist attacks? He speaks of "serious accidents which led to the death of a young man." He thereby enjoyed the chance to comment ironically on Carreyrou's lack of attention when Carreyrou asked, "Don't you think that in speaking about incidents, you are actually behind what took place?" Le Pen replied, "I said accident, but you heard incidents." At the end of this exchange, the roles were inverted; Le Pen is a man who weighs his words, whereas Carreyrou became a devious and intolerant interlocutor. This entire interaction contributed to the image of a victim of the media that Le Pen cultivates. When, for example, they discussed the National Front political program, Carreyrou adopted the citational strategy of "the confession" (Mouillaud & Tetu, 1989), which consists of attributing comments to the other that would work against him. And each time, Le Pen caught him on it, for instance, in their dialogue relating to immigration:

Carreyrou: Mr. Le Pen, let's talk in concrete terms, you would like to expel three million immigrants over how many years, five, seven? . . . That means hundreds of thousands per year. That means tens of thousands per month. Explain to me how you would do this, Mr. Le Pen.

Le Pen: They have come, they can very well leave.

Carreyrou: You would open up concentration camps to concentrate them.

Le Pen: Yeah, right, with the SS and dogs . . . this can be done . . . by a whole series of measures which do not have the caricatural character you have described with the concentration camps.

Carreyrou: You know what concentration means. It means to concentrate in one space.

Le Pen: I also know what the image of a concentration camp evokes.

Here, Le Pen does not confuse etymology and semiology. He has learned his lessons well from the bad press following his previous declarations about camps and gas chambers.

CONCLUSION AND DISCUSSION

The force of Le Pen as a debater is the result of a combination of at least three elements, which I studied separately, although they are intimately linked: (1) diverting of the usual argumentative techniques to the advantage of a manipulative strategy, which consists in framing a debatable claim as one founded on reason and common sense; (2) considerable skills in playing off generally accepted ideas and current stereotypes; and (3) a great capacity to handle interlocutive standoff and to thwart the traps of his interlocutor, which makes his image more advantageous.

The strength and the danger of Le Pen's argumentation is therefore, in my opinion, the consequence of a surprising association of two aspects of political discourse which are a priori antithetical. The first is the pamphleteer aspect. Angenot (1982) defines pamphleteer "discourse as discourse of ideological rupture that follows sudden ruptures in the social field between a set of values and concrete practices." Moreover, "his discourse is based on principles ensured in the law by his adversary, which he betrays." Le Pen criticizes the claim of the elite and the political establishment to embody the values of France and proposes an ethical and political restoration. One can also find in Le Pen's discourse what Angenot (1982) describes as "appeal to feelings," "real-life experience," "eye-witnessing," or relying on "figures of inversion."

The second aspect is dialogic. Contrary to what Angenot writes about the *exotopos* of pamphleteers, such as Georges Bernanos and Louis-Ferdinand Celine, who asserted their ideological marginality and enclosed themselves in narcissistic isolation, in which no addressee whatsoever was acceptable to them, Le Pen situates himself at the very center of the world that he wishes to transform. Attentive to the "putting into words" and the "worlds of others," in the terms of François (1994: 16), he constructs his argument in a dialectical interaction with dominant representations, sometimes relying on them and at other times subverting them. He does the same with his direct interlocutor, Carreyrou, who becomes a veritable partner in the construction of his discourse and image.

Le Pen is both a pamphleteer and a polemicist (Angenot, 1982). His discourse has the force of the pamphlet (amalgamations, assertions, obvious observations, argumentative inversions, denunciations, circularity, and upsets). But it also has the flexibility of polemical discourse because it plays on the beliefs and formulas of others in order to impose his own.

REFERENCES

Amossy, R. (1994). Les dessous de l'argumentation dans le débat politique télévisé [Beneath the argument in televised political debates]. *Littérature*, 93, 31–47.

Angenot, M. (1982). *La parole pamphlétaire* [The words of satirical pamphlets]. Paris: *Payot*.

Birenbaum, G., & François, B. (1987, December). Le Front National joue les ambiguïtés [The national front playing with ambiguity]. *Projet*, p. 208.

Bonnafous, S. (1991). *L'immigration prise aux mots* [Immigration taken in words]. Paris: Editions Kimé.

Bonnafous, S. (1996). La gestion de l'incertain par les médias contemporains dans la crise yougoslave [The method of dealing with uncertainty of the contemporary media in the Yugoslav crisis]. *Mots*, 47, 7–21.

Bonnafous, S. (1997). Òu sont passés les immigrés? [Where have the immigrants gone?]. *Cahiers de la Méditerranée moderne et contemporaine.*

Chibane, M. (1994). *Hexagone* [Hexagon] (Film). Paris: Ciné Classic (distributor).

François, F. (1994). *Morale et mise en mots* [Morality and words]. Paris: L'Harmattan.

Gosselin, A. (1995). Les attributions causales dans la rhétorique politique [Causal attributions in political rhetoric]. *Hermes*, 16, 153–66.

Honore, J. P. (1985, April). Jean-Marie Le Pen et le Front National: Description et interprétation d'une idéologie identitaire [Jean-Marie Le Pen and the National Front: A description and interpretation of an identitarian ideology]. *Les Temps Modernes*, 465.

Honore, J. P. (1986). La hierarchie des sentiments: Description et mise-en-scène du Français et de l'immigré dans le discours du Front National [The hierarchy of sentiments: The description and presentation of the French and the immigrant in the discourse of the National Front]. *Mots*, 12, 129–57.

Kassovitz, M. (1995). La Haine [Hatred] (film). France: MKV pour Lazonnec Diffusion.

Le Gall, Gerard (1996). "La tentation du populisme" [The Temptation of demagogy]. *L'état de l'opinion*, 187–211.

Le Pen, J. M. (1984). *Les Français d'abord* [The French first]. Paris: Carrere Lafon.

Leroux, P. (1993). 7/7 ou la célébration répétée d'une admiration mutuelle [7/7 or the recurrent celebration of mutual admiration] *Politix*, 23, 113–24.

Mayer, N. & Perrineau, P. (Eds.) (1996). *Le Front National à découvert* [The National Front revealed]. Paris: Presses de la FNSP.

Miller, G. (1992). *Malaise* [Disaster]. Paris: Editions de Seuil.

Mouchon, J. (1995). Espace public et discours télévisé [Public space and televised discourse]. In I. Pailliard (Ed.), *L'espace public et l'emprise de la communication* [The public space and the influence of communication] (pp. 177–91). Grenoble: Ellug.

Mouillaud, M., & Tetu, J. L. (1989). *Le journal quotidien*. Lyon: Presses Universitaires de Lyon.

Perelman, C. (1970). *Traité de l'argumentation* [Treaty on argumentative reasoning] (4th ed.). Brussels: University of Brussels.

Schnapper, D. (1995). Penser la préférence nationale [Thinking through national preference]. In D. Martin-Castelnau (Ed.), *Combattre le Front National* [Fighting the National Front] (pp. 201–10). Paris: Vinci.

Soudais, M. (1996). *Le Front National en face* [Facing the National Front]. Paris: Flammarion.

Sternhell, Z. (1978). *La droite révolutionnaire* [The revolutionary right]. Paris: Editions de Seuil.

Taguieff, P. A. (1984). La rhetorique du national-populisme: Les règles élémentaires de la propagande xénophobe [The rhetoric of national-populism: The basic rules of xenophobic propaganda]. *Cahiers Bernard Lazare*, 109, 19–38.

TF1: 7/7 (television program). (1995). "Gérard Carreyou reçoit Jean-Marie Le Pen, President du Front National" [Gérard Carreyou receives Jean-Marie Le Pen, Front National President]. February 26.

Taguieff, P. A. (1991). *Face au racisme* [Faced with racism]. Paris: La Découverte.

Taguieff, P. A. (1996). La métaphysique de Jean-Marie Le Pen [The metaphysics of Jean-Marie Le Pen]. In N. Mayer & P. Perrineau (Eds.), *Le Front National à découvert* [Discovering the Front National] (pp. 173–94). Paris: Presses de la FNSP.

Trois cents mesures pour la renaissance de la France, programme de gouvernement [Three hundred measures for the renaissance of France, government program] (1993). Paris: Editions Nationales.

CHAPTER 10

The Media, the Markets, and the Crash: A Consideration of Financial Press Narratives

MATTHEW G. SORLEY

INTRODUCTION

Recent years have witnessed a dramatic proliferation in the number of financial news services available to investors. A visit to the local newsstand would reveal a host of financial newspapers and magazines from which to choose. Similarly, television broadcasters have developed a series of financial programs that chronicle the market action. With the recent development of television specialty channels, one can obtain information from a variety of networks exclusively devoted to financial matters. The media maintain a continuous and extensive presence in the market. In fact, with the exception of the weather and sports, few if any other domains of activity receive such extensive media coverage (Snow & Parker, 1984: 153). Despite the pervasiveness of the media in the financial markets, few investigators have adopted this presence as a focus of examination.

In chronicling the financial events of the day, it is the responsibility of the financial media to identify, collect, package, and disseminate economic news. Through the rendering of narrative accounts of market phenomena, the financial press constructs a version of economic, social, and political reality. Through techniques such as discourse analysis, it is possible to demystify the epistemological base on which such social accounts rest and to deconstruct the discursive practices that are employed. This chapter presents a consideration of the discursive practices of the financial media through a discourse analytic examination of financial press accounts of the 1987 stock market crash. With a focus on news frames, two themes are addressed: (1) the function and construction of investor categories and (2) the rhetoric of regulation. The feasibility of and implications for future research in this area are discussed. In this this chapter, reconsideration of the 1987 stock market crash is made from a decidedly noneconomic perspective. Further, the chapter represents a foray into the political implications of economic communication.

A number of researchers have studied the influence of the media on market trading (e.g., Andreassen, 1987, 1990; Klein & Prestbo, 1974). Such efforts have demonstrated the powerful effect of news in stimulating stock price movements. Snow and Parker (1984: 170) examined the portrayal of the market by the media and concluded that not only are the market and the news about it inextricably interconnected, but that the market's viability is partly contingent on the way it is portrayed by the media. The authors contend that the media present a distorted picture of the market, which functions to perpetuate and sustain certain beliefs and practices that are critical to the market's functioning. In essence, the financial media serve a most vital function in the legitimation, production, and reproduction of the markets.

Of specific relevance to the current project is the small body of research spawned by the market events of October 19, 1987. On this date, a massive stock market meltdown swept across the trading floors of the world. This panic would erode more than 22 percent of the Dow Jones Industrial Average (arguably the world's most identifiable and quoted statistic), which would dramatically eclipse the 12.8 percent decline witnessed on "Black Tuesday" in 1929. Similarly, the market declines in London, Hong Kong, Toronto, and Sydney each exceeded 10 percent. In a consideration of media account construction, Metz (1988) offers a chronological account of how the story of the crash was developed by the media, including the editorial and article placement decisions made at the *Wall Street Journal*. In the ethnographic tradition, Warner and Molotch (1993: 194) examine the financial press accounts of the crash tendered by market participants in order to determine how they made sense of the event. In conclusion, the authors "presume that participants' accounts become the basis for media coverage. Media and market practices thus reinforce one another in a recursive, structurating fashion. The market reality is constituted through people's judgments about sentiment and social structure."

The vast majority of research pertaining to the crash of 1987, however, has originated from within the field of economics. For example, such projects focus on the influence of computer-program trading, the futures market, securities regulation, and other economic phenomena (e.g., Antonious, 1993; Dwyer & Hafer, 1990; Kamphuis, Kormendi & Watson, 1989; McClain, 1988; Moser, 1994).

This chapter focuses on the role of the financial press in socially constructing the 1987 crash through discourse. It attempts to demystify the epistemological base on which the media accounts rest and to deconstruct the discursive practices and processes in their natural breeding ground, namely the social text. The financial pages are a powerful social text and represent a robust source of data for qualitative researchers. Placed within the field of social discourse, the financial press does more than merely describe economic events or offer realistic accounts of economic phenomena. As noted by Potter and Wetherell (1987), social texts do not merely *reflect* or *mirror* objects, events, and categories preexisting in the social and natural world. Rather, they actively construct a version of those things. "They do not just describe things; they do things. And being active, they have social and political implication" (Potter & Wetherell, 1987: 6).

The media accomplish their constructive work by framing or promoting particular aspects of perceived reality. That is, a series of selection and exclusion decisions are made with respect to the events of the day. The media establish the agenda of their audience by identifying which issues and which aspects of those issues will be reported. Therefore, the media play an influential role in defining what is to count as news and how the news is to be interpreted. In essence, they offer a linguistic rendering of events that is typically perceived as a proxy for an objective reality.

According to Gamson (1985: 617), "News frames are almost entirely implicit and taken for granted. They do not appear to either journalists or audiences as social constructions but as primary attributes of events that reporters are merely reflecting." Given that media productions are perceived as objective representations of reality, they attain a truth status that enhances their legitimacy and ascendancy over alternative accounts. Foucault (1980) argues that once ideas are afforded a truth status, they become normalizing in the sense that they construct societal norms around which people are compelled to pattern or constitute their existence. In doing so, nonprivileged groups might suffer the subjugating effects of power and contribute to the maintenance of those bodies of knowledge that make truth claims.

Discourse analysis affords us an opportunity to turn the lens of examination on the social text itself, so that one can ponder the structure and organization of discourse. The framework allows for a consideration of text function and the possible consequences of the use of particular versions in the text. In discourse analysis, the focus is directed to the language, which is viewed as structured to reflect and perpetuate current power relations, structure ideology, and define the dominant version of subjective reality. Discursive practices are those that reproduce societal institutions, and discourse analysis allows identification of which institutions are reinforced and which institutions are censured when a particular discourse is employed.

When the media produce an account of a stock market event, who benefits and who does not? As Parker (1992: 21) notes, from this information, one can speculate as to "who would want to promote and who would want to dissolve the utilized discourse... an analysis can show how the discourse allows the dominant group in a society to tell their narrative about the past in order to justify the present, and prevent those who use subjugated discourses from making history." Therefore, the media may be conceptualized as a conduit through which the elites of society transmit their versions of events. Through influential social texts, it is possible to "define the framework within which collective social reality is perceived, and consequently to shape the basis of social action" (Adoni & Mane, 1984: 331). To date, no discourse analytic investigation has focused on media accounts of such major financial events as the 1987 stock market crash. This chapter addresses the impoverishment of the literature in this area and represents a movement to consider the discursive functions of financial reporting.

THE ANALYTIC ARCHIVE

The sample source consists of the October 20, 1987, editions of the *Wall Street Journal* and the *New York Times*. These editions represent the first opportunity for the two newspapers to offer their accounts of the market action of the previous day. Both newspapers enjoy high levels of international prestige, respect, and circulation and are deemed to represent influential social texts. As indicated by Warner and Molotch (1993: 169), surveys have consistently ranked the *Wall Street Journal* as the most trusted publication in the United States. In addition, it represents one of the handful of U.S. publications that is routinely consulted by journalists working for other media, which means it influences content across publications. Of the *New York Times*, Gans (1979: 126) notes, "The size and quality of its editorial and reporting staff are taken as guarantors of the best professional judgment." The analyses were initiated by selecting from both newspapers all articles concerning the behavior of the market on October 19. An effort was made to be inclusive in the development of the analytic archive. Several themes emerged during the analyses, two of which, presented here, relate to the issues of (1) the function and construction of investor categories and (2) the rhetoric of regulation. What follows is a modest selection of extracts and their associated analyses. The initial phases of the analytic enterprise were reported in Sorley (1996).

INVESTOR CATEGORIZATIONS: BIG AND LITTLE

The financial world and financial pages are especially rich contexts in which to examine people's use of categorizations. Specifically, discussions and representations of those deemed to be large and small investors occupy a considerable portion of the newspaper accounts. The discourse utilized in such representations plays an active role, in that it does not just describe investors; rather, it has a hand in constructing investor categories and making assumptions about those deemed worthy of inclusion into such categories. The accuracy of these judgments is not within the focus of this chapter. As noted by Potter and Wetherell (1987: 160), "The concern is exclusively with talk and writing itself and how it can be used, not with descriptive acuity." The following extract is from an article titled "Big Investors Say They Knew Better Than to Overstay":

Extract 1: They told you so! Some investors predicted the end of the bull market before the past week's collapse, or sold off big positions within the past few months. They include real-estate tycoon Donald Trump, corporate raider Asher Edelman, and private investor Jim Rogers. . . . "I sold all my stock over the last month," said Mr. Trump. "The timing was no different than the Grand Hyatt—what do you think of it?" The Grand Hyatt was a successful hotel project Mr. Trump undertook in Manhattan in the late 1970's at the tail end of New York City's fiscal crisis. One market source says Mr. Trump made about $175 million during the stock market's move up, partly by playing such takeover targets as Allegis Corp. and Holiday Corp., but has sold most of his $500 million portfolio. (Smith, 1987)

The use of the term *overstay* in the title implies that a normative rule was contravened by those who maintained a position in the marketplace. Simply, it is considered rude and an expression of ignorance if one overstays a welcome. The "big" investors "knew better" than to violate this market norm. "They told you so," plus the exclamation point, is a powerful statement that, in combination with the headline, sets a righteous tone for the forthcoming text. Donald Trump serves as an exemplar of the large investor community, as he enjoys all the rights and privileges of being identified with the elite group of American society. Therefore, it is not surprising that his thoughts were available for print and that his explanations were deemed worthy of repetition and distribution throughout the world.

As evidence of Trump's predictive prowess, a comparison is made with a past instance of extreme profit and astute decision making. The passage creates an image of one who can time the market with great success and navigate nimbly between investment adventures. The nature of the profits is clearly specified, and this quantification is presented as further evidence of large-investor market savvy. Trump accomplished his fortune by *playing*, a term indicating that investing successfully is simple. The title and extract combine to suggest that "big" is synonymous with knowledge, foresight, and intelligence. This is important in that members of the elite group enjoy enhanced investment opportunities in the marketplace through the manipulation of information, regulations, and media accounts. In addition, exactly what constitutes a "big" investor is not specified; thus, the category remains relatively amorphous.

The following extract is from an article titled "The Market Rouses Worst

Fears of Little Investors: Many Are Beginning to Talk in Terms of Doomsday; Big Investors Are Braver," and pertains to the small-investor category:

Extract 2: Robert C. McCollum, an elementary school principal in Galena Park, Texas ... says, that about eight days ago, he considered taking his "sweet" profit in Compaq Computer shares, which had tripled in value since he bought them—but he decided against selling. Then, over the weekend, he considered unloading stocks—but again decided to stay in. "I thought that reason would take over and it would stabilize," he says. "That was my gamble." ("The Market Rouses," 1987: 17)

The title of the article focuses on internal constitution and personality characteristics as determining investor reaction to the crash. "Little" investors are characterized in terms of their "fears," whereas the "big investors are braver." A clear demarcation line between investor categories is developed, a matter to which I return shortly. This extract reads like a story of missed opportunities and heartbreak. The narrative description is highly effective in creating a graphic and vivid account, in retrospect, of an ill-advised investment strategy. Quantification of the investor's losses is chronicled—losses experienced in common with other small investors. The speculative episode is deemed to consist of several phases, each of which would have resulted in "sweet" profits. The recency of the opportunities and near sell decisions leave the story even more emotionally alluring.

However, these gains are dramatically vanquished in the "gamble" of greed. The conceptualization and presentation of the market as a game of chance, like gambling, indicate that the small investor is apt to be burned by the probabilities. Without the predictive prowess and sophistication of the larger investors, the small investor can look upon the market only as a gamble; or so the text would have one believe. The "big" investors are typically depicted in terms of their gains, whereas "little" investors are represented in terms of their losses. Further, the actions of big investors *prior* to the crash are focused on, and the reactions of little investors *after* the event are presented. In addition, the big investors are depicted as having recently liquidated their holdings and realizing tremendous profits in the process. Meanwhile, the little investor is shown to have gambled away the opportunity and thus is a victim of his or her own greed.

The construction of these diametrically opposed investor categories allows for the location of responsibility within the personal characteristics of investors. As suggested by Potter and Wetherell (1987: 116), "categories are flexibly articulated in the course of certain sorts of talk and writing to accomplish particular goals, such as blamings or justification." Simply, the "little" investor deserved to sustain such heavy losses in view of his or her irrationality and lack of sophistication and market savvy. In essence, the image of the small investor "becomes typified and reified into a social category" (Potter & Wetherell, 1987: 113), known as the "little" or "unsophisticated" investor. By virtue of this categorization, the situation of the small investor can be dismissed or ignored because the "little" investor is fully explained by his or her supposed personality characteristics. The function of category development is the maintenance and protection of the status quo.

Although the following extract does not pertain exclusively to the aforementioned investor distinction, it elucidates additional information regarding the big-investor category, as presented by the media:

Extract 3: Referring to the current U.S. trade deficit, Mr. Trump explained, "The U.S. cannot afford to lose $200 billion a year while Japan and Saudi Arabia are making tremendous profits and the U.S. is paying totally for their defense." (Smith, 1987)

Trump does not "state" or "say," rather, he "explains." The utilization of such a term imparts to Trump the role of lecturer or educator. Therefore, it is expected that his words be afforded the respect that such a position deserves. In presenting the "$200 billion" trade deficit figure, Trump uses quantification to confer legitimacy to his forthcoming attempt to locate responsibility for the recent market turmoil. In contrast to small investors, the large investors are provided with speaking space to communicate their political and social commentaries. In Extract 3, this communication takes the form of assigning blame. In times of domestic upheaval and financial crisis, it is not uncommon to attempt to locate a scapegoat for negative events. In the past, this has been used to unite an otherwise divided community through the identification of a common enemy, one realized in a foreign country or minority group. The chosen discourse creates the image of hard-earned American dollars being virtually stolen by those in foreign countries. Trump goes further to assert that these countries are being granted free defense by the United States.

Although a true discourse analysis is not primarily concerned with the accuracy of an account, such a statement is curious because Japan and Saudi Arabia have been traditionally regarded by American policy makers to be of strategic significance, both geographically and economically. The use of a "charity discourse" in this instance implies that the benevolent American state is protecting foreign countries just to be nice. The sentence also contains a tone of rejection—despite the best efforts of the United States, its efforts just aren't appreciated. This is designed to provoke anger toward the foreign countries and arouse sympathy for the United States. The utilization of this discourse further insulates the elite group from serious critical inquiry in the post-crash environment.

THE RHETORIC OF REGULATION

From the earliest writings of Adam Smith comes the metaphor of the "invisible hand," a metaphor rich in history and tradition for economics. Allowed to operate unfettered and unimpaired by governmental regulations, the market is seen to be relatively self-policing and virtuous in its own right. With financial crises comes the inevitable questioning of the invisible hand as a guiding principle for the markets. The narratives produced by the financial press contain a variety of accounts pertaining to regulations or lack thereof.

The following extract is from an article titled, "Stocks Plunge 508 Points amid Panicky Selling:

Extract 4: Although Washington took no action yesterday, some analysts and officials said the market collapse could ultimately spark more securities regulation. "It's tough to predict what shape it will take, but you will see a lot of responses from the regulatory agencies," said Gregg Jarrell, the SEC's [Securities and Exchange Commission's] chief economist until last year. "You want to do some serious moves—unprecedented moves—to show you're in charge." (Metz, Murray, Ricks, & Garcia, 1987: 22)

In the body of the extract, "Washington" connotes more than just a geographical region; it also connotes a sense of power, respect, patriotism, duty, and responsibility. The use of "Washington" affords a sense of legitimacy to the forthcoming comments. The phrase "although Washington took no action yesterday" might function as a justification for inaction and the maintenance of the status quo; or it might function as a postponement of the use of acknowledged power.

Given that the statements come from "some analysts and officials," this speculation acquires additional legitimacy. As the extract continues, what is for most people an esoteric economic concept, securities regulation, is introduced as a possible solution to the market turmoil. Invoking such terms in combination with "Washington" establishes the illusion of a government and economic system working in concert to resolve the crisis. The use of vague terms, such as *tough, a lot*, and *serious*, is noteworthy, for these terms serve as substitutes for actual action, institutional examination, and change. The use of "you" in "you want to do some serious moves" implies that any reasonable individual would want to do the same thing. The function of this discourse is to warrant and justify whatever moves such regulatory agencies deem appropriate in the future. In essence, it affords the market policy makers an early strike at taking command over whatever change, in fact, does occurs. In effect, this discourse defines the very terms of the ensuing debate over regulation and establishes the righteousness of the elite groups in supervising the post-crash environment. This represents a most effective attempt at managing and diffusing any potential threats to this control. The regulatory agencies are framed in a parental discourse, as if they are about to enter the romper room and restore a sense of sanity to a world gone mad.

The use of the word "spark" implies a quick response, in contrast to the Washington that "took no action." A calming, pacifying tone is established by this extract. Perhaps the function of this discourse is just that: to pacify the critics of the system by developing a vague and unspecified plan of action. Market officials, economists, and politicians are seen to utilize a brand of discourse intended to calm the turbulent market. Indeed, the invisible hand is a guided hand.

Attempts to exert a calming effect were also embedded within justifications for inaction and the maintenance of the current regulatory framework. The following extracts are representative of such efforts:

Extract 5: Mr. Stigler, like other economists, stresses that today's financial system and economic policy mechanisms provide considerably more protection against the type of cascading economic collapse that crippled the nation during the Depression, which lasted from 1929–1933. (Bacon, 1987: 1)

Extract 6: There are many safeguards in place today—some instituted directly in response to the Depression that would tend to prevent the cascading financial collapse that characterized the crash, impoverishing millions of Americans. (Gelman, 1987: 1)

In Extract 5, "Mr. Stigler, like other economists," establishes the forthcoming statements as being synonymous with the prevailing wisdom of economics. His comments are "stressed," which establishes the earnest nature of the appeal. A comforting discourse is utilized in both accounts, as active words, such as "protection," "prevent," and "safeguards," are employed. Both extracts utilize the Depression of the 1930s as an extreme case formulation (a concept further explored by Potter and Wetherell, 1987) that serves as a comparison with the current situation. By invoking the images of that financial disaster, the current meltdown appears far less harsh by comparison. The event that "crippled" and "impoverished millions" is compared with the present situation, which is described by using a comforting discourse. Should one look to officials for reassurance that total financial meltdown is improbable because of already existing regulations, this possibility is provided. Through the media, a rhetoric of regulation is established with the function of producing and reproducing the sociopolitical realm that is the marketplace. In addition, the persistent use of esoteric economic concepts and terminology in financial press accounts is evident. Few individuals are well versed in the intricacies of SEC regulatory procedures and trade deficits; therefore, the reader has little choice but to validate the claims of those who profess expertise. By locating the source of the crash in a diversity of esoteric economic concepts, the current political arrangement is, in effect, reproduced and immune from serious critical inquiry.

CONCLUDING REMARKS

The discourses utilized by the media in describing and explaining the market crash of 1987 serve to disempower noninstitutional investors. Elite publications, such as the *Wall Street Journal* and the *New York Times*, produce narratives of financial experience that reinforce and reproduce the existing social order. Nonprivileged groups are situated in stories that emphasize their incompetence and lack of influence in the financial realm. Such narratives perpetuate current social relations by minimizing the sense of personal agency that nonprivileged groups experience in their financial dealings. Simply, having one's experience located in failure-saturated stories has the ultimate effect of reducing investor self-efficacy (see White & Epston, 1989, for a discussion of personal stories).

In essence, a world of limited possibilities is constructed and offered as reality. Central to the telling of the dominant story is the construction of investor categories. The demarcation line between categories need not be rigid to be influential. An uncritical reading of influential social texts results in the construction and proliferation of these stories as the dominant versions of financial events. In this manner, such constructions are afforded a truth status and endowed with a supposedly objective perspective that purports to render an accurate representation of reality. The comments of analysts, economists, politicians, and other professionals help to cast the financial press as objective purveyors of reality. Economists are certainly well versed in scientific discourse and are undoubtedly aware of the ascendancy of "science talk" over other forms of speaking (McCloskey, 1985).

Discourse analysis provides an opportunity to critique the dominant versions offered by the media and to identify the subjugating effects of such discourses. Therefore, research of this variety represents a potentially emancipatory activity. Once investors are able to deconstruct the terms in which they are characterized, a more informed investment community is an inevitable result. Indeed, "one of the positive fruits of discourse analysis is to promote an informed critical attitude to discourse . . . to be more aware of its constructive nature and the close connection between the way textual versions of the world are put together and specific policies and evaluations are pushed" (Potter & Wetherell, 1987: 174–75). Therefore, an applied and pragmatic possibility for this research may be realized through a more informed investor. The discourse analytic framework is not intended as a replacement for modernist methodologies, such as those utilized in the previously conducted research. Rather, such projects can complement and supplement those methodologies by adopting a positivist view of phenomena.

At the end of 1995, the total value of the world's equities was approaching $20 trillion (Fishman, 1997). This vast amount of capital represents the ultimate prize for the elite-controlled investment industry. With investment performance expectations running high and the massive inflow of capital apt to continue, further research into the discourse employed in financial newsletters, broker statements, and sales pitches would be of a practical nature. For example, Clark, Drew, and Pinch (1994) examined how salespersons manage the objections raised by customers during telephone sales calls. In addition, a consideration of television and the Internet in contributing to the construction of investment stories is warranted. Further, the symbiotic relationship forged between the investment analyst and the media should serve as fodder for future research. Given the recent proliferation of investment fraud and scandal, the role of the media in promoting certain stock issues should be the subject of critical inqiry. Female investors have typically indicated lower levels of investor confidence in comparison to their male counterparts (Estes & Hosseini, 1988).

The media might be implicated in the production and reproduction of this arrangement through differential presentation of male and female investors; however, the manner in which female investors are characterized by the financial media has received only scant research attention (e.g., Sorley, 1996). Finally, given the nature of relationships among the economy, optimism, and electoral success, provocative results might be obtained by analyzing the statements of politicians in the financial pages. By examining the role of a variety of actors in the financial press, one can better appreciate the politics of economic communication.

REFERENCES

Adoni, H., & Mane, S. (1984). Media and the construction of reality: Towards an integration of theory and research. *Communication Research*, 11, 323–40.

Andreassen, P. B. (1987). On the social psychology of the stock market: Aggregate attributional effects and the regressiveness of prediction. *Journal of Personality and Social Psychology*, 53, 490–96.

Andreassen, P. B. (1990). Judgmental extrapolation and market overreaction: On the use and disuse of news. *Journal of Behavioral Decision Making*, 3, 153–74.

Antonious, A. (1993). To what extent did stock index futures contribute to the October 1987 stock market crash? *Economic Journal*, 103, 1444–61.

Bacon, K. H. (1987, October 20). A repeat of '29? Depression in '87 is not expected. *Wall Street Journal*, pp. 1, 24.

Clark, C., Drew, P., & Pinch, T. (1994). Managing customer objections during real-life sales/negotiations. *Discourse and Society*, 5, 437–62.

Dwyer, G. P., Jr., & Hafer, R. W. (Eds.) (1990). The stock market: Bubbles, volatility, and chaos (Proceedings of the Thirteenth Annual Economic Policy Conference of the Federal Reserve Bank of St. Louis). Boston: Kluwer.

Estes, R., & Hosseini, J. (1988). The gender gap on Wall Street: An empirical analysis of confidence in investment decision making. *Journal of Psychology*, 122, 577–90.

Fishman, T. C. (1997, February). The joys of global investment: Shipping home the fruits of misery. *Harper's*, pp. 35–42.

Foucault, M. (1980). *Power/knowledge: Selected interviews and other writings.* New York: Pantheon.

Gamson, W. A. (1985). Goffman's legacy to political sociology. *Theory and Society*, 14, 605–22.

Gans, H. (1979). *Deciding what's news.* New York: Vintage.

Gelman, E. (1987, October 20). Does 1987 equal 1929? *New York Times*, pp. 1, 34.

Kamphuis, R. W., Jr., Kormendi, R. C., & Watson, J. W. H. (Eds.). (1989). *Black Monday and the future of financial markets.* Homewood, Ill.: Dow Jones-Irwin.

Klein, F., & Prestbo, J. A. (1974). *News and the market.* Chicago: Henry Regnery.

The market rouses worst fears of little investors: Many are beginning to talk in terms of doomsday; big investors are braver. (1987, October 20). *Wall Street Journal*, pp. 1, 17.

McClain, D. (1988). *Apocalypse on Wall Street.* Homewood, Ill.: Dow Jones-Irwin.

McCloskey, D. N. (1985). *The rhetoric of economics.* Madison: University of Wisconsin Press.

Metz, T. (1988). *Black Monday: The catastrophe of October 19, 1987 . . . and beyond.* New York: William Morrow.

Metz, T., Murray, A., Ricks, T. E., & Garcia, B. E. (1987, October 20). Stocks plunge 508 amid panicky selling. *Wall Street Journal*, pp. 1, 22.

Moser, J. (1994). A note on the crash and the participation in stock index futures. *Journal of Futures Markets*, 14, 117–19.

Parker, I. (1992). *Discourse dynamics: Critical analysis for social and individual psychology.* London: Routledge.

Potter, J., & Wetherell, M. (1987). *Discourse and social psychology: Beyond attitudes and behaviour.* London: Sage.

Smith, R. (1987, October 20). Big investors say they knew better than to overstay. *Wall Street Journal*, pp. 22.

Snow, D. A., & Parker, R. (1984). The media and the market. In P. A. Adler & P. Adler (Eds.), *The social dynamics of financial markets.* Greenwich, Conn.: JAI Press.

Sorley, M. G. (1996, July). *The social construction of a stock market crash: A discourse analysis.* Paper presented at the Nineteenth Annual Scientific Meeting of the International Society of Political Psychology, Vancouver, Canada.

Warner, K., & Molotch, H. (1993). Information in the marketplace: Media explanations of the '87 crash. *Social Problems*, 40, 167–88.

White, M., & Epston, D. (1989). *Literate means to therapeutic ends.* Adelaide, Australia: Dulwich Centre.

CHAPTER 11

The Political Rhetoric of a Unified Europe

CHRIST'L De LANDTSHEER

This chapter presents a political-semantic analysis of metaphorical discourse within the European Parliament (1981–1993). These analyses of political processes by means of the study of political style are called political-semantic studies (De Landtsheer, 1994; Lasswell, 1949a). The term *political semantics* refers to the political study of meaning or the study of meaning in politics (De Landtsheer, 1994). Holsti's (1969: 634, 636) reliability hypothesis for content analysis (according to Holsti's definition this political-semantic analysis can be considered as a content analysis) states that variables must meet the criterion of popularity to infer aspects of culture and cultural change.

The rhetoric in the European Parliament is public discourse, and the mass media increasingly report on this (Eurobarometer); however, it does not, meet this popularity criterion. My results only partly mirror feelings of European identity among European citizens. The challenge of measuring these feelings among the delegates, however, was big enough. The rhetoric of 700 delegates (directly elected since 1979) to the European Parliament in 1996 is affected by their national culture (the collective programming of the mind, which distinguishes one category of people from another [Hofstede, 1989: 193]) or their identity (the perception of similarities among the members of one group and dissimilarities to those outside the group [Kerremans, 1997] 303–14). Nevertheless, delegates are influenced by the growing power of the European Union. Even though, until now, the European Parliament has had only advisory power, it has considerable influence on the policy of the European Union; it is the Union's only democratic institution (Commission of the European Communities, 1992).

The parliamentary territory itself functions as an integrating factor

(Lang, 1993: 39); the European Parliament creates a new European culture. Rhetoric certainly is an essential feature of culture, and the Parliament creates a European discursive space (Bonham, Jonsson, Persson, and Shapiro, 1987). European parliamentary rhetoric informs one about common cultures and common identities. Political rhetoric, itself, of course, plays a role in creating national (or other) cultures and identities. Literature (Kerremans, 1997) correctly emphasises the importance of subjectivity in these feelings of common identity or culture. This is why the study of political style (the arrangement of the parts of communication, which may be simple or complex elements composed of signs, symbols, or symbol-signs [Lasswell, 1949b], seems appropriate to investigate feelings of national and European identities among the members of the European Parliament, who directly represent the 345 million citizens of Europe (Eurostat, 1996).

Institutional analyses by policy scholars and surveys by opinion researchers indeed focus on manifest aspects of the European unification process. Political style analysis, certainly, is a method more adapted to examine the subconscious level, in particular the collective mental processes that are part of European integration (De Landtsheer, 1994; De Sola Pool, 1956; Weinberger, 1995). Style in the language of politics varies according to basic features of the power situation (Lasswell, 1949b). As a consequence, delegates in the European Parliament increasingly address the European citizens. Their immediate contact with delegates from other European countries who speak other languages places them in a European communicative situation; they transfer their messages systematically into other, culturally different regions in order to reach audiences of different nationalities (Dobrzynska, 1995).

In addition, the Parliament is organized according to political factions (instead of national delegations). These political cultures, which transcend the borders of nation-states, possess a common style in their political language. Together, they represent a regional European culture that cuts across traditional nations. In the parliament of a unified Europe, political identities are more important than national identities (Weinberger, 1995); rhetorical style of political groups surpasses the national rhetorical style. Political messages, thus, are formulated in view of a European audience and, as a whole, should be equipped with associations similar to those of this audience (Dobrzynska, 1995; Weinberger, 1995). If, for instance, a gendered (political) culture exists, the rhetorical style of the European Parliament reflects it (Krizcova, 1994). This European rhetoric should, as a whole (in order to generate the sense intended by the delegates), also reflect the mental needs of the European audience. These needs of European citizens are assumed to depend on various factors (e.g., socioeconomic, political, and cultural) that might affect social stress (De Landtsheer, 1994; Fritzsche, 1984; Gaus, 1981).

This chapter thus examines the supranational programming (Hofstede,

1989: 193) of the European discursive space (Bonham et al., 1987) by mapping out the debates held in the European Parliament, according to its delegates' national, political, gender, and socioeconomic programming.

PROCEDURE

Eurodelegates use their native language during parliamentary debates, if possible, because their speeches are simultaneously translated in the Union's official languages (English, French, German, Dutch, Danish, Italian, Greek, Spanish, and Portuguese) and later published in the *Official Journal of the European Union*. Members of the audience (e.g., other delegates) thus actively or passively participate in their own languages; delegates thus can communicate directly with their parliamentary audience and accordingly formulate their speeches. This rhetorical analysis takes advantage of conditions (e.g., translation facilities) peculiar to the European Parliament. In its ideal form, this analysis would extend the coding procedure by having native speakers examine speeches produced in their own languages. Language in itself indeed reflects, in a unique way, vital information (e.g., social, cultural, political) that cannot be captured by translations. I had to content myself with a less detailed, but nevertheless acceptable, coding procedure in which native speakers of Dutch and English coded the entire Dutch and English proceedings. In addition to extensive samples selected with care and seemingly refined research instruments, five conditions support validity for this reduced procedure.

First, debates were simultaneously coded because pilot study conclusions recommend this procedure (De Landtsheer, 1995b). Second, speeches were formulated and translated in view of an international audience. Dobrzynska (1995) justly remarks that an immediate interaction with an interlocutor who speaks another language obviously differs from the translation of a written text, originally created with no intent of adjusting it to another cultural consciousness, that is now functioning outside its original communicative context. Third, translations were of excellent quality. Fourth, encoders examined speeches in their native languages. Fifth, and most important, my focus was on rhetorical style and not on codes, which are more language sensitive (Dudley, 1984).

Sample

I used a 621,012-word sample (298,036 words for the English proceedings and 322,976 words for the Dutch proceedings) of parliamentary debates held between 1981 and 1993. Starting from 1979 (the year in which the first direct elections of the European Parliament took place), I selected two to three debates for each two calendar years. Debate issues—agricultural prices (A), women and employment (W), and transport (T)—were chosen on the basis of their relative importance within the Union's policy (Commission, 1992), continuity, fair distribution of words, and fair representation of both sexes within the sample period (see the Appendix).

Metaphors (Why?)

This analysis focuses on metaphors (figures of speech), in which a word or phrase symbolizes an idea by the use of an implicit comparison, rather than by directly stating the idea (metaphors are detailed below). The following construction metaphor of the European house, which symbolizes the unification process of Europe, was stated by Jacques Delors, former president of the European Commission, at the French Bishops Conference in Lourdes, October 27, 1989: "We have laid the economic foundations and started on the ground floor. But the first and second stories still have to be built, and it will take more than one architect to see the project through." (Commission, 1992: 7). Empirical research at both the individual level (Opfer and Anderson, 1992) and the societal level (De Landtsheer, 1994; De Sola Pool, 1956; Lasswell, 1949a, 1949b) supports this conclusion. This metaphor exemplifies the stylistic, pragmatic, semantic, communicative, universal, affective, and cultural features of metaphors that are relevant in view of this political-semantic investigation of European culture and identity.

This common example is enough to demystify the metaphorical concept in order to clear up the arguments for my choice, which refer to metaphors as elements of style, political argumentation, and communication and as subconscious, affective, semantic, cultural, and universal products.

1. *Stylistic Elements.* Style is simply the order and movement that politicians give to their thoughts (Lasswell, 1949b: 21). Metaphorical analysis thus deals with linguistic strategies, contrary to a semiotic analysis that focuses on linguistic codes (De Landtsheer, 1994; Ricoeur, 1975: 274). Indeed, one does not have metaphorical words but metaphorical usage (Lepschy, 1976: 64), and the interpretation of metaphor is based within a theory of language use, not a theory of grammar (Fraser, 1984: 184). The difference between signs within a sign system (Fraser, 1984: 184) is not important but the reference to the real word is important. Because metaphors are figures that transgress or manipulate grammar (Dudley, 1984: 158), it is possible to study metaphors cross-linguistically.

2. *Elements of Political Argumentation.* Weinberger (1995) adequately describes political argumentation as pragmatic argumentation, which, contrary to objective argumentation (that deals only with the relation of arguments to the probandum), looks at the subjective reactions of the audience. Because it has the intention to influence people's behavior, the relation between the arguing person and the addressee(s) is an essential part of political rhetoric (Weinberger, 1995). European delegates select meta-

phors not only with a view to the sense conveyed but also with a view to the listener (e.g., their international audience) (Dobrzynska, 1995: 596). Even translated into foreign languages, their metaphors should be relevant. This assumption supports a cross-cultural study of metaphors, in which, under certain conditions, translations also can be examined.

3. *Communicative Elements.* Listeners should have associations similar to those of the speaker, as this is prerequisite for generating the sense intended by the speaker (Dobrzynska, 1995: 596). Metaphorical analysis can test emphatic (e.g., communicative, democratic) abilities of European delegates toward their European audience.

4. *Subconscious Products.* Rather than content analysis, language is an objective source of information because of its unconscious character (Sapir, 1962: 432–433).

5. *Affective Products.* These engage, besides cognition, imagination, and feelings (Dobrzynska, 1995: 597; Ricoeur, 1975). Because of this function, (political) metaphors are a powerful source of information regarding collective mental processes, such as European unification. Empirical research at both the individual level (Opfer and Anderson, 1992) and the societal level (De Landtsheer, 1994; De Sola Pool, 1956; Lasswell, 1949a, 1949b) supports this conclusion.

6. *Semantic Products.* Metaphors are a direct representation of meaning (Dudley, 1984: 158).

7. *Cultural Products.* These products are based on broader cultural cognitive structures (Sweetser, 1995). Thus, metaphors are appropriate in the study of national culture in relation to other cultures and to the broader regional culture.

8. *Universal Products.* Regardless of language or nationality, people show a natural ability to recognize these universal products (Mooy, 1976), even in a familiar foreign language, as can be concluded from my pilot study (De Landtsheer, 1994).

Metaphorical Analysis (How?)

Metaphors belong to ornamental and symbolic style (contrary to sign-oriented or factual style), which is assumed to infect political discourse during severe political or economic crises (De Landtsheer 1994; De Sola Pool, 1956; Lasswell, 1949a, 1949b). An acceptable explanation for this states that the need for emotion dominates economic crisis (Gaus, 1981), and that metaphors predominantly belong to the emotive component of language (as far as this component can be separated from the cognitive) (Dobrzynska, 1995: 597; Ricoeur, 1975). The interaction theory explains that the production of a metaphorical expression implies an actual subject of discussion and an idea from a different sphere of life that is literally used to describe the subject. The interaction between these two generates a new, figurative meaning and a new emotive view on the subject; the metaphorical process involves the transmission of the subject from the cognitive path onto the emotive path of thought (De Landtsheer, 1994). Similarities are not considered metaphors because little mental interaction takes place between the subject of discussion and the idea to which this subject is compared (Lodewick, Coenen, & Smulders, 1983, 57). The present case study applies my previously developed metaphorical model, which indicates that the metaphorical power of political rhetoric (metaphorical coefficient C) increases during economic crises because metaphors symbolize *social stress* (term introduced by Fritzsche [1994]). A case study in political semantics (De Landtsheer, 1994) details this method, which combines a social-scientific reference frame (De Sola Pool, 1956; Lasswell, 1949b; Gaus, 1981) and a linguistic one (Ricoeur, 1975; Schaff, 1960). The model assumes that metaphors are predominantly emotive symbols that fulfill several functions, such as self-reassurance (in simplifying complex situations) and relaxation (through evasion from reality and exhaustion of repressed feelings) (Edelman 1977: 35; Koeller, 1975: 222; Mooy, 1976: 16). Because metaphors simplify, comfort, reassure, and relax the audience, politicians and political journalists tend to express themselves more metaphorically when anxiety levels in society increase. Political metaphors should accordingly be considered as indicators of social stress (Fritzsche, 1994). This stress can be due to restrictions put upon people by culture and by severe economic or political crises (De Landtsheer, 1995a; De Sola Pool, 1956; Lasswell, 1949b). I express the metaphorical power of discourse in a metaphorical coefficient (C), which is the product of metaphorical frequency (F), intensity (I), and content (D). To calculate these variables, metaphors should be defined. The pilot study (De Landtsheer; 1995b) indicates that most definitions still allow for personal interpretation, even when specifications (e.g., no comparisons, no soft [dead] images, no strong literary language) are given.

The subjective criterion by Mooy (1976: 17), the strangeness or surprise of a metaphorical expression in its context, was experienced as applicable to identification of metaphors. Its reliability increases when coding results of at least two equally well-instructed, separately and consistently, operating encoders are confronted. In fact, my native English encoder (e) used a broad metaphorical concept (Karatza, 1997) based on figurative language. Figures are those twists and complications in discourse that mark out a difficulty in the path of meaning, such as metaphors, parallelism, disjunctions (Dudley, 1984: 158). The native Dutch encoder (d) used a limited metaphorical concept (Willemsen, 1996) based on direct transfer of name because of similarity, contrary to metaphors in a broad sense, which include, besides the above-mentioned restricted metaphors, allegories, concretizing (of abstract subjects), and synesthesia (Lodewick et al., 1983).

Variables are calculated as follows (detailed in De Landtsheer, 1994):

- The frequency variable (F) is the number of metaphors (calculated as above) per 100 words.
- The intensity variable (I) is calculated on the basis of a five-point scale. It consists of the sum of weak (w, value 1), normal (n, value 2), strong (s, value 3) metaphors, and in-between ones (values 1.5 and 2.5), divided by the total number of metaphors (t). Values refer to strength of reference to the literary meaning (Mooy 1976: 121) and to the difference between conventional and original metaphors (Koeller, 1975: 233–41).
- The content variable (D) is calculated on the basis of a six-point scale. Values are based on the weighing of the content categories in function of the specific metaphoric effects. D constitutes the sum of popular metaphors (p, value 1), metaphors referring to nature (n, value 2), political and intellectual metaphors (po, value 3), metaphors referring to death and disaster (d, value 4), metaphors referring to sports and games (sp, value 5), and metaphors referring to illness (m, value 6), divided by the total number of metaphors (t).

Political discourse testifies to social stress as it uses more metaphors (F), more intense or innovative metaphors (s), and more pessimistic or aggressive metaphors (d and m). Low unemployment rates (U) provide a country with a socially relaxed environment, and thus generate few (low F values) and less surprising (w) political metaphors that tend to express materialism and optimism (p, n) (De Landtsheer, 1994). This metaphorical model was, according to the above procedure, applied to the sample of European Parliamentary discourse (1981–1993). Metaphorical power of the delegates' political language is assumed to depend on (1) their political orientation, (2) their nationality, (3) their language, (4) their gender, and (5) on the Union's economic situation (e.g., unemployment rates). The following hypotheses were tested:

1. Right-wing extremist politicians produce speech with high C scores (metaphorical power is strong) compared to other politicians. Right-wing extremist rhetoric uses more propaganda strategies (e.g., stylistic means [Koeller, 1975]), and it accelerates popular anxiety, while abusing socially stressful economic situations (e.g., Gaus, 1981). This commonly accepted theory, for which empirical evidence is hard to find, together with my pilot study inspired, this hypothesis.
2. Politicians representing countries with less stressful conditions (e.g., prosperous economy) produce speech with low C scores (metaphorical power, on average, is low compared to speech by politicians of less prosperous countries). Empirical evidence is available on the fact that political speech more closely resembles everyday speech as stressful conditions disappear or diminish.
3. The European languages represented in the sample have similar C scores (metaphorical power is equal). Because of the similar origin of European languages (common genetic relationship, long cultural contacts) I do not expect languages to differ as such. Dissimilarity, of course, could be expected with geographically and consequently culturally separated languages (Druckman, Benton, Ali, &

Bagur, 1976). Lackner (1995: 77–88) characterizes political language in China as wooden language—language full of stereotyped metaphors.

4. Male political speech has higher C scores than female political speech (male politicians produce speeches with higher metaphorical power than female colleagues). Literature describes a female political culture with its female political language (Kahn, 1994). Krizkova (1994) concluded in her discourse analysis of four 1993 European Parliamentary debates (Social Dimension of Maastricht, Creation of Jobs for Women, Arms Industry, and Embargo against Cuba) that male delegates, more than females, tend to use rhetorical means (modals, repetition, emphasising, I-forms, rhetorical questions, and metaphors). Empirical evidence on this view, commonly accepted among scholars in cultural studies and women's studies, is hard to find.

5. C scores in European parliamentary rhetoric (as a whole) positively correlate with the Union's unemployment rates (U) (metaphorical power [social stress] in the delegates' speech corresponds with the feelings of European citizens, who are affected by socioeconomic conditions). The existence of this particular relationship (already confirmed for a particular nation) in a European sample would confirm European identity (nationality).

POLITICAL GROUP RESULTS

Average 1981–1993 speech percentages of the ten political groups (ranging from extreme left to extreme right) into which I categorized the factions in the European Parliament are (English [e] and Dutch [d] proceedings):

1. Socialists (S) 24.29 (e) and 25.46 (d); 2. Christian Democrats (CH) 23.70 (e) and 24.50 (d); 3. Conservatives (CON) 17.16 (e) and 16.05 (d); 4. Liberals (LIB) 8.38 (e) and 8.44 (d); 5. Extreme Left (EXL) 7.95 (e) and 6.99 (d); 6. Greens (G) 5.58 (e) and 4.89 (d); 7. Left (L) 3.71 (e) and 3.44 (d); 8. Independents (I) 3.08 (e) and 3.99 (d); 9. Technicals (T) 3.61 (e) and 3.80 (d); 10. Extreme Right (EXR) 2.55 (e) and 2.44 (d).

C scores of 1981–1993 speeches by these groups are:

(e): 1. Left 19.37; 2. Extreme Left 19.06; 3. Right-wing extremism 18.52; 4. Greens 17.99; 5. Independents 17.18; 6. Liberals 16.94; 7. Conservatives 16.46; 8. Christian Democrats 15.27; 9. Socialists 14.07; 10. Technical Faction 12.71.

(d): 1. Extreme Right 6.45; 2. Technical Faction 5.08; 3. Extreme Left 4.49; 4. Independents 4.05; 5. Greens 3.30; 6. Conservatives 3.25; 7. Liberals 3.19; 8. Socialists 2.80; 9. Christian Democrats 2.65; 10. Left 2.51.

Considerable (e) and (d) C differences are due to F rates (3.19, e, and 0.61, d), because I rates (1.63, e, and 1.77, d) and D rates (3.09, e, and 2.94, d) are comparable. Correlation between (e) and (d) average values series (number of metaphors, number of words, F, D, I, C; n 1, ... n 60) for political groups (EXL, L, G, S, CH, LIB, CON, EXR, T, I) is 0.99.

Political groups with 1981–1993 average C scores that are equally above the 16.54 (e) average and the 3.78 (d) average are Extreme Right, Independents, and Extreme Left; those with C scores that are equally below the (e) and (d) averages are Socialists, Christian Democrats, and Conservatives.

COUNTRY RESULTS

Twelve European countries are represented in the 1981–1993 Eurorhetoric sample (the Netherlands, Belgium, Germany, France, Ireland, United Kingdom (UK), Denmark, Italy, and Greece, 1981–1993; Luxembourg, 1983, 1987, 1991, 1993; Spain and Portugal, 1987–1993). Their average percentages of speech during 1981–1993 are:

1. Germany 14.19 (e) and 15.02 (d); 2. France 13.42 (e) and 12.40 (d); 3. UK 12.03 (e) and 13.37 (d); 4. the Netherlands 11.92 (e) and 10.94 (d); 5. Spain 10.30 (e) and 11.76 (d); 6. Italy 10.55 (e) and 10.24 (d); 7. Ireland 7.02 (e) and 6.54 (d); 8. Portugal 5.92 (e) and 5.38 (d); 9. Greece 4.71 (e) and 5.70 (d); 10. Denmark 4.83 (e) and 3.15 (d); 11. Belgium 4.35 (e) and 4.92 (d); 12. Luxembourg 1.33 (e) and 1.37 (d).

Average C scores for 1981–1993 are:

1. France 20.02 (e) and 4.22 (d); 2. Portugal 17.7 (e) and 3.38 (d); 3. Belgium 16.60 (e) and 4.35 (d); 4. Italy 16.44 (e) and 3.44 (d); 5. the Netherlands 15.63 (e) and 3.43 (d); 6. Greece 15.16 (e) and 2.43 (d); 7. Spain 15.11 (e) and 2.31 (d); 8. Denmark 14.91 (e) and 2.97 (d); 9. Luxembourg 14.70 (e) and 2.86 (d); 10. Ireland 14.42 (e) and 3.54 (d); 11. UK 14.22 (e) and 3.31 (d) 12. Germany 14.32 (e) and 2.56 (d).

Average unemployment rates (U) for all countries (years represented in the samples, Organization for Economic Cooperation and Development (1995) statistics) are:

Spain 18.69, Ireland 14.66, Belgium 11.09, Italy 10.60, Denmark 9.77, France 9.57, UK 9.19, the Netherlands 7.56, Greece 7.43, Germany 7.21, Portugal 6.60, Luxembourg 1.56.

Correlations between the series of countries' average U rates and the series of countries' average C rates are 0.59 (e) and 0.51 (d) and between U rates and D rates, 0.63 (e) and 0.59 (d) (Spain and Portugal not included). Except for Portugal (represented in only part of the sample), countries with high unemployment rates (Belgium, Italy, and France) are those with the highest C rates in political speech, and reversed (Germany, Luxembourg). Correlation between (e) and (d) average values (n 1 ... n 72) series for all countries is 0.99.

Delegates whose C scores are equally above the 1981–1993 average 15.72 (e) and 3.23 (d) scores represent France, Belgium, Italy, and Portugal; those whose C scores are equally below the (e) and (d) averages represent Germany, Luxembourg, and Denmark.

LANGUAGE RESULTS

Nine official languages were spoken in the 1981–1993 European Parliament: English: UK, Ireland; French: France, Belgium, and Luxembourg; German: Germany; Dutch: the Netherlands, Belgium; Danish: Denmark; Italian: Italy; Greek: Greece; Spanish: Spain; Portuguese: Portugal).Their speech percentages on a yearly average are:

1. English 17.41 (e) and 20.15 (d); 2. French 16.15 (e) and 15.04 (d); 3. German 14.70 (e) and 15.62 (d); 4. Dutch 15.04 (e) and 13.83 (d); 5. Spanish 10.22 (e) and 11.82 (d); 6. Italian 9.75 (e) and 9.22 (d); 7. Danish 8.00 (e) and 3.17 (d); 8. Greek 4.95 (e) and 5.72 (d); 9. Portuguese 3.77 (e) and 5.41 (d).

Average 1981–1993 C scores in parliamentary speech are:

1. French 20.67 (e) and 3.89 (d); 2. Greek 16.57 (e) and 2.43 (d); 3. Portuguese 16.38 (e) and 3.38 (d); 4. Italian 6.05 (e) and 3.34 (d); 5. Dutch 15.18 (e) and 3.73 (d); 6. Spanish 15.07 (e) and 2.31 (d); 7. Danish 14.75 (e) and 2.97 (d); 8. English 14.67 (e) and 3.19 (d); 9. German 14.42 (e) and 2.65 (d).

Correlation between (e) and (d) series of average values (n 1 ... n 54) for all languages is 0.98 (d). Only French and Portuguese (represented in only part of the sample) have C scores above the average scores 15.97 (e) and 3.15 (d).

GENDER RESULTS

Average speech percentages during the 1981–1993 sample are: male delegates, 69.88 (e) and 68.58 (d); female delegates, 30.12 (e) and 31.42 (d).

Average C-rates in parliamentary speech during 1981–1993 are: up to 15.88 (e) and 3.14 (d) a year; males score 16.28 (e) and 3.28 (d); females score 15.26 (e) and 3.05 (d).

Correlation between series of average values (n1—n12) for male and female rhetoric is 0.99. Male politicians' speech, on average, is slightly more metaphorical than female political speech. Gender socialization processes and the resulting condition that women are still less politically skilled than men could be responsible for this relatively more content-oriented and less rhetorical way that females express themselves in politics.

SOCIOECONOMIC RESULTS

Average C scores during 1981–1993 are: 1981, 16.52 (e) and 2.66 (d); 1983, 14.83 (e) and 4.02 (d); 1985, 13.44 (e) and 4.03 (d); 1987, 14.85 (e) and 3.3 (d); 1989, 17.98 (e) and 2.41 (d); 1991, 16.95 (e) and 3.25 (d); 1993, 16.62 (e) and 2.54 (d).

Average U rates for the European Union (countries represented in all sample years) are: 1981, 7.57; 1983, 10.08; 1985, 10.56; 1987, 10.05; 1989, 8.83; 1991, 8.74; 1993, 10.63.

Correlations between U and C and between U and D, respectively, are 0.60 (e) and 0.48 (d), and 0.32 (e) and 0.77 (d).

Results of (d) coding indicate that metaphorical power (C) as a social stress component of Europarliamentary rhetoric corresponds with social stress among the Union's population, which is influenced by unemployment rates (U). This holds true in particular for D, whose coding is less affected by both translation operations and coding subjectivity than F and I (and thus also less than C). Whereas (e) coding is based on a broader metaphorical concept (nonliterally language use) than (d) scores (Karatza, 1997: 16; Willemsen, 1996), (e) variables are more ambiguous than (d) variables, and (e) results tend to be less productive than (d) results. Lindblad (1984: 161) explains how low correlations between obviously unrelated variables can be meaningful. D results, however, seem to hold unconditionally.

CONCLUSION

In the European Parliament, political orientations flourish—more so than national feelings and remarkably more so than linguistic awareness. A gendered political culture, however, seems to be real. Moreover, the initial economic unification of the Union's members has definitely entered the political sphere, as Europarliamentarians' speeches do empathize with the economic sorrows of European citizens.

This is the picture that can be drawn from this metaphorical analysis of a 621,012-word sample of European Parliamentary speech (1981–1993); metaphorical variables that express social stress in political speech lead to this promising conclusion. The coding of these variables (for identical debate samples) by native speakers in English and Dutch Europarliamentary proceedings, indicates that a restricted metaphorical concept (as the one practiced by the Dutch encoder) is the most productive and that metaphorical content is the most appropriate variable to overcome limitations posed by translations and subjective interpretations.

Confronting and interpreting Dutch and English linguistic coding further results in the detailed conclusions that follow.

Hypothesis 1 is confirmed. Pronounced political cultures testify to the European Parliament's political and, thus, European reality. Indeed, speeches by members of distinguished political factions differ from speeches by political opponents in their metaphorical power. Moreover, metaphorical power for all speeches from left to center-right political groups differs from right-wing and left-wing extremist speeches (see Figure 11.1). The most active political factions (Socialists [S] and Christian Democrats [CH]) produce speeches with the least social stress components (metaphorical power). The least active political factions (the pronounced Right-wing

Figure 11.1
Metaphorical Power in European Parliamentary Rhetoric by Political Groups, 1981–1993 (Dutch Proceedings)

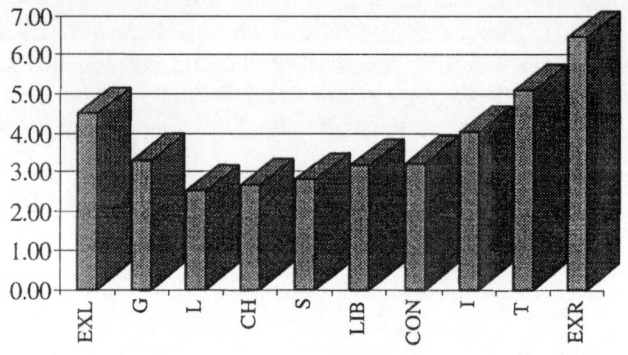

Factions were grouped into the following political orientations (for further explanation consult the Appendix): Extreme Left (EXL), Green (G), Left (L), Christian Democrats (CH), Socialist (S), Liberals (LIB), Conservatives (CON), Independants (I), Technicals (T), Extreme Right (EXR).

Extremist (EXR) and the Technical [T] and Independent [I] factions, with members of varied, mostly right-wing orientation) produce speeches that, on average, are considerably more stress-composed (metaphorically). To this hypothesis, however, could be added that not only right-wing extremist rhetoric but also left-wing extremist rhetoric stands out from rhetoric by other democratic political orientations.

Hypothesis 2 is confirmed. Nationality still exists within the Union. Among the twelve countries represented in the sample, prosperous ones, such as Germany and Luxembourg, generate parliamentary speech that is less metaphorical (has a lower social stress component), whereas delegates from France, Italy, and Belgium, countries with suffering economies (high unemployment rates), produce highly metaphorical rhetoric that scores high on social stress.

Hypothesis 3 is confirmed. From the nine official languages in the sample, metaphorical power, or social stress scores by separate languages, does not significantly differ except for France and Portugal (which is represented in only part of the sample). Most French in the Parliament, however, is spoken by delegates from France and Belgium, countries with highly stressful socioeconomic conditions.

Hypothesis 4 is confirmed. Social stress scores for the speech of female politicians are slightly lower than those for male speech. My interpretation is that females are still less politically skilled as a consequence of traditional socialization processes.

Hypothesis 5 is more or less confirmed. Members of the European Parliament seem to incorporate the collective mental needs of European citizens in their speeches, as they adapt social stress components, such as metaphorical content, of their speeches to their European audience's socioeconomic conditions (e.g., unemployment rates) that affect these needs. This ability of European parliamentarians to empathize with European citizens testifies to the political, and thus democratic, qualities of the European Parliament.

The conclusions that European identity and European culture exist, at least in the European Parliament, and that this parliament possesses political and democratic legitimacy should inspire policy makers in the Union. Perhaps the rhetorical arrears (Clarke, 1987) that have been noted for 1981–1993 European female politicians will progressively diminish as more females enter European politics. Or maybe one can hope for a more content-oriented political rhetoric because of a larger female political participation, both active and passive.

DISCUSSION

Data from this metaphorical analysis can be compiled in more detail; connections among the political, national, linguistic, and gender mappings of linguistic data can be further elaborated, as can the temporary fluctuations within the 1981–1993 sample. Also, results can be interpreted more intensively; social-democratic rhetoric, Christian-democratic rhetoric, liberal rhetoric, conservative rhetoric, extremist rhetoric, environmentalist rhetoric, and female political rhetoric are concepts that deserve further explanation and investigation. This also holds for the particular style characteristics of European languages, for the particular (cultural) stress conditions of European nations (e.g., religious, linguistic, and political problems), and for the conditions particular to the European Parliament (translation modalities).

In addition, a metaphorical analysis under more favorable conditions, such as using samples of only original speeches (no translations), each coded by at least two native speakers, could be conducted. Meanwhile, one can consider the current analysis as a more positive start.

APPENDIX

1. Debates dealing with Agricultural Prices (A) and Women and Employment (W) were selected for all sample years; debates on Transport (T) were added for 1985, 1989, and 1993. The Dutch sample (d) of 322,976 words included, on average, 46,139 words a year, or 53,993 words for 1981 (A & W), 48,721 words for 1983 (A & W), 41,697 words for 1985 (A, W, & T), 43,509 words for 1987 (A & W), 36,978 words for 1989 (A, W, & T), 37,465 words for 1991 (A & W), and 60,613 words for 1993 (A, W, & T). The English sample (e) of 289,036 words included, on average, 42,576 words a year, or 57,485 words for 1981 (A & W), 46,258

words for 1983 (A & W), 32,646 words for 1985 (A, W, & T), 48,706 words for 1987 (A & W), 33,131 words for 1989 (A, W, & T), 40,320 words for 1991 (A & W), and 39,490 words for 1993 (A, W, & T).

2. Speeches in the 1981–1993 sample consisted of 298,036 words (English version, e) and 322,976 words (Dutch version, d), with a yearly average of 42,576 (e) and 46,139 (d) words.

3. Factions were grouped into the following political orientations: 1. Extreme Left (EXL): Communists, Left Coalition (CG) and the Party for a United European (Left) (GUE). 2. EXL rhetoric counts 25,424 (e) and 24,446 (d) words, with an average of 3,632 (e) and 3,492 (d) words a year (1981–1993) 2. Left (L): Rainbow Faction (ARC), a coalition of independent members of the left. L rhetoric counts 10,196 (e) and 8,586 (d) words, with an average of 1,699 (e) and 1,717 (d) words a year (1985–1993) 3. Green (G): The Greens (V). G rhetoric counts 5,109 (e) and 4,881 (d) words, with an average of 2,554 (e) and 2,440(d) words a year (1991, 1993). 4. Socialists (S): Socialist Parties. S rhetoric consists of 77,822 (e) and 88,980 (d) words; on average, 11,117 (e) and 12,711 (d) words a year (1981–1993). 5. Christian Democrats (CH): European Peoples Party (PPE). CH rhetoric consists of 75,949 (e) and 85,628 (d) words; on average, 10,849 (e) and 12,232 (d) words a year (1981–1993). 6. Liberals (LIB): Liberal and Democratic Party (L/LDR). LIB rhetoric consists of 26,846 (e) and 29,511 (d) words; on average, 3,835 (e) and 4,215 (d) words a year (1981–1993). 7. Conservatives (CON): European Democrats (ED), DEP, RDE. CON rhetoric consists of 54,980 (e) and 56,090 (d) words; on average 7,854 (e) and 8,012 (d) words a year (1981–1993). 8. Technicals (T): Technical Faction (CDI). T rhetoric (mostly right-wing) consists of 4,964 (e) and 7,592 (d) words (1981–1983); on average, 1,654 (e) and 1,898 (d) words a year. 9. Independents (I): delegates are of various, mostly right-wing orientation. I rhetoric consists of 9,888 (e) and 13,943 (d) words (1981–1993); on average, 1,412 (e) and 1,991 (d) words a year. 10. Right-wing extremism (EXR): The European Right Party (DR). EXR rhetoric consists of 7,009 (e) and 6,104 (d) words; on average, 1,168 (e) and 1,220 (d) words a year (1985–1993).

4. Average D (content variable) scores for speech of political groups are the following: Right-wing extremism, 3.39 (e) and 3.68 (d); Independents, 3.14 (e) and 2.93 (d); Technicals, 2.93 (e) and 3.28 (d); Extreme-Left, 3.15 (e) and 3.20 (d); Christian Democrats, 3.13 (e) and 2.86 (e); Conservatives, 3.11 (e) and 3.05 (e); Liberals, 3.10 (e) and 2.90 (e); Socialists, 3.05 (e) and 2.80 (d); Left, 3.04 (e) and 2.79 (d); Greens, 2.86 (e) and 2.57 (d).

5. Number of words by countries in the debates are the following: The Netherlands, 38,415 (e) and 38,382 (d) words; on average, 5,487 (e) and 5,483 (d) words. Belgium, 14,033 (e) and 17,250 (d) words; on average, 2,004 (e) and 2,464 (d) words. Germany, 45,733 (e) and 52,704 (d) words; on average, 6,533 (e) and 7,529 (d) words. France, 43,243 (e) and 43,507

(d) words; on average, 6,177 (e) and 6,215 (d) words. Ireland, 22,630 (e) and 22,958 (d) words; on average, 3,232 (e) and 3,279 (d) words. United Kingdom, 38,786 (e) and 46,924 (d) words; on average, 5,540 (e) and 6,703 (d) words. Denmark, 15,581 (e) and 11,064 (d) words; on average, 2,225 (e) and 1,580 (d) words. Italy, 31,474 (e) and 33,075 (d) words; on average, 4,496 (e) and 4,725 (d) words. Greece, 15,839 (e) and 19,985 (d) words; on average, 2,262 (e) and 2,855 (d) words. Spain, 18,974 (e) and 23,584 (d) words; on average, 4,743 (e) and 5,896 (d) words. Portugal, 10,902 (e) and 10,791 (d) words; on average, 2,725 (e) and 2,697 (d) words. Luxembourg, 2,454 (e) and 2,752 (d) words; on average, 613 (e) and 688 (e) words.

6. Rhetoric produced in various languages includes the following number of words: English, 55,683 (e) and 70,339 (d); on average, 7,954 (e) and 10,048 (d). French, 51,654 (e) and 52,482 (d); on average, 7,379 (e) and 7,497 (d). German, 47,021 (e) and 54,504 (d); on average, 6,717 (e) and 7,786 (d). Dutch, 48,091 (e) and 48,265 (d); on average, 6,870 (e) and 6,895 (d). Italian, 31,202 (e) and 32,202 (d); on average, 4,457 (e) and 4,600 (d). Danish, 25,541 (e) and 11,064 (d); on average, 3,648 (e) and 1,580 (d). Spanish, 18,686 (e) and 23,584 (d); on 1987–1993 average, 4,671 (e) and 5,896 (d). Greek, 15,839 (e) and 19,988 (d); on average, 2,262 (e) and 2,855 (d). Portuguese, 6,891 (e) and 10,791 (d); on 1987–1993 average, 1,722 (e) and 2,697 (d).

7. Male delegates produced 29,756 (e) and 31,638 (d) words of the samples; on yearly average, 4,250 (e) and 4,519 (d). Female delegates produced 12,819 (e) and 14,500 (d) words of the samples; on yearly average, 1,831 (e) and 2,071 (d).

ACKNOWLEDGMENT

The author wishes to thank her students, Carola Willemsen and Debby Karatza, for their collecting of linguistic data and for their helpful comments, partly reflected in their theses.

REFERENCES

Bonham, G. M., Jonsson, C., Persson, S., & Shapiro, M. J. (1987). Cognition and international negotiation: The historical recovery of discursive space. *Cooperation and Conflict*, 22, 63–80.

Clarke, J. (1987). Woman and political leadership. Paper presented at the ninth annual scientific meeting of the International Society for Political Psychology, San Francisco.

Commission of the European Communities. (1992). *From single market to European union: Europe on the move*. Luxembourg: Office for Official Publications Unit of the European Communities.

De Landtsheer, C. (1994). The language of prosperity and crisis: A case study in political semantics. *Politics and the Individual*, 4 (2), 63–85.
De Landtsheer, C. (1995a). Political communication. *Politics, Groups and the Individual*, 2 (Special issue), 1–20.
De Landtsheer, C. (1995b). Political metaphors as ideological meaning objects in cross-cultural parliamentary rhetoric. Case study: The European parliament debates xenophobia. Paper presented at the Conference Sprache des Parlaments und Semiotik der Demokratie, Tutzing, Germany
De Sola Pool, I. (1956). Variety and repetition in political language. In H. Eulau et al. (Eds.), *Political behavior: A reader in theory and research* (pp. 217–31). Washington, D.C.: Library of Congress.
Dobrzynska, T. (1995). Translating metaphor: Problems of meaning. *Journal of Pragmatics*, 24, 595–604.
Druckman, D., Benton, A. A., Ali, F., & Bagur, J. S. (1976). Cultural differences in bargaining behavior: India, Argentina and the United States. *Journal of Conflict Resolution*, 20, 413–48.
Dudley, A. (1984). *Concepts in film theory*. Oxford: Oxford University Press.
Edelman, M. (1977). *Political language: Words that succeed and policies that fail*. Orlando, Fla.: Academic Press.
Eurostat yearbook: A statistical eye on Europe. (1996). Luxembourg: Office for Official Publications of the European Committee.
Fraser, B. (1984). The interpretation of novel metaphors. In A. Ortony (Ed.), *Metaphor and Thought* (pp. 172–85). New York: Cambridge University Press.
Fritzsche, P. (1994). Social stress: A new approach to explain xenophobia. Paper presented at the 8th Conference of the Dutch Society of Political Psychology, Amsterdam.
Gaus, H. (1981). *Menselijk gedrag in perioden van langdurige economische recessie. Een schets* [Human behavior during long-term economic recessions. An outline]. Malle, Belgium: De Sikkel.
Hofstede, G. (1989). Cultural predictors of national negotiating styles. In F. Mautner-Markhof (Ed.), *Processes of international negotiations* (pp. 193–201). Boulder, Colo.: Westview.
Holsti, O. (1969). Content analysis. In G. Lindsey and E Aronson (Eds.), *The handbook of social psychology* (2nd ed., Vol. 2). 596–692. Reading, Mass.: Addison-Wesley.
Kahn, K. F. (1994). Gender differences in campaign messages: The political advertisements of men and women candidates for the US Senate. *Political Research Quarterly* (January), 481–503.
Karatza, D. (1997). *The semantics of European Parliamentary debates*. Unpublished master's thesis, Communication Department, University of Amsterdam.
Kerremans, B. (1997). The Flemish identity: Nascent or existent? [Special issue on media and nationalism]. *Res Publica*, 34 (2), 303–14.
Koeller, W. (1975). *Semiotik und Metaphor* [Semiotic and metaphor]. Stuttgart: Metzlersche Verlagsbuchhandlung.
Krizkova, M. (1994). Male and female political rhetoric in the European Parliament. Paper ACCESS [International Programme Faculty of Political] and ECS [Social-Cultural Sciences], University of Amsterdam.

Lackner, M. (1995). Des termes subtils porteurs d'un grand message: Remarques a propos de quelques particularits linguistiques du discours politique en Chine [Subtle terms carriers of big messages: Remarks on peculiarities of Chinese political discourse]. *Relations Internationales*, 81, 77–88.

Lang, W. (1993). A professional view. In G. O. Faure & J. Z. Rubin (Eds.), *Culture and negotiation* (pp. 38–46). Newbury Park, Calif.: Sage.

Lasswell, H. D. (1949a). The language of power. In H. D. Lasswell, Nathan Leites et al. (Eds.), *Language of politics: Studies in quantitative semantics* (pp. 3–19). New York: George W. Stewart.

Lasswell, H. D. (1949b). Style in the language of politics. In H. D. Lasswell, Nathan Leites et al. (Eds.), *Language of politics: Studies in quantitative semantics* (pp. 20–39). New York: George W. Stewart.

Lepschy, G. (1976). Interpretation and semantics. *Cahiers de Lexicologie*, 29, 64.

Lindblad, J. T. (1984). *Statistiek voor historici* [Statistic for historians]. Muiderberg, the Netherlands: Dick Coutinho.

Lodewick, H., Coenen, P., & Smulders, A. (1983). *Literaire kunst* [Literary art]. Den Bosch, the Netherlands: Malmberg.

Mooy, J. J. (1976). *A study of metaphor: On the nature of metaphorical expressions with special reference to their reference*. Amsterdam: North Holland.

Opfer, Joseph, & Anderson, Peter A. (1992). Explaining the sound bite: A test of a theory of metaphor and assonance. Paper presented at the Western Speech Communication Association Convention, Boise, Idaho.

Ricoeur, P. (1975). *La metaphore vive* [The lively metaphor]. Paris: Editions du Seuil.

Sapir, E. (1962). *Selected writings in language, culture and personality*. Berkeley, Calif.: Mandelbaum.

Schaff, A. (1960). *Introduction la sémantique* [Introduction to semantics]. Paris: Anthropos.

Sweetser, E. (1995). Metaphor, mythology, and everyday language. *Journal of Pragmatics*, 24, 585–93.

Weinberger, O. (1995). Argumentation in law and politics. *Communication and Cognition*, 28 (1), 37–54.

Willemsen, Carola (1996). *De retoriek van het Europees Parlement* [Rhetoric in the European Parliament]. Unpublished master's thesis, Communication Department, University of Amsterdam.

PART III

Methods in the Study of Political Discourse

CHAPTER 12

Political Interviews: Television Interviews in Great Britain

PETER BULL

INTRODUCTION

In the age of television, televised interviews have become one of the most important means of political communication. The first such interview in the United Kingdom appears to have taken place in 1951 when Anthony Eden, a senior member of Winston Churchill's government, was interviewed by British Broadcasting Corporation (BBC) announcer Leslie Mitchell; however, it was all so stage-managed that Cockerell (1988), in his history of television in British politics, refers to it as a "cod interview." During the the early 1950s, the BBC still had a monopoly in broadcasting, and a highly deferential style of interviewing was employed at that time (Day, 1989). With the introduction of the commercial channel Independent Television (ITV) in 1955, however, the political interview was transformed from what has been referred to as the "pat-ball" interview to a more aggressive and challenging encounter.

The most prominent exponent of this new style was Sir Robin Day, who had originally trained as a barrister. He writes in his autobiography, "The sixties was the period when the television interview became established as a new branch of journalism, as part of the political process, and increasingly as a political event in its own right" (Day, 1989: 142). By the 1980s, Day claimed that interviewing had become harder as politicians had become progressively more at ease in set-piece interviews. Politicians had become much more professional in the way they handled television: they gave greater attention to impression management, to interview technique, to the rules of engagement under which interviews were conducted, and even to the interview set itself (Jones, 1992). Indeed, it began to appear to some commentators, including Sir Robin Day, that the political interview had been effectively neutralized (Jones, 1992).

The televised political interview has also become the theme of a substantive research literature, focused specifically on the nature of the interaction that takes place. To some extent, this interaction is a kind of illusion: what appears to be a conversation is, in fact, a performance transmitted to an overhearing audience potentially of millions (Heritage, 1985). It is also a performance governed by its own special set of rules, in which the type of conversation that takes place is quite distinctive.

Characteristic features include the pattern of turn-taking, the frequent occurrence of both interruptions and equivocation, and the central role of self-presentation and face management. It is the purpose of this chapter to review research on these distinctive features, to consider to what extent the research provides a basis for evaluating the interview performance of both interviewers and politicians, and to discuss possible implications for the pessimism concerning the future of the political interview reported by the commentators above (Day, 1989; Jones, 1992).

TURN-TAKING

A number of observers have commented on the distinctive nature of turn-taking in political interviews. Typically, the interviewer both begins and ends the interview; he or she is also expected to ask questions, and the interviewee is expected to provide replies (e.g., Clayman, 1989; Greatbatch, 1988; Heritage, Clayman, & Zimmerman, 1988). Even when the interviewer departs from the question-and-answer format, for example, by making a statement, the statement is typically followed with a question or concluded with a tag in the form of "isn't it?" or "wasn't it?" Indeed, it has been argued that the question-and-answer format is the principal means used by the participants to create and sustain talk (Schegloff, 1989), although interviewers may engage in nonquestioning actions in order to open and close interviews (Heritage & Greatbatch, 1991).

The way in which news interviews are terminated is significantly affected by the pattern of turn-taking, according to Clayman (1989). Given that interviewees are not expected to speak unless the interviewer has asked them to do so, termination can be accomplished in a unilateral fashion by the interviewer; this is in contrast to ordinary conversation, where it is jointly managed by the participants. The opening sequence of a news interview also differs from ordinary conversation in a number of important respects, Clayman (1991) maintains. In particular, the primary task of the opening is to project the agenda for the interview, whereas topics in ordinary conversation are not predetermined but negotiated during the course of the interaction.

Turn-taking in political interviews can break down if interruptions are excessive, and one of the most well-known studies was concerned with this theme (Beattie, 1982). A detailed analysis was made of two political interviews in the 1979 British general election: one between Margaret Thatcher (leader of the Conservative Opposition, 1975–1979) and Denis Tuohy, and the other between James Callaghan (Labour prime minister, 1976–1979) and Llew Gardner. It was found that whereas the interviewer interrupted Thatcher almost twice as often as she interrupted him, the pattern for Callaghan was the reverse: he interrupted the interviewer more than he was interrupted. Beattie claimed that Thatcher was often interrupted following the display of turn-yielding cues, in particular at the ends of clauses associated with drawl on the stressed syllable and a falling intonation pattern. According to Beattie, Thatcher was excessively interrupted because these turn-yielding cues were misleading, giving the interviewer the impression that she had completed her utterance. The interviewer then attempted to take over the turn, whereupon Thatcher continued speaking.

Another intensive study of interruptions in political interviews, this time based on the 1987 British general election, was carried out by Bull and Mayer (1988). They compared Thatcher (prime minister, 1979–1990) and Neil Kinnock (leader of the Labour Opposition, 1983–1992). They found no significant difference in the extent to which the party leaders either interrupted or were interrupted; indeed, the pattern of interruptions between the two leaders was markedly similar and correlated at a highly significant level. The results were quite contrary to what might have been expected from the study by Beattie (1982), who claimed that Thatcher was excessively interrupted because she gave misleading turn-yielding cues. Where the politicians did differ was in the frequency with which Thatcher explicitly protested at being interrupted, with comments such as ". . . please let me go on" or ". . . may I now and then say a word in my own defense." On at least two occasions, she objected to being interrupted when there was no sign of an interruption, the interviewer (Jonathan Dimbleby) even openly protesting on one occasion that he was not about to interrupt! The frequent use of such comments could have given the misleading impression that Thatcher was being excessively interrupted, although the objective evidence showed that this was not the case.

EQUIVOCATION

In the Bull and Mayer (1988) study, a content analysis was also conducted of the reasons for interrupting in political interviews; it showed that the most frequent reason was to reformulate questions. This suggested that interruptions might be directly linked to equivocation. If a politician talks at length while failing to answer a question, the interviewer must be able to interrupt effectively in order to pursue an appropriate reply. Hence, a further study was conducted in order to provide some basic information on equivocation in political interviews (Bull & Mayer, 1993).

Results showed that Thatcher replied to only 37 percent of the questions put to her and Kinnock to only 39 percent. They are directly comparable to the results of an independent study by Harris (1991), who found in an analysis of a different set of political interviews (principally with Thatcher and Kinnock) that the politicians gave direct answers to just over 39 percent of the questions asked. By way of comparison, it is interesting to consider the reply rate in televised interviews for other leading public figures who are not politicians. For example, it was found that Diana, Princess of Wales, in an interview with Martin Bashir (November 20, 1995), replied to 78 percent of the questions put to her (Bull, 1997). Thus, the studies by Bull and Mayer and by Harris both provide empirical evidence in support of the popular view that politicians do not reply to a large proportion of questions in political interviews.

Bull and Mayer (1993) also devised a typology of non-replies to questions, that showed a highly significant correlation of 0.93 betwen Thatcher and Kinnock across 11 superordinate categories. Making political points was by far the most frequent form of non-reply used by both politicians; the second most frequent was attacking the question. The 11 superordinate categories were further subdivided into 30 subordinate categories, which did show some stylistic differences between the two politicians. Whereas Thatcher inhibited awkward questions by making personal attacks on the interviewers, Kinnock's style was much more defensive; he sometimes answered in the negative (e.g., stating at length the policies that the Labour Party would not follow), thereby simply inviting further questioning on the same topic while also making himself appear evasive.

In spite of these stylistic differences between Thatcher and Kinnock, what is more striking is the broad degree of similarity between them, both in the proportion of questions to which they failed to reply and in the manner of their non-replies. This might simply support the popular view that one politician is very much like another and that each tends to evade most of the questions asked by interviewers. An alternative view comes from the work of Bavelas, Black, Chovil, and Mullett (1990) on equivocation. They are critical of the notion that politicians are intrinsically evasive and point out that it might be something to do with the communicative situation. Bavelas and colleagues have developed a theory of equivocation, according to which people in general (i.e., not only politicians) typically equivocate when placed in what is referred to as an avoidance-avoidance conflict, where all of the possible replies to a question have potentially negative consequences but where, nevertheless, a reply is still expected. The underlying argument is that although it is an individual who equivocates, it is not he or she who is the cause of the equivocation; rather, equivocation is the result of the individual's communicative situation.

Bavelas et al. (1990) further argue that the political interview is particularly prone to the avoidance-avoidance conflicts that they regard as responsible for equivocation. As far as politicians are concerned, a common source of conflict is that there are many controversial issues on which there is a divided electorate. Direct replies supporting or criticizing either position would offend a substantial number of voters and are therefore to be avoided. Another set of conflicts does not involve policy issues but is created by the interview process itself. One such conflict is the pressure of time limits. If the politician is asked about a complex issue but is forced to answer briefly, he or she has a choice between two unattractive alternatives: reducing the issue to a simple incomplete answer or appearing long-winded, circuitous, and evasive.

Again, if the candidate lacks knowledge of the issue being addressed, he or she faces the unfortunate choice of acknowledging ignorance, improvising, or fabricating an answer. Finally, there may be instances of interpersonal conflict between politician and interviewer. If the interviewer is very aggressive, there are costs to pay from either a counterattack or a meek acceptance.

It is important to note that, with the exception of being well prepared on every conceivable issue, the politician can do little about other sources of conflict. Inevitably, voters will be divided; parties, candidates, and constituencies will disagree; there will always be occasions when brief replies are required in political interviews; candidates will have to keep secrets; and reporters will ask aggressive questions. Most important of all, the public and press are waiting to seize on any mistake. Bavelas et al. (1990) interviewed a number of politicians, and they stressed again and again that the goal of a campaign is to avoid making mistakes. They told familiar horror stories of highly publicized mistakes that ended political careers—in short, elections are lost, not won.

ISSUES OF FACE

Although Bavelas et al. (1990) present a large number of reasons why avoidance-avoidance conflicts occur in political interviews, they do not identify any common underlying theoretical explanation for this phenomenon. In this context, one interesting observation is made by Jucker (1986: 71), who states: "It is clear that what is primarily at issue in news interviews is the interviewee's positive face." The term *positive face* refers to the desire to be approved of by others, whereas the term *negative face* refers to the desire to have autonomy of action (Brown & Levinson, 1978: 66). Jucker (1986: 71) argues that maintaining positive face in news interviews is particularly important for democratically elected politicians because their political survival ultimately depends on the approval of a majority of people in their own constituency.

According to the highly influential paper "On Face-work" by Goffman (1955), concerns with face are salient in virtually all social encounters. Not only do people defend their own face in social interaction, Goffman points out, but they also have an obligation to defend the face of others. In the context of a political interview, politicians might seek to support the face of political colleagues and allies; at the same time, they would not wish to support the face of negatively valued others, such as their political opponents. In many relationships, Goffman further observes, the members come to share a face so that, in the presence of third parties, an improper act on the part of one member becomes a source of acute embarrassment to other members. This is especially true of the British party political system, where the party is paramount; typically, the politician appears on television as the representative of that party to defend and promote its collective face.

Consequently, on the basis of Goffman's observations, it can be argued that politicians must concern themselves with three different aspects of face: their own individual face, the face of significant others, and the face of the party that they represent (Bull, Elliott, Palmer, & Walker, 1996). Thus, there are a number of good reasons for arguing that face is of central importance in political interviews; further, the concept also can be used to provide an underlying rationale for the avoidance-avoidance conflicts identified in political interviews by Bavelas and colleagues, as described above. For example, Bavelas et al. (1988) point out that politicians equivocate because there are many controversial issues on which there is a divided electorate; in this case, politicians are seen to be protecting face by not espousing opinions that a substantial body of voters might find offensive or unacceptable.

Another set of conflicts is created by the time limits of the interview. Again, it is the politician's own face which is at stake, since he or she does not wish to appear either incompetent (by reducing the issue to a simple, incomplete answer) or devious (by appearing long-winded, circuitous, or evasive). In the case where the candidate lacks sufficient knowledge of the issue being addressed, the risk to the politician's face is either appearing incompetent (by admitting ignorance) or putting his or her face at risk in the future, if subsequently it can be shown that the answer was less than adequate.

In short, issues of face arguably underlie all the avoidance-avoidance conflicts identified by Bavelas and colleagues as being responsible for equivocation in political interviews. Indeed, not only can the phenomenon of equivocation be explained in terms of face, it also can be used to explain when and why politicians do reply to questions. For example, if a politician is asked to justify a specific policy, failure to offer some kind of rationale might raise doubts either about the politician's professional competence or about the validity of the policy, or perhaps about both.

Hence, the concept of face offers the possibility of a theory of question-response sequences in political interviews. In order to conduct an empirical test of this theory, a new typology of questions in political interviews was devised in order to analyze questions in terms of their face-threatening properties; this typology was based on a set of eighteen interviews with the leaders of the three main political parties in the 1992 British general election (Bull et al., 1996). The typology distinguishes between nineteen different types of face-threat, divided into the three superordinate categories of face that politicians must defend—personal face, the face of the party that they represent, and the face of significant others. On the basis of this analysis, two types of question were distinguished: (1) the type in which each of the principal modes of response was considered to present some kind of threat to face, and (2) the type in which a nonthreatening response was considered possible.

Some questions (40.8 percent of the 557 used in the interviews) were so tough that each of the principal modes of response open to the politicians was considered to present some form of face-threat (referred to as Bavelas-type because they are hypothesized to create an avoidance-avoidance conflict). For example, Sir Robin Day posed this kind of problem to Neil Kinnock, when he asked him whether, under a Labour government, the trade unions would recover much of their pre-Thatcher power. If Kinnock answered yes to this question, he would run the risk of offending that proportion of the electorate who are opposed to trade unions and are fearful of their excessive influence. If he replied no, he would risk offending that proportion of the electorate who favor trade unions, as well as offending the trade unions themselves and their supporters within his own party. If he failed to reply, he might simply be seen as evasive. Thus, each of the principal response options presents some kind of threat to face; in the event, Kinnock made the best of a bad job by simply stating Labour Party trade union policy, without indicating whether or not this meant that the unions would recover much of their pre-Thatcher power under a Labour government.

Not all questions, however, pose this kind of dilemma to politicians. It was considered that there were some questions to which politicians could respond without necessarily threatening face, in the sense that it was possible to produce responses that did not incur any of the nineteen face-threats specified in the coding system. Where it was considered that such a response could be made, that response option was coded as "no necessary threat." It is important to note that this coding was used, regardless of whether or not such a response actually occurred. It is also important to note that a "no necessary threat" response can take the form of either a reply or a non-reply.

Some questions are so favorable that they give the politician an open invitation to make positive statements about himself or herself and the party that the politician represents. For example, Day asked John Major (Conservative prime minister, 1990–1997):

Why do you deserve... why does the Conservative Party deserve under your leadership what the British people have never given any political party in modern times—a fourth successive term of office?

In replying to this question, Major was given the opportunity to present both himself and the Conservative Party in a favorable light. Failure to reply would be extremely face-threatening because it would imply that neither he nor the Conservative Party deserved a fourth term of office.

Questions for which a "no necessary threat" response was judged possible comprised 59.2 percent of the questions in all eighteen political interviews. This type of question is of particular importance because it allows a direct test of the main tenet of the face model: that politicians, in responding to questions, will opt for a "no necessary threat" response. The results of the analysis provided overwhelming support for this hypothesis; in most cases where it was possible to choose a "no necessary threat" response, this was the response chosen by the politicians, either directly or by implication. The most frequently occurring type of question was couched in what is referred to as a *yes-no* format (Quirk, Greenbaum, Leech, & Svartvik, 1985: 387–394). Given that there are three principal modes of responding to such questions (confirm, deny, equivocate), the probability of a "no necessary threat" response occurring by chance is 33 percent; in fact, the total proportion of "no necessary threat" responses to yes-no questions was 87 percent.

EVALUATING THE INTERVIEW PERFORMANCE OF POLITICIANS

The face model is not only predictive but also potentially evaluative. Given an adversarial political system in which politicians must seek to present the best face, their interview performances could be considered unskilled if they produce face-damaging responses when a "no necessary threat" option is available. On this basis, an evaluation was conducted of the interview performances of the three principal party leaders with respect to what are called avoidable face-damaging responses (Bull & Elliott, 1994).

For example, Sir Robin Day asked Paddy Ashdown (leader of the minority Liberal Democrats since 1988), "You promised to put an extra penny on the standard rate of tax for education and training. Can you call this courageous and honest when very few people think you're ever going to be in a position to do that?" Ashdown did not reply to this question; instead, he attacked it. In fact, he could have given a reply in the affirmative. He could have argued for the possibility of a hung Parliament and maintained that, in such circumstances, the Liberal Democrats would use all their influence to get this measure through the House of Commons. By not replying to the question, Ashdown gave the impression that he does not really believe that he can substantiate the stance that this policy is courageous and honest, thereby undermining the face of his party.

In the 1992 British general election, Major produced the lowest proportion of avoidable face-damaging responses and Kinnock the highest. Thus, where a "no necessary threat" response was possible, Major nearly always selected this option (90.4 percent of questions); Kinnock selected it for 83.0 percent and Ashdown for 87.2 percent of the questions (Bull & Elliott, 1994). This is interesting, given the extensive criticism that Major's communicative style attracted in the media; however, this analysis would suggest that critics might have underestimated his communicative skills in terms of the actual content of what he says.

EVALUATING THE INTERVIEW PERFORMANCE OF INTERVIEWERS

A further application of the face model is based on the proposition that Bavelas-type questions are "tougher" than those questions that allow at least one type of response that is not intrinsically face-threatening. Hence the relative proportion of Bavelas-type questions in an interview can be used as a measure of toughness, referred to as "level of threat."

Level of threat also can be compared across interviews with politicians from different political parties as a means of assessing interviewer neutrality (Bull & Elliott, 1995). In addition, level of threat provides a means of evaluating differential reply rates to questions. For example, Ashdown answered significantly more questions than Major. Was this because Ashdown was simply asked easier questions? In fact, his reply rate was much greater, irrespective of whether he was responding to "no necessary threat" or Bavelas-type questions, which would suggest this was not the case.

The proposition that politicians tend to find Bavelas-type questions problematic is borne out by the finding that they typically equivocate in response to this type of questioning. Most of the Bavelas-type questions in the Bull et al. (1996) data (87 percent) were couched in a yes-no format. Given that there are three principal modes of responding to such questions (confirm, deny, equivocate), the probability of an equivocal response occurring by chance is 33 percent; in fact, the total proportion of equivocal responses to yes-no questions was 66 percent. The fact that equivocation occurs at twice the rate expected by chance alone would suggest that the politicians found difficulty with this kind of question and were unsure how to tackle it. A high proportion of Bavelas-type questions would therefore constitute a tough form of interview and make the politician appear evasive.

In terms of level of threat, of the six interviewers studied in the 1992 general election, Brian Walden emerged as the toughest, with almost half (49.4 percent) of his questions carrying a threat in every direction, almost twice as many as those for David Frost, who emerged as the softest interviewer with only 28.9 percent of Bavelas-type questions carrying threats. The results also showed an interesting trend in that most of the interviewers gave the toughest interviews to Major in terms of the relative proportion of Bavelas-type questions; the one exception to this trend was David Frost, who gave his softest interview to John Major. Thus, not only was David Frost the softest interviewer overall, he was also the only interviewer to give his softest interview to the leader of the governing party.

CONCLUSIONS

Studies of political interviews have identified a number of characteristic features of discourse in this situation: the distinctive pattern of turn-taking, the high frequency of interruptions and equivocation, and the importance of face management and self-presentation.

To a large extent, the direction of a politician's response to a question is predictable from its face-threatening structure, and it has been argued that the concept of face can be used to evaluate the interview skills of both interviewers and politicians.

The salience of face management and issues of self-presentation might also underlie the recent pessimism about the future of the political interview (Day, 1989; Jones, 1992). Given an adversarial political system in which no politician can afford to lose face, a politician's skills in face management in interviews become of central importance. But to the extent that the direction of a politician's response is largely predictable from the face-threatening structure of questions, responses will be uninformative, and the main interest of the interview becomes whether the politician makes any "mistakes"—that is, whether they produce any face-damaging responses to questions. Indeed, it is arguable that the adversarial style, which has become such a hallmark of British political interviews, simply exacerbates this trend toward face-saving on the part of the politician. Nevertheless, televised political interviews in Britain show no sign whatsoever of decreasing in frequency. In the 1997 British general election, they played as prominent a role as ever and, as such must continue to be considered one of the most important and characteristic means of political communication in contemporary British politics.

REFERENCES

Bavelas, J. B., Black, A., Bryson, L., & Mullett, J. (1988). Political equivocation: A situational explanation. *Journal of Language and Social Psychology*, 7, 137–45.

Bavelas, J. B., Black, A., Chovil, N., & Mullett, J. (1990). *Equivocal communication*. Newbury Park, Calif.: Sage.

Beattie, G. W. (1982). Turn-taking and interruptions in political interviews—Margaret Thatcher and Jim Callaghan compared and contrasted. *Semiotica*, 39, 93–114.

Brown, P., & Levinson, S. C. (1978). Universals in language usage: Politeness phenomena. In E. Goody (Ed.), *Questions and politeness* (pp. 56–310). Cambridge: Cambridge University Press.

Bull, P. E. (1997). Queen of hearts or queen of the arts of implication? Implicit criticisms and their implications for equivocation theory in the interview between Martin Bashir and Diana, Princess of Wales. *Social Psychological Review*, 1, 27–36.

Bull, P. E., & Elliott, J. (1994, September 21). Is John Major a major face-saver? An assessment of televised interviews with the party leaders during the 1992 British General Election. Paper presented at the Annual Conference of the Social Psychology Section of the British Psychological Society, Downing College, University of Cambridge.

Bull, P. E., & Elliott, J. (1995, 14 September). "Probing the political interviewer"—An evaluation of television interviewers during the 1992 British General Election. Paper presented at the Annual Conference of the Social Psychology Section of the British Psychological Society, College of Ripon & York St. John, York.

Bull, P. E., Elliott, J., Palmer, D., & Walker, L. (1996). Why politicians are three-faced: The face model of political interviews. *British Journal of Social Psychology*, 35, 267–84.

Bull, P. E., & Mayer, K. (1988). Interruptions in political interviews: A study of Margaret Thatcher and Neil Kinnock. *Journal of Language and Social Psychology*, 7, 35–45.

Bull, P. E., & Mayer, K. (1993). How not to answer questions in political interviews. *Political Psychology*, 14, 651–66.

Clayman, S. E. (1989). The production of punctuality: Social interaction, temporal organization and social structure. *American Journal of Sociology*, 95, 659–91.

Clayman, S. E. (1991). News interview openings: Aspects of sequential organization. In P. Scannell (Ed.), *Broadcast talk* (pp. 48–75). London: Sage.

Cockerell, M. (1988). *Live from number 10: The inside story of prime ministers and television*. London: Faber & Faber.

Day, Sir R. (1989). *Grand inquisitor: Memoirs*. London: Weidenfeld & Nicolson.

Goffman, E. (1955) On face-work: An analysis of ritual elements in social interaction. *Psychiatry*, 18, 213–31. Reprinted in E. Goffman (1967), *Interaction ritual: Essays on face to face behaviour* (pp. 5–45). Garden City, N.Y.: Anchor.

Greatbatch, D. (1988). A turn-taking system for British news interviews. *Language in Society*, 17, 401–30.

Harris, S. (1991). Evasive action: How politicians respond to questions in political interviews. In P. Scannell (Ed.), *Broadcast talk* (pp. 77–99). London: Sage.

Heritage, J. C. (1985). Analyzing news interviews: Aspects of the production of talk for an overhearing audience. In T. van Dijk (Ed.), *Handbook of discourse analysis* (Vol. 3) (pp. 95–117). New York: Academic Press.

Heritage, J. C., Clayman, S. E., & Zimmerman, D. (1988). Discourse and message analysis: The micro-structure of mass media messages. In R. Hawkins, S. Pingree, & J. Weimann (Eds.), *Advancing communication science: Merging mass and interpersonal processes*. Newbury Park, Calif: Sage.

Heritage, J. C., & Greatbatch, D. L. (1991). On the institutional character of institutional talk: The case of news interviews. In D. Boden & D. Zimmerman (Eds.), *Talk and social structure* (pp. 93–137). Cambridge: Polity Press.

Jones, W. (1992). Broadcasters, politicians and the political interview. In W. Jones & L. Robins (Eds.), *Two decades in British politics* (pp. 53–78). Manchester: Manchester University Press.

Jucker, J. (1986). *News interviews: A pragmalinguistic analysis*. Amsterdam: Gieben.

Quirk, R., Greenbaum, S., Leech, G., & Svartvik, J. (1985). *A comprehensive grammar of the English language*. London: Longman.

Schegloff, E. A. (1989). From interview to confrontation: Observations on the Bush/Rather encounter. *Research on Language and Social Interaction*, 22, 215–40.

CHAPTER 13

Functions of Recent U.S. Presidential Slogans

HERBERT BARRY III

This chapter discusses slogans that summarize the promises or policies of presidential administrations. The four most recent presidents are selected. Two, Jimmy Carter and William J. Clinton, are Democrats. The other two, Ronald Reagan and George Bush, are Republicans. Two of the presidents, Reagan and Clinton, were elected for two terms. The other two were elected for a single term.

ATTRIBUTES OF POLITICAL SLOGANS

A *political slogan* is defined as a catchword or rallying motto distinctly associated with a political party or other group. Although a slogan generally originates with the president or a member of the administration, its effectiveness depends on acceptance and use by the public. Slogans to describe a presidential administration have become increasingly prominent in recent years, especially beginning with Woodrow Wilson's proposal for "the new freedom" in 1912. The increase in oral communications, by radio and television, has magnified the effectiveness of *sound bites*, defined as brief, memorable statements. Some sound bites become slogans that characterize a presidential administration.

Slogans are generally brief statements of a single idea. They are therefore easy to remember and repeat. An extreme example is a slogan of three one-syllable words, such as "the square deal" (Theodore Roosevelt), "the new deal" (Franklin D. Roosevelt), "the fair deal" (Harry Truman), "just say no" (Reagan), and "war on drugs" (Bush).

Slogans with multiple ideas and more numerous words are often abbreviated in repetitions by journalists and other members of the public. An example is Wilson's slogan for his reelection campaign in 1916, "With honor, he kept us out of war." It was abbreviated to "He kept us out of war." Franklin D. Roosevelt, in his acceptance speech for the Democratic presidential nomination in 1932, stated, "I pledge you, I pledge myself, to a new deal for the American people." That statement was quickly abbreviated to "the new deal." A more recent example is Carter's statement in 1977, "energy crisis—the moral equivalent of war." Most repetitions by the public were limited to the first two words: "energy crisis."

The slogan needs to be a distinctive phrase that the president offers and the public accepts as a valid promise or policy. Association of a slogan with a presidential administration depends on three conditions. First, the group of words is not used frequently in other contexts. Second, the slogan is proposed multiple times by the president or by a member of the administration. Third, the slogan is repeated many times by journalists and other commentators. The public may therefore determine whether the president continues to use a slogan and act in accordance with it. The influence of public sentiment on decisions by the leader is discussed by deMause (1982), using the slogan "group fantasy," and by Barry (1991), using the slogan "group governance."

METHODS FOR IDENTIFYING PRESIDENTIAL SLOGANS

The present chapter considers multiple slogans associated with Carter, Reagan, Bush, and Clinton. Slogans associated with presidents can express their intentions for their administrations and the reactions to them by journalists and other commentators.

Preparation of this chapter began by compiling for each president a list of potential slogans included in campaign promises, speeches, and written documents. The sources include reproductions printed in newspapers, magazines, and books.

Two electronic files were also used. One electronic file is a CD-ROM disk of *The Presidential Papers* (United States, Presidents, 1995). It indicates the frequency of use of slogans by the president and his administration. The majority of the text consists of speeches by each president. Some of the text reproduces printed documents, such as proposed legislation, and statements by the president's press secretary, by cabinet members, by other people in dialogues with the president, and questions by reporters in press conferences. The information on Clinton is limited to part of his first term. The other electronic file is a collection of CD-ROM disks of the text of the *New York Times*, one disk for each year from the beginning of 1991 to the end of 1996 (*New York Times*, 1996). These disks indicate how frequently a slogan was used in news reports and articles in that newspaper during a limited time span after the presidencies of Carter and Reagan.

Information on frequency of use of the slogans was obtained from

Functions of Recent U.S. Presidential Slogans   163

Table 13.1
Slogans by President Carter

Text of Slogan	Type of Slogan
A government as good as the people	Domestic conciliation
I will never lie	Specific promise
Panama Canal Treaty	Foreign conciliation
Energy crisis	Domestic aggressiveness
Decontrol of gasoline prices	Domestic program
Deregulation of airlines	Domestic program
Environmental protection	Domestic program
Camp David Accords	Foreign conciliation
Human rights	General conciliation

searches for occurrences of the slogans in both electronic files. A search command for the specified phrase obtained a count of the number of occurrences. A further procedure in some cases was to determine the context by reading the text before and after the specified phrase.

MULTIPLE SLOGANS

Tables 13.1–13.4 identify slogans associated with the presidencies of Carter (1977–1981), Reagan (1981–1989), Bush (1989–1993), and Clinton (beginning in 1993).

The slogans for each president are listed in the approximate sequence of their initial appearance. Each slogan is accompanied by an adjective and a noun that identify its principal characteristics. The adjectives are "specific," "general," "domestic," and "foreign." The nouns are "promise," "program," "conciliation," "aggressiveness," and "novelty."

Carter Slogans

The slogans most distinctively associated with Carter (Table 13.1) are moralistic declarations, "a government as good as the people" and "I will never lie." The nine slogans include four conciliations and only one aggressiveness. The aggressiveness of "energy crisis" is emphasized in the original, longer statement, "energy crisis—the moral equivalent of war."

The slogans associated with Carter have not been repeated frequently by journalists and other commentators since his single term as president. The most persistent Carter slogans are general statements made also by other presidents but associated more strongly with Carter because he stated them

Table 13.2
Slogans by President Reagan

Text of Slogan	Type of Slogan
Get the government off the backs of the people	Domestic aggressiveness
Supply side economics	General promise
Reduce government spending	Domestic promise
Tax reduction	Domestic program
The new American revolution	Domestic novelty
Strategic Defense Initiative	Specific program
The evil empire	Foreign aggressiveness
It's morning in America	Domestic promise
Just say no	General aggressiveness

more frequently or emphatically. Examples are "environmental protection" and "human rights."

Reagan Slogans

The nine slogans associated with Reagan in Table 13.2 include three classified as aggressiveness and none as conciliation. Several slogans associated with Reagan became very popular in accordance with the frequent characterization of Reagan as "the great communicator." The first slogan, "get the government off the backs of the people," was an unusually lengthy campaign promise in 1980.

Early in the Reagan administration, two frequently repeated domestic promises were "tax reduction" and "reduce government spending." These are general statements that did not originate in Reagan's administration. They are associated with Reagan because of his frequent repetitions of these domestic promises.

The slogan, "supply side economics," was adopted rather than originated by Reagan. An unusual development was that journalists and other commentators often substituted the slogan "Reaganomics," although this slogan of a single word was not originated or approved by Reagan.

One of the most frequently repeated Reagan slogans is the specific program, "strategic defense initiative." Even more frequently repeated is a different phrase for the same program, "star wars." This rival slogan was not approved by Reagan, but the two common words of a single syllable gave it a crucial advantage over "strategic defense initiative."

Another frequently repeated Reagan slogan is the domestic campaign

Table 13.3
Slogans by President Bush

Text of Slogan	Type of Slogan
A thousand points of light	General conciliation
I want a kinder, gentler America	Domestic conciliation
No new taxes	Domestic promise
The education president	General promise
War on drugs	Domestic aggressiveness
Operation Desert Storm	Foreign aggressiveness
The new world order	Foreign novelty

promise in 1984, "it's morning in America." Another type of popular slogan is the vague advice, "just say no," which was originated by the president's wife, Nancy. The initial statement of this advice was more specific by adding ". . . to drugs and alcohol."

A different category of Reagan slogan is "the new American revolution." The word "new" conveys the idea of novelty and therefore desirable progress. The principal slogan of many previous presidents has also contained the word "new" (Barry, 1990, 1996).

Bush Slogans

The seven slogans associated with Bush in Table 13.3 include two that express conciliation in domestic policy and two that express aggressiveness. A different type of slogan is "the new world order." The phrase pertains to foreign policy and contains the word "new." This slogan originated in 1991, in the second half of Bush's four-year term, but became the most frequently repeated Bush slogan.

A frequently repeated but embarrassing Bush slogan is "no new taxes," a campaign promise stated in his acceptance speech for the Republican nomination for president. The original phrase was "read my lips: no new taxes." Two years later, the promise was broken in an agreement with the Democratic majority in Congress on a tax bill.

Clinton Slogans

The nine slogans associated with Clinton are listed in Table 13.4. Only one pertains to foreign policy, "North American free trade agreement." The first three slogans were campaign promises in 1992. The last, "bridge to the 21st century," was a campaign promise in 1996.

The first slogan, "the new covenant," seldom has been repeated by jour-

Table 13.4
Slogans by President Clinton

Text of Slogan	Type of Slogan
The new covenant	General novelty
Reinventing government	Domestic promise
Putting people first	General promise
North American Free Trade Agreement	Foreign conciliation
Health care reform	Domestic program
End welfare as we know it	General promise
AmeriCorps	Domestic program
The era of big government is over	General promise
Bridge to the twenty-first century	General promise

nalists and others in spite of several repetitions by Clinton. A more successful effort by Democratic President Clinton to attract support from Republicans is indicated by three conservative, rather than liberal, slogans, "reinventing government," "end welfare as we know it," and "the era of big government is over."

DISCUSSION OF POLITICAL SLOGANS

Political slogans are prominent and frequently repeated attributes of recent presidential administrations. The use of slogans for political purposes has a long history. Choice of a slogan is influenced by the personality of the president. The effectiveness of slogans is partly attributable to the association of a presidency with a brief, attractive, distinctive phrase.

History of Political Slogans

Some political slogans are not associated with a president or other political leader. Early examples are "give me liberty or give me death" by Patrick Henry in 1775 and "all men are created equal" in the Declaration of Independence by Thomas Jefferson in 1776. Bailey (1976) offers an extensive collection of and commentary on slogans in the United States.

Slogans associated with the earlier presidents of the United States were usually personal descriptions of the individual rather than statements of his administration's promises or purposes. Examples are "father of his country" (George Washington), "old hickory" (Andrew Jackson), "young hickory" (James Polk), "the rail splitter" (Abraham Lincoln), and "the rough rider" (Theodore Roosevelt). Popular slogans for some recent presidents also have been personal descriptions, such as "tricky Dick" (Richard Nixon) and "the Teflon president" (Reagan).

The most frequently repeated slogans of recent presidents have generally referred to promises or programs of a president's administration rather than his personal characteristics. Two recent changes might account for the recent focus of slogans on performance rather than personality. The first change is the frequent exposure of the public to the presidents in televised news reports and speeches. People are therefore more aware of the complexity and variability of the president's personal characteristics. The second change is the greatly enlarged federal government bureaucracy. The president is less likely to be regarded as the personification of the entire government.

Slogans as Personality Expressions

The type of slogan associated with a president may be determined partly by the individual personality. Barry (1990, 1996) reports that the word "new" was contained in the principal slogan associated with each of six presidents: "the new freedom" (Wilson), "the new deal" (Franklin D. Roosevelt), "the new frontier" (John F. Kennedy), "the new Federalism" (Nixon), "the new American revolution" (Reagan), and "the new world order" (Bush). The middle name of each of these presidents was the mother's premarital surname. Possible effects of this unusual linkage with the mother are discussed by Barry (1990, 1996). Each of these six presidents grew up in a family with one or more older brothers or sisters. Harris (1964), Barry (1979), and Sulloway (1996) discuss effects of birth order in the childhood family on adult personality.

Brevity and Distinctiveness of Slogans

The 34 slogans listed in Tables 13.1 through 13.4 indicate that slogans are generally brief phrases. The majority are either three or four words. Only eight of the slogans are longer than four words. Longer statements are less memorable and less likely to be repeated often enough to become established as slogans. Some of the slogans in Tables 13.1 through 13.4 are abbreviated versions of the original statements.

If brevity were the only qualification, most slogans would be a single word. Instead, Tables 13.1 through 13.4 contain only one slogan that is a single word and only three slogans that consist of two words. It is difficult for a phrase of one or two words to become distinctively associated with a single presidential administration. The single word "AmeriCorps" (Clinton) combines two words, "America" and "Corps." The three slogans of two words, "energy crisis" and "human rights" (Carter) and "tax reduction" (Reagan) are phrases used in many contexts. Therefore, these slogans do not fully satisfy the criterion of distinctive association with a single president.

Because slogans generally attempt to elicit strong emotional responses, the majority of them contain words that are frequently used and familiar to most people. In Tables 13.1 through 13.4, the longest word is "environmental" (Carter). The slogans contain many words that designate strong emotions. Examples are "good" and "rights" (Carter); "revolution," "defense," and "evil" (Reagan); "kinder," "gentler," and "war" (Bush); "health," "reform," and "welfare" (Clinton); and "new" (Reagan, Bush, and Clinton). The principal emotional effect of slogans is due to the combination of words, such as "morning in America" (Reagan), "a thousand points of light" (Bush), and "putting people first" (Clinton).

Human languages contain a large number of familiar words. Many millions of phrases are combinations of three or four words. There is no shortage of brief slogans that are distinctively associated with a single individual or product. New brief slogans will become distinctively associated with future presidencies.

Effectiveness of Slogans

The purpose of a political slogan is to increase acceptance of a presidential proposal by associating it with a brief, memorable phrase. It is hard to prove the efficacy of a slogan because the slogan and the proposal are inextricably associated with each other. Acceptance of the proposal, accompanied by the slogan, cannot be compared with the fate of the same proposal at the same time in the absence of the slogan.

I believe that a slogan often makes a crucial difference. A slogan is a vivid stimulus repeatedly associated with the proposal. Public opinion is approximately equally divided for and against many controversial proposals. An attractive, popular slogan can easily change the outcome from rejection to acceptance by members of the public and their representatives in Congress. Examples might be "strategic defense initiative" (Reagan) and "North American free trade agreement" (Clinton).

Political slogans that advertise a presidency have the same purpose as commercial slogans that advertise a product. Distinctive slogans are associated with some products, such as "the pause that refreshes" and "fly the friendly skies." Corporations spend millions of dollars to publicize these and other slogans because they contribute to public acceptance of their products.

REFERENCES

Bailey, T. A. (1976). *Voices of America*. New York: Free Press.
Barry, H., III. (1979). Birth order and paternal namesake as predictors of affiliation

with predecessor by presidents of the United States. *Political Psychology*, 1 (2), 61–66.

Barry, H., III. (1990). Intensified maternal identification among recent presidents of the United States. In P. H. Elovitz (Ed.), *Historical and psychological inquiry* (pp. 26–40). New York: International Psychohistorical Association.

Barry, H., III. (1991). National group governance in presidential elections: Fact and fantasy. In J. Offerman-Zuckerberg (Ed.), *Politics and psychology: Contemporary psychodynamic perspectives* (pp. 23–41) New York: Plenum Press.

Barry, H., III. (1996, June 30). Psychological antecedents of presidential slogans. Paper presented at 19th Annual Scientific Meeting of the International Society of Political Psychology, Vancouver, British Columbia.

deMause, L. (1982). *Foundations of psychohistory*. New York: Creative Roots Press.

Harris, I. D. (1964). *The promised seed: A comparative study of eminent first and later sons*. New York: Free Press.

New York Times. (1996). *The New York Times* (Computer Files, CD-ROM, 1991–1996). Ann Arbor, Mich.: University Microfilms International.

Sulloway, F. J. (1996). *Born to rebel: Birth order, family dynamics, and creative lives*. New York: Pantheon.

United States, Presidents. (1995). *The Presidential Papers* (Computer Files, CD-ROM). Provo, Utah: CDex Information Group.

CHAPTER 14

Political Language in an Environmental Controversy: Integrative Complexity and Motive Imagery in Advocacy Propaganda and the Press

PETER SUEDFELD, LORAINE LAVALLEE,
AND JENNIFER BROUGH

INTRODUCTION

Controversy has plagued forest management in Clayoquot Sound, an area located on the west coast of Vancouver Island, Canada (for details, see Lavallee & Suedfeld, 1997). The ongoing dispute has attracted local, regional, national, and even international attention. The Sound is a beautiful and pristine rain forest watershed, one of British Columbia's most popular tourist destinations. It is home to about 2,000 people, more than half of whom live in the town of Tofino and about half of whom belong to one of five aboriginal groups; another 29,000 people live in the immediate vicinity. Tofino is now primarily a center for ecotourism, but two other communities in the area (Ucluelet and Port Alberni) depend on the forest industry.

In conflicts over environmental policy, negative communication spirals seem to be the norm (Lange, 1993). As controversy escalates, participants increasingly ignore the complexity of the issues and the views of others. Derogatory epithets and rigid positions characterize the debate (Satterfield, 1996), and the possibility of mutually acceptable solutions becomes remote.

Two psychological processes may be responsible for the bitterness of such debates (Lange, 1993): (1) communication devoted to defeating opponents evokes similarly competitive and simplistic responses (see also Kelley & Stahelski, 1970; Miller & Holmes, 1975; Pearce, 1989; Pearce & Cromen, 1980; Pearce, Littlejohn, & Alexander, 1987); and (2) when opposing groups perceive their own particular goals as the only benevolent and legitimate ones, the results include an escalation of conflict and a rejection of compromise solutions (Deutsch, 1969).

Theory from the domain of political psychology provides a framework for understanding these tendencies. The cognitive manager model (Suedfeld, 1992) posits that problem solvers use the lowest level of integratively complex reasoning that they judge to be needed to reach their goals. Low integrative complexity is evidenced by a lack of awareness that there are legitimate alternative ways of looking at an issue and by categorical, right-or-wrong thinking in which potential ambiguity or conflict is not tolerated or even noticed.

High complexity is characterized by pluralistic reasoning, in which relationships among differing perspectives or goals are explicitly considered, with decisions based on syntheses of various alternatives. It requires more time, energy, concentration, and information-seeking and assessing mechanisms, and may lead to the neglect of other problems.

It follows that if a problem is seen as solvable through simple strategies, such strategies will be adopted. This is the case, *inter alia*, when only one's own values are seen as worthy of concern or when only one motive is activated. Conversely, value or motive pluralism and accountability to a diverse constituency enhance integratively complex reasoning (e.g., Tetlock, 1986).

In this chapter, we assess both value pluralism and motive pluralism related to the needs for Power, Affiliation, and Achievement (Atkinson, 1958; McClelland, 1961, 1975). *Power*, which corresponds to the goal of asserting influence identified by Lange (1993), is a desire for control, prestige, impact, or influence over others; *Affiliation* is the need to establish, maintain, or restore friendly relations among persons, groups or nations; and *Achievement* is a concern for excellence, improvement, and unique accomplishment. Motive pluralism suggests, for example, that groups having an intrinsic need to be both influential (Power) and liked (Affiliation) and recognizing that these two motives may dictate incompatible strategies will try to design arguments and solutions that will be more complex than those of groups motivated by either motive alone.

The information which we present in this chapter is based on a study that examined information campaigns and newspaper coverage concerning the Clayoquot land-use debate for the presence of motivational and cognitive factors that could influence the quality of forest land-use discussions and intergroup relations. First, we assessed the integrative complexity of published materials from source groups involved in the debate and from newspapers. Integrative complexity is defined by two cognitive variables, *differentiation* (the recognition of various components relevant to, and/or various legitimate viewpoints about, an issue) and *integration* (the development of conceptual connections among differentiated components) (e.g., Suedfeld, Tetlock, & Streufert, 1992).

Second, we applied a system developed by Winter (1992) to score need for Power, Achievement, and Affiliation reliably in archival materials. Winter's scoring system can be used on any text that is, at least in part, aspirational or that contains statements about goals, actions, or wishes.

Third, we coded the values endorsed by source groups to assess value overlap. We used Rokeach's (1979) definition of values as the beliefs about desired end states of existence (e.g., freedom, equality, happiness) or qualities implying preferred modes of conduct (e.g., ambitious, honest, independent).

Fourth, we analyzed newspaper coverage of the conflict for *balance*, defined as the presentation of the views of various major parties to the dispute without dismissing them as incorrect or otherwise not legitimate.

ROLE OF THE MASS MEDIA IN THE DISPUTE

It is quite likely that reports in the mass media affect policy disputes, including those about environmental policy. Many people look to newspapers as a source of information in trying to understand complex issues; balanced, complex coverage encourages nuanced, integrative, tolerant perspectives and support for creative resolutions.

Discussing an event in a dramatized fashion reduces readers' complexity in thinking about the event as well as their recall of factual information about it (Milburn & McGrail, 1992). We scored newspaper editorials for the same motive imagery factors as were analyzed in the public information materials of the disputants. Such analyses indicate motive richness (beyond mere factual description) in the editorials and compare the motives underlying explicitly partisan arguments with those of the purportedly nonpartisan media.

GROUPS INVOLVED IN THE CLAYOQUOT SOUND DEBATE

The following source groups were included in this study:

1. Three environmentalist groups: Friends of Clayoquot Sound, a local group established in Tofino; the Sierra Club of Western Canada and the Western Canadian Wilderness Committee (WCWC), based in urban centers
2. MacMillan Bloedel, Canada's largest forest company, with the largest land holdings in the Sound
3. Share Clayoquot Sound, a forestry community group based in Ucluelet (just outside the Sound), associated with "Share B.C." groups that have emerged in forestry-dependent communities to symbolize the use of contested areas for multiple purposes, definitely including forestry
4. The government of British Columbia

5. The Scientific Panel for Sustainable Forest Practices in Clayoquot Sound (referred to as Advisory Panel), appointed by the government to make recommendations on forestry in Clayoquot Sound and consisting of native leaders and independent scientists and forestry experts

We scored articles and editorials from one newspaper (referred to as local) published in Vancouver, the nearest large city; two newspapers (referred to as national), published in distant Canadian cities; and eight foreign, mostly American, newspapers published in major cities.

Environmentalist groups and forest industry advocacy groups defend the interests of different, and often opposing, constituents. The government and advisory groups, in contrast, are responsible for combining forestry activities with environmental values. Newspapers supposedly take a relatively balanced view, although they vary in their support for environmentalism versus industrial activity. Our newspaper sample also varied in how seriously the conflict and its possible resolutions would affect the newspaper's owners, editors, reporters, advertisers, and readers.

METHOD

Source Groups

Materials were solicited from thirteen groups involved in the Clayoquot debate and were received from nine groups. Two of these did not provide sufficient material for motive imagery coding, thus leaving seven source groups in the study. The materials analyzed for the Advisory Panel are taken from its first report (*Scientific Panel*, 1994), which describes its general guiding principles.

Newspapers

We selected newspaper articles and editorials from available library and Internet sources. The local newspaper is the Vancouver *Sun*, and the national newspapers are the Toronto *Globe and Mail* and the Halifax *Chronicle Herald*. Foreign newspapers included the *San Francisco Chronicle, Washington Post, New York Times, Dallas Morning News, Chicago Tribune, Los Angeles Times, Christian Science Monitor*, and *Manchester* (England) *Guardian*. This number of foreign sources was necessary because each reported relatively little about the Clayoquot Sound debate, and we also wanted to ensure a range of political orientations, national and international standing, readership, and other factors.

Straight news articles were scored for balance by counting the number of lines that referred to or quoted the views of various disputants as legitimate or worthy of consideration. These views were categorized as environmentalist, industry, government, and native. Editorials were scored for integrative complexity and for motive imagery; because no foreign paper published any editorials on the Clayoquot issue, the latter scores were derived solely from local and national editorials.

Scoring Systems

Integrative Complexity. Qualified scorers coded the information campaigns and editorials following the Conceptual/Integrative Complexity Scoring Manual (Baker-Brown, Ballard, Bluck, de Vries, Suedfeld, & Tetlock, 1992). The basic scoring unit is a passage (usually a paragraph) that focuses on one idea. For the editorials, the entire editorial was used as the scoring unit. At least five randomly selected scorable units are needed to provide a reliable score.

The coding system uses a 1–7 ordinal scale. A score of 1 reflects no differentiation; 3, moderate to high differentiation, but no integration; 5, moderate to high differentiation and low to moderate integration; and 7, high differentiation and high integration. Scores of 2, 4, and 6 identify transition points where properties of the next higher score are implied but not explicitly stated. Qualified scorers must participate in a workshop lasting three to five days, be familiar with the scoring manual (Baker-Brown et al., 1992), and maintain at least r = 0.85 with expert scoring.

Motive Imagery. The Achievement, Affiliation, and Power motive scoring systems were originally developed to code the brief imaginative stories that people tell or write in a Thematic Apperception Test (TAT) (Atkinson, 1958). We followed the training and scoring procedures as modified for use in archival studies (Winter, 1992).

Motive scores are the mean number of times that imagery related to the particular motive is present in 1,000 words of text. Five source groups provided at least two sets of 1,000 words each, and two sets of scores were obtained for each motive. Only one set of 1,000 words was available and scored for the WCWC and the Sierra Club.

Values. The values endorsed by the source groups were recorded from the material used for motive imagery coding. In order for a statement to be coded as endorsing a value, it had to express the source's explicit concern about, preference or need for, or intention to achieve a certain outcome or end state (e.g., "We need to ensure biodiversity."). Schwartz's (1992) value survey was used as a guide to help identify commonly held values.

Table 14.1
Average Integrative Complexity Levels for Source Groups

Source Groups	Complexity Score
British Columbia Government	2.11
Share Clayoquot Sound	1.86
Advisory Panel	1.84
Western Canadian Wilderness Committee	1.73
MacMillan Bloedel	1.69
Sierra Club	1.42
Friends of Clayoquot Sound	1.29

RESULTS

Complexity

Table 14.1 presents the mean levels of complexity for each source group. There were only low differentiation and no integration even in the most complex texts.

Each of the groups was then assigned to one of three categories: environmentalist, forest industry, or government/Advisory Panel. A one-way analysis of variance (ANOVA) was computed using the conservative critical value for N = 7 rather than the actual number of paragraphs. Complexity scores differed significantly across groups, $F(2, 4) = 7.70$, $p < .005$; Tukey's tests showed significantly higher complexity for the government/Advisory Panel than for the environmental advocacy groups, M = 1.96 versus 1.49, $t(2) = 3.82$, $p < .005$ (one-tailed). The complexity score of the industry advocacy groups (M = 1.80) was between the other two and did not differ reliably from either.

Editorials in local (M = 1.9) and national (M = 1.7) newspapers showed about equal levels of complexity. Both means were well within the complexity range of the source groups and showed implicit, rather than clear, differentiation. Thus, editorials were not strikingly better than partisan materials in recognizing legitimate alternative viewpoints or dimensions of the argument, much less in drawing conclusions that would integrate differing positions.

Motive Profiles

Total level of motive imagery (motive richness [Suedfeld, Bluck, Ballard, & Baker-Brown, 1990]) was quite low (Table 14.2). Overall, power imagery far exceeded levels of Affiliation and Achievement imagery in the

Table 14.2
Motive Imagery Scores

	Power	Affiliation	Achievement	Total
Western Canadian Wilderness Committee	4.00	0.00	0.00	4.00
Sierra Club	0.00	1.00	0.00	1.00
Friends of Clayoquot Sound	1.00	0.00	0.00	1.00
British Columbia Government	4.00	1.00	0.50	5.50
Advisory Panel	0.50	0.50	1.00	2.00
Share Clayoquot Sound	0.00	0.00	0.00	0.00
MacMillan Bloedel	2.00	0.00	0.00	2.00
Total Source Groups	**11.50**	**2.50**	**1.50**	
Local newspapers	1.25	1.75	0.75	3.75
National newspapers	0.00	0.00	0.33	0.33
Total Newspapers	**1.25**	**1.75**	**1.08**	

materials of the source groups. Using a repeated measures ANOVA, levels of imagery were found to differ significantly, $F(1, 2) = 3.9$, $p = 0.05$. Because these were within-subject comparisons, we used paired t-tests to assess paired differences. The difference between the levels of Power imagery ($M = 1.64$) and Achievement imagery ($M = 0.21$) approached conventional levels of significance, $t(6) = -2.02$, $p = 0.08$. The same analysis with Affiliation ($M = 0.36$) was less reliable, $t(6) = -1.89$, $p = .11$. These findings provide some support for Lange's (1993) contention that groups involved in land-use debates are focused on asserting influence and lack other goals that might facilitate discussions (i.e., Affiliation and Achievement). This conclusion, however, is qualified by differences observed in motive imagery among the different groups.

One-way ANOVAs compared the levels of each type of imagery among the three group categories. The only reliable difference observed was in Achievement imagery, $F(1, 2) = 12.86$, $p = 0.02$. Tukey's tests indicated that the government/Advisory Panel displayed significantly ($p < 0.05$) higher Achievement imagery (0.75) than the environmentalist groups and the forest industry (both = 0) categories. No reliable intergroup difference was found for Power and Affiliation.

Table 4.2 also shows motive imagery in newspaper editorials. Again, there was generally low motive richness, but local newspaper items were significantly higher than national items, $F(1, 5) = 29.3$, $p = 0.003$. We did not find the same predominance of Power as in source group materials.

Rather, the local newspaper had a high score on Affiliation, which indicated a concern about relations among the various participants in the dispute. Despite the very small sample size, the difference in Affiliation between the local and national newspapers approached significance, $t(5) = 2.35$, $p < 0.07$, two-tailed. The local newspaper also showed a tendency toward higher Power imagery ($p = 0.14$). Neither Affiliation nor Power appeared in the national editorials at all.

Value Profiles (Source Groups Only)

The degree to which the concerns of other groups are accepted as legitimate can be assessed by the extent to which the values endorsed by one group overlap with those of another (Table 14.3). Consistent with our predictions, we found no clearly overlapping values between the environmental and industry advocacy groups.

The government endorsed the widest range of values: environmental protection, local economic stability, and the economic prosperity of the province. The values of the Advisory Panel reflected its membership: the guiding value was to sustain the productivity and natural diversity of forest ecosystems, and the cultural values of Native First Nations, with other values endorsed to the extent that they did not undermine the guiding value.

Associations among Variables

The small number of groups prohibits statistical analyses of association among the motivational and cognitive variables examined in this study. Consistent with predictions that derive from Tetlock's value pluralism model (1986), however, the texts of the group that displayed the widest range of values, those of the British Columbia government, were also the most complex. The relation between complexity and motive pluralism—or, indeed, any measure of motive imagery—was less apparent.

Newspaper Coverage

Table 14.4 shows the distribution of news coverage that presented as legitimate (although not necessarily supporting) the viewpoints of various disputants. The views of the British Columbia government received attention from local and national Canadian newspapers and were virtually ignored by foreign ones; conversely, the views of native groups received more play in foreign than in Canadian articles. In spite of the small sample, both of these differences approached traditional levels of significance, $F(3, 26) = 2.6$, $p < 0.10$ and $F = 2.95$, $p < 0.07$, respectively.

Table 14.3
Values Endorsed by Source Groups

Western Canadian Wilderness Committee
  Preservation of old growth forests
  Rights of Native First Nations to Clayoquot lands

Sierra Club
  Protect the continued existence of all wildlife and plant species
  Aesthetic values of nature
  Rights of Native First Nations to Clayoquot lands

Friends of Clayoquot Sound
  Protection of wilderness and ecosystems
  Rights of Native First Nations to Clayoquot lands

British Columbia Government
  Preservation of wilderness
  Economic stability for communities
  Sustainable forestry
  Local participation in resource decision making
  Economic prosperity of the province

Advisory Panel
  Sustain the productivity and natural diversity of the region
  Human respect for the land and sea, and all the life and life systems they support
  Healthy economy for current and future generations through sustaining ecosystems
  Clayoquot Native First Nations' cultural (including spiritual) values
  Aesthetic and recreational values of region

Share Clayoquot Sound
  Forests devoted to resource extraction (working forest land base)
  Strong economy
  Corporate freedom
  Economic prosperity for small communities
  Recreational opportunities in the environment
  Support and compensation for workers displaced by conservation

MacMillan Bloedel
  None

Table 14.4
Newspaper Coverage of Participants' Positions

Mean % of Coverage Presenting

Newspapers	Environmentalists	Industry	Natives	Government
Local	41	26	10	23
National*	42	20	5	34
Foreign	36	26	30	8

*Figures do not total 100 percent due to rounding.

DISCUSSION

As conflicts over old-growth forests and other environmental issues escalate, we need a better understanding of factors that will decrease polarization and improve the quality of discussions and solutions. The diverse interests involved in forest land-use decisions require a movement toward pluralistic reasoning, in which complex decisions provide a synthesis of multiple goals without compromising important social, environmental, and economic values.

Consistent with Lange's (1993) research, the Clayoquot campaigns reflected relatively low levels of complexity and a focus on Power motivation. This pattern is characteristic of mutually hostile, uncompromising positions, and in studies of international crises has been found to precede the outbreak of war (Winter, 1993). Thus, the persuasive materials of the various disputants were not compatible with nonconfrontational resolutions. Although it can be argued that such materials might deliberately simplify to give a public impression of firm conviction (e.g., Lange, 1993), such deliberate manipulation of complexity (unlike the manipulation of content) appears to be limited where it exists at all (e.g., Guttieri, Suedfeld, & Wallace, 1995; Tetlock & Tyler, 1996). But regardless of the cause (Tetlock, 1981), a competitive public communication spiral can undermine the quality and eventual outcome of the debate.

The fact that newspaper editorials are no more complex than the inherently partisan statements of the source groups implies that not much help can be expected from those media in the search for generally acceptable integrative solutions. This is especially true when influential international media focus on dramatic, high-profile components of the event and ignore attempts to defuse the situation and develop acceptable compromises, thus encouraging continued intractability among disputants.

The groups trying to combine forestry activities with environmental values and accountable to the public at large (Tetlock, Skitka, & Boettger, 1989)—that is, the government and the Advisory Panel—displayed the highest complexity. To look at the data in another way, the defenders of existing policy (the government and the industry advocates) and the planners of new policy (the Advisory Panel, whose high score on achievement motivation reflects this goal) evidenced higher complexity than did policy critics (the environmentalists), a pattern compatible with earlier findings in both revolutionary and electoral politics (Suedfeld & Rank, 1976; Tetlock 1981; Tetlock, Hannum, & Micheletti, 1984).

The forest company texts contained the same total amount of imagery as the Advisory Panel; however, all of that imagery was focused on Power. Similarly, the very high motive richness of the environmental group WCWC consisted totally of Power imagery. Power imagery also dominated government texts, which had relatively low levels of Achievement and Affiliation.

Although the overall pattern of high Power, low Affiliation, and low Achievement imagery was consistent with Lange's hypothesis, there was considerable variability in Power imagery among the source groups. Regarding our prediction that the texts of advocacy groups would contain more Power and less Affiliation and Achievement imagery than those of the government/Advisory Panel, only the prediction for Achievement imagery was supported. The local advocacy groups on both sides (Friends of Clayoquot Sound and Share Clayoquot Sound), the Sierra Club, and the Advisory Panel displayed little or no Power imagery; MacMillan Bloedel showed low motive imagery, all of it Power. The government and WCWC displayed the strongest motives to influence others. The balance of motives in the Advisory Panel report suggests that the panel was guided by all three motives, a pattern that might facilitate satisfactory solutions.

Previous research has suggested that groups viewing only their own values as benevolent and legitimate are unlikely to engage in highly complex thinking about the issue (Tetlock, 1983) and might create negative spirals of destructive strategies and tactics (Deutsch, 1969). Indeed, Lange (1993) hypothesized that the negative communication spirals between forest industry advocacy groups and environmental advocacy groups was in part due to the conflict of values between these groups. As hypothesized, we found no overlapping values between the environmental and forest industry groups.

Environmentalists and people living in forestry-dependent communities have significant common interests, and the conflict might have less to do with differences in environmental concerns and values than with rural forest workers' concerns that their livelihoods are being dictated by urban outsiders, whether environmentalists or forest company managers (Dunk, 1994). The lack of shared values expressed in our data reflects hostility between people in forestry-dependent communities and environmental activists, which could be responsible for deflecting the discussion from the depletion of the resource, a central concern of both groups. Newspaper coverage did not remedy the situation: Canadian newspapers devoted two to three times as much space, and foreign newspapers ten times as much, to the opposing advocates as to the broader views of the government and its advisors.

As hypothesized, the wide range of values endorsed by the government and the Advisory Panel, which attempted to combine forestry and environmental values, overlapped with those of both advocacy groups. The Advisory Panel provides an example of an alternative approach to compromise solutions. Although it identified guiding values, it also endorsed other values—a healthy economy, aesthetic and recreational values—as long as pursuing them did not compromise the core value, respect for ecosystem sustainability.

Value and Motive Pluralism and Integrative Complexity

The cognitive manager model makes explicit predictions about value and motive pluralism and integrative complexity. Unfortunately, because of the small number of groups involved in any one land-use dispute, analyses of association among these variables are difficult. Some trends, however, deserve further attention. The groups with the three highest complexity scores—the government, Share Clayoquot Sound, and the Advisory Panel—endorsed the most diverse set of values, a finding consistent with the value pluralism hypothesis. The texts of the government and Advisory Panel contained all three forms of motive imagery, providing some support for the motive pluralism hypothesis. In contrast, however, the texts of Share Clayoquot Sound contained no motive imagery at all. The extent to which value and motive pluralism facilitate complex reasoning and prevent vilification of other groups requires more research.

Low complexity, a combination of the high need for Power with no concern for Affiliation or Achievement and the lack of shared values, predicts the continuation of forest wars, coercive attempts, and disruption. In the summer of 1997, the forestry labor union blockaded several environmentalist camps and boats, and the verbal conflict escalated further. The media have been unwilling or unable to suggest alternative approaches, and the government has had little success. Unless the patterns identified in this report are recognized and changed, we see little hope for peaceful resolution of Clayoquot and similar conflicts.

NOTE

This research was made possible by an operating grant from the Social Sciences and Humanities Research Council of Canada to the first author, and a Doctoral Fellowship from the same agency to the second author. We are grateful to Erin Soriano, who scored the source group materials for integrative complexity. Correspondence about the study should be addressed to the first two authors at the

Department of Psychology, University of British Columbia, 2136 West Mall, Vancouver, B.C. V6T 1Z4.

REFERENCES

Atkinson, J. (Ed.) (1958). *Motives in fantasy, action and society.* Princeton, N.J.: Van Nostrand.

Baker-Brown, G., Ballard, E. J., Bluck, S., de Vries, B., Suedfeld, P., & Tetlock, P. E. (1992). The conceptual/integrative complexity scoring manual. In C. P. Smith (Ed.), *Personality and motivation: Handbook of thematic content analysis* (pp. 401–18). Cambridge: Cambridge University Press.

Deutsch, M. (1969). Conflicts: Productive and destructive. *Journal of Social Issues,* 25, 7–41.

Dunk, T. (1994). Talking about trees: Environment and society in forest workers' culture. *Canadian Review of Sociology and Anthropology,* 31, 14–34.

Guttieri, K., Suedfeld, P., & Wallace, M. D. (1995). The integrative complexity of American decision-makers in the Cuban Missile Crisis. *Journal of Conflict Resolution,* 39, 595–621.

Kelley, H. H., & Stahelski, A. J. (1970). The inference of intentions from moves in the prisoner's dilemma game. *Journal of Experimental Social Psychology,* 6, 401–19.

Lange, J. I. (1993). The logic of competing information campaigns: Conflict over old growth and the spotted owl. *Communication Monographs,* 60, 239–57.

Lavallee, L., & Suedfeld, P. (1997). Conflict in Clayoquot Sound: Using thematic content analysis to understand psychological aspects of environmental controversy. *Canadian Journal of Behavioural Science,* 29, 194–209.

McClelland, D. C. (1961). *The achieving society.* Princeton, N.J.: Van Nostrand.

McClelland, D. C. (1975). *Power: The inner experience.* New York: Irvington.

Milburn, M., & McGrail, A. B. (1992). The dramatic presentation of news and its effects on cognitive complexity. *Political Psychology,* 13, 613–32.

Miller, D. T., & Holmes, J. G. (1975). The role of situation restrictiveness on self-fulfilling prophecies: A theoretical and empirical extension of Kelley and Stahelski's triangle hypothesis. *Journal of Personality and Social Psychology,* 31, 661–73.

Pearce, W. B. (1989). *Communication and the human condition.* Carbondale: Southern Illinois University Press.

Pearce, W. B., & Cronen, V. E. (1980). *Communication, action, and meaning: The creation of social realities.* New York: Praeger.

Pearce, W. B., Littlejohn, S. W., & Alexander, A. (1987). The new Christian right and the humanist response: Reciprocated diatribe. *Communication Quarterly,* 35, 171–92.

Rokeach, M. (1979). *Understanding human values: Individual and societal.* New York: Free Press.

Satterfield, T. A. (1996). Pawns, victims, or heroes: The negotiation of stigma and the plight of Oregon's loggers. *Journal of Social Issues,* 52, 71–83.

Schwartz, S. H. (1992). Universals in the content and structure of values: Theoretical advances and empirical tests in 20 countries. *Advances in Experimental Social Psychology,* 25, 1–65.

Scientific Panel for Sustainable Forest Practices in Clayoquot Sound (1994, January). Review of current forest practice standards in Clayoquot Sound. Victoria, B.C.

Suedfeld, P. (1992). Cognitive managers and their critics. *Political Psychology*, 13, 435–54.

Suedfeld, P., Bluck, S., Ballard, E. J., & Baker-Brown, G. (1990). Canadian federal elections: Motive profiles and integrative complexity in political speeches and popular media. *Canadian Journal of Behavioural Science*, 22, 26–36.

Suedfeld, P., & Rank, D. A. (1976). Revolutionary leaders: Long-term success as a function of changes in conceptual complexity. *Journal of Personality and Social Psychology*, 34, 169–78.

Suedfeld, P., Tetlock, P. E., & Streufert, S. (1992). Conceptual/integrative complexity. In C. P. Smith (Ed.), *Personality and motivation: Handbook of thematic content analysis* (pp. 393–400). Cambridge: Cambridge University Press.

Tetlock, P. E. (1981). Pre-to post-election shifts in presidential rhetoric: Impression management or cognitive adjustment? *Journal of Personality and Social Psychology*, 41, 207–12.

Tetlock, P. E. (1983). Accountability and complexity of thought. *Journal of Personality and Social Psychology*, 45, 74–83.

Tetlock, P. E. (1986). A value pluralism model of ideological reasoning. *Journal of Personality and Social Psychology*, 50, 819–27.

Tetlock, P. E., Hannum, K., & Micheletti, P. (1984). Stability and change in senatorial debate: Testing the cognitive versus rhetorical style hypothesis. *Journal of Personality and Social Psychology*, 46, 979–90.

Tetlock, P. E., Skitka, L., & Boettger, R. (1989). Social and cognitive strategies for coping with accountability: Conformity, complexity, and bolstering. *Journal of Personality and Social Psychology*, 57, 632–41.

Tetlock, P. E., & Tyler, A. (1996). Churchill's cognitive and rhetorical style: The debates over Nazi intentions and self-government for India. *Political Psychology*, 17, 149–70.

Winter, D. G. (1992). Content analysis of archival materials, personal documents, and everyday verbal productions. In C. P. Smith (Ed.), *Personality and motivation: Handbook of thematic content analysis* (pp. 110–25). Cambridge: Cambridge University Press.

Winter, D. G. (1993). Power, affiliation, and war: Three tests of a motivational model. *Journal of Personality and Social Psychology*, 65, 532–545.

CHAPTER 15

Post-Realism, Just War, and the Gulf War Debate

FRANCIS A. BEER AND ROBERT HARIMAN

REALISM AND POST-REALISM

Realism is the traditional, historical theory of international relations, reformulated in recent years as neorealism. It includes important narratives, among which are stories of itself and of the world. Realism presents itself as the primary actor in the world of theory, with greater power than other theories. Its taut story of world politics includes the following important elements:

1. Nation-states are the primary characters of world politics.
2. Nation-states are ranked by their power, measured mostly in terms of material capabilities, especially military force.
3. Nation-states conduct their foreign policies on the basis of national interest defined in terms of power. They calculate and compare benefits and costs of alternative policies and use all available means, including war.
4. The competition for power is permanent and ubiquitous. The story of realism continues indefinitely, often with consequences that are tragic in human terms.

With the end of the cold war and the transformation of the international environment, critics have increasingly attacked this view. They believe that realism has serious deficiencies as positive theory, thus failing fully and accurately to describe, explain, and predict international behavior. Post-realism makes the same charge and goes on to challenge the very positivistic bases on which realism rests. Post-realism takes a linguistic turn and suggests that realism is not only scientific positivistic theory but also—more significantly—a form of rhetoric representing itself as scientific positivistic theory. Realist theory is thus not only detached scientific observation but also speech action. As realism describes, explains, and predicts the world, it also constructs, shapes, forms, and controls it (Beer and Hariman, 1996).

Post-realists go beyond criticism to construct world politics persuasively in other ways. There is more to the story than realists admit, and post-realists supply missing parts of the tale. Elements of the post-realist narrative include the following:

1. Nation-states are not the only important characters in international relations. International organizations, such as the United Nations; domestic political factions; public opinion; and individuals all affect global events.

2. Power does not just grow from the barrel of a gun. International interactions are complex, and nonmaterial capabilities can be significant. Power is difficult to generalize and project and has very important dimensions that are embedded in specific issues and places.

3. Foreign policy cognition is thicker, denser, and hotter than realism believes. There is more to decision making than simple motivations of national interest defined in terms of power, benefits, costs, ends, and means. National elites have singular memories of history and its lessons; unique perceptions shape their views of policy situations and their political decisions. They are concerned with the legal, ethical, and moral rules of their communities, and they can be emotional.

4. Decision makers are not necessarily bound by realist narrative or by its characterization or plot. Decision makers appear in many different forms; they can construct themselves in many different ways. They can and do make a difference.

Post-realism, like realism, recognizes logic and facts; unlike realism, post-realism also recognizes rhetoric. Taking a linguistic turn, it emphasizes narrative as an important means of persuasion, with realist narrative being a primary example. Post-realism relies on criticism and the formulation of alternatives. It involves deconstruction and reconstruction, a rereading of texts, and a rewriting of concepts and practices to achieve a thorough revision of realist discourse. The turn into post-realism also involves an emancipatory dynamic; a renewed emphasis on agency, action, and freedom; a belief that a post-realist can affect his or her world. While sensitive to the claims of objective science, with its determinant structures, and processes, post-realism sees, at the same time, that these are human creations, the resultants, the emergent properties, of scientific and political practice. Post-realists broaden scientific inquiry to include a complex field of analytical frameworks. These frameworks are shaped in such a way that they are suitable for analyzing not only an objective "Other" but also the more important subjective "Self." Post-realism thus implies reflexivity; it suggests self-awareness that is enhanced by a heightened sensitivity to speech. Finally, post-realism combines strategy and ethics, power and prudence, cultural context and interpretation, and persuasion and psychology. These combinations emerge more clearly from a reconsideration of the realist doctrine of strategy, to which we now turn.

Post-realism incorporates these concerns in a three-tiered pyramid model of strategic action that includes competition, control, and criticism (Hariman, 1989). The first level, and the broadest, is the competitive calculus. The actor in this primitive situation is similar to Hobbes's natural man, driven by basic needs or instincts or drives. In the state of nature, where "man is a wolf to man," the actors compete with each other for scarce resources. This level is pure realism, with its heavy reliance on self-interest and the strategic interaction of self-interested actors as they are typically represented in rational choice and game theoretic formulations.

The second level is control, particularly self-control. Whereas the first level of competition emphasizes interaction with the Other, the second level of control emphasizes the construction of the Self. The Self, like Niccolo Machiavelli's Prince, recognizes the chaos and unpredictability of the competitive situation in the guise of *fortuna*. In response, he or she focuses on controlling what is most controllable: the persona or virtu of the ruler or decision maker (Hariman, 1995: 398). This persona is always calculating, manipulating, reacting to the competitive environment and—first and foremost—constructing itself as an imposing and intimidating character whom others will obey. It is better for the prince to be feared than to be loved, believes Machiavelli. Self-control is the attribute of this character that is essential to produce this outcome.

The argument to this point reflects and is consistent with classical and modern realist discourse. The third level of strategic action, critical judgment, takes one into new territory, well beyond modern realism's comfort zone. It is the critical turn, the defining move of post-realist strategy. It draws upon the work of strategist Karl von Clausewitz and particularly his elaboration of the importance of *Kritik*, which can be roughly translated as *criticism*. As Clausewitz defines it, *Kritik* is the process of moving strategic analysis through a hierarchy of perspectives that incorporate ever more diverse criteria and standards for judgment. The application of *Kritik* does not deny the validity of lower level analyses, but it does allow the strategist to reintroduce previously bracketed considerations. Further, from the perspective of *Kritik*, no account of the action is ruled irrelevant simply because it does not fit with a lower-level analysis. Thus, this form of critical thinking, which seems unnecessary to explain actions in simple competitive situations, allows one to compare and translate different, perhaps incommensurable, accounts that may question the very nature of such situations.

This idea develops more fully when it is restated as part of the linguistic turn. After the move to the highest level, strategic thinking becomes explicitly a form of interpretation. The strategist has to be able not only to assess the array of forces and to gauge political objectives and constraints but also to understand different accounts of the situation stated in different ways. Instead of presuming that outcomes are determined by the logic of a primitive strategic situation and the natural laws of coercion in a static political environment, the strategist presumes that the meanings of strategic conflicts are not easily predicted from any one set of variables. Instead of an autonomous mode of analysis and a single language of calculation, the strategist recognizes that different languages offer different realities, different meanings, and different means for motivating reactions. Thus, the strategist has to be able to translate, learn from, and perhaps act in accord with discourses that reflect different cultural practices and communal interests than those explicitly represented in the typical formulations of grand strategy.

Law, ethics, and religion become more serious concerns at the highest level of strategy because they are now understood in a different way. Where realists saw irrelevant distractions, post-realists recognize important and accurate maps of complex social formations. This wide screen also captures previously neglected discourses of the peoples caught in the field of conflict, whether they are there as enemies, collaborators, or bystanders, regardless of their level of civilization. One cannot presume that any of their perspectives is inadequately informed or inconsequential, but one has to look to each for knowledge, symbolic resources, and constraints potentially at work in the situation. Likewise, one cannot rule that an argument is not sufficiently military or geopolitical, for the strategist has to consider whether success on those terms could be damaging to broader political, social, or ecological objectives.

In short, there are many levels of discourse impinging upon the strategic situation, and the strategist will be more likely to succeed by recognizing how the horizontal means-end calculus within any account of the situation also has to be matched by a vertical attempt to gain maximum interpretive power. One's thinking always will be bracketed; questions of utility and effectiveness, speed and impact will be paramount. But the genius lies in the ability to discern which discourses for interpreting the scene shall be maximized and which set aside at any particular time.

This formulation reevaluates the normative dimension of world politics. From their bracketed, marginal position in realist theory, values, ethics, and morality now emerge as significant parallel discourses, the return of the repressed. Normative discourse has its own important strategic implications, depending on the actors, the situation, and number of people who believe it to be important.

Normative discourse exists in the mind in schema form, to use the vocabulary of contemporary psychology. Schemata are internal cognitive frames that are embedded in people's minds. As traces of past experience, they provide guides to future action. They help actors to interpret environmental cues and frame current issues of peace and war within a particular context of previously learned meaning. The cognitive process begins when initial cues from the environment stimulate or prime the actors to recall a particular schema. The schema frames events in a particular structure of perception and interpretation that leads to specific policies, decisions, and actions. Sound strategic analysis recognizes the critical importance of such cognitive processes, and of alternative cognitive schemata, in the heuristics of decision making.

JUST WAR

The doctrine of just war is a clear example of an alternative cognitive schema at work in the formulation of foreign policy. This doctrine provides a different schema or framework for structuring the global struggle for power and the massive violence that goes with it and for indexing a complex network of related narratives. Public speakers articulate and evoke these narratives in public discourse to reflect and shape public consciousness of political issues. They frame these issues to give them a particular intention and meaning, a sense and direction, and a goal and purpose.

Just war has deep and broad historical roots. Some of its sources lie in the work of non-Western scholars, for example, the classical Islamic scholar Shaybani. Western origins include the classical churchmen and lawyers, whose Latin words index many of the terms in contemporary usage (see Beer, 1987, 1981; Walzer, 1977). The doctrine of the just war has two major branches: (1) justification for going to war, *jus ad bellum*, and (2) justifiable acts in wartime, *jus in bello*. The justification for going to war, jus ad bellum, in turn, depends on four principal elements: (1) proper authority, (2) just cause, (3) right intent, and (4) peaceful end (Johnson, 1975: 26). Once war actually begins, international law helps to define its limits. Contemporary limits on war-fighting violence, articulated through the doctrine of *jus in bello*, include two major elements: (1) proportionality and (2) discrimination (Johnson, 1975: 26). Despite claims of military necessity, the doctrine of *jus in bello* helps in determining whether the means are appropriate to the ends.

Modern proponents of just war suggest that it serves as a set of international norms or rules that are part of the prevailing international legal and ethical regime. Yet the political mechanisms through which just war theory lives in the real world have not been well developed. For just war theory to be politically effective, actors must bring the theory to the concrete level of politics. International decision makers and attentive international publics must have a material interest in promoting it, believe that it is important, be well informed about it, and attempt to apply it in specific international situations.

This happens in policy discourse. Proponents and opponents of particular policies related to peace or war use elements of just-war doctrine to support their own policy positions and attack those of political opponents. The motivation to use the doctrine of just war comes not only from the abstract, a general desire to rein in international violence, but also as part of the rhetorical weaponry of policy argument.

The rhetorical use of just war is talk, but it is also more than that. One can never be certain that words accurately reflect the real thoughts of the speakers nor that all important motivations for action are spoken; yet, one can safely assume that public rhetoric reflects what is in somebody's mind. Speakers would not say the words if they did not believe that an audience would properly receive and appreciate them. Political actors speak theory to maintain and mobilize support, to articulate and refresh the beliefs of supporters, to neutralize or convert opponents, and to construct and dissolve domestic and international coalitions.

THE GULF WAR DEBATE

Between January 10 and 12, 1991, the United States Congress conducted the most extensive public peace/war debate in American history. Most members of the House and the Senate spoke in plenary session about the Gulf War decision. All of this is in a compact body of text that is self-contained and locally accessible.

Preliminary investigation has revealed an outline of how the speakers used arguments asserting claims and counterclaims that are traceable to elements of the *jus ad bellum*. For example, one facet of the debate concerned the proper authority of the president to undertake war against Iraq and the role that Congress should play in that decision. Senator George Mitchell (D-Me.) succinctly described the conflict between presidential and congressional authority. On the one hand, he noted the president's valid claim to authority. "The Constitution designates the President as Commander in Chief of the Armed Forces," he said. "With that designation comes the authority to direct the deployment of those forces." On the other hand, he advanced a counterclaim to limit presidential authority. "The Constitution also grants to the Congress," he said, "the authority to raise and support armies and to declare war" (ll. 104–09).[1]

The proper authority of the United Nations was also important. Senator Patrick Leahy (D-Vt.) noted that "President [George] Bush's leadership in securing a United Nations authorization of the use of force if necessary to compel Iraq to leave Kuwait is a triumph for the role and authority of the United Nations in establishing collective security as a basis for international relations" (ll. 554–57).

Some Senators challenged Iraqi President Saddam Hussein's proper authority to wage war. His claim hinged partly on the acceptance or rejection of his historical claim that Kuwait was properly a part of Iraq and therefore within Iraq's sphere of sovereign internal action. Senator Patrick Moynihan

(D-N.Y.) implicitly recognized Saddam's argument. "Iraq as such," he noted, "is an artifact of the Treaty of Sevres which ended the First World War with Turkey and the allies in 1920. The precise borders of Iraq were drawn in a tent in 1925 by a British colonial official" (ll. 1141–43).

Most U.S. senators did not believe that Iraq had a reasonable historical claim to Kuwait. They asserted, instead, that Kuwait was indeed a proper, independent sovereign state and that, therefore, Iraq did not have proper authority under international law to use military force. Senator Jesse Helms (R-N.C.) asserted that "The principle of national sovereignty is the very basis of our independence and national survival. It follows from the rule of national sovereignty that legitimate governments have the right not to be disturbed by foreign aggression." By itself, this statement might have served to justify the proper authority of Iraq to use force within its sovereign borders, including Kuwait. Senator Helms, however, explicitly rejected this claim when he asserted Kuwaiti sovereignty. "These principles are of particular importance to the United States," he said, "when the victim whose sovereignty is violated is a country such as Kuwait, which has a key role in economic and diplomatic relationships with the United States" (ll. 40658–64).

Iraq's lack of fundamental democratic processes also raised the question of Saddam's own legitimacy as leader, which further undermined his claim of proper authority. This issue, however, was complicated by Kuwait's own lack of the political, economic, and social freedoms that Americans take for granted. Senator Kent Conrad (D-N.D.) did not favor military intervention. He tried to lighten the challenge to Iraq's proper authority by claiming that "the sovereignty of Kuwait is a secondary issue. A well-crafted compromise can restore Kuwaiti independence. Freedom, at least as Americans understand it," he continued, "is not an issue in the Gulf. Americans serving there aren't free to observe their religious holidays nor enjoy their favorite beverages" (ll. 27509–14).

The questions of just cause and right intent hinged partly on resolution of the prior issue of proper authority. As noted, Saddam's argument rested on his reading of the history of the British Empire. If Saddam did not have proper authority or just cause, as U.S. and allied decision makers insisted, the legitimacy of the *casus bellum*, of the United States case for war, was stronger. It was also implicit that Americans and their allies had just cause and right intent because the U.S. effort was part of a collective self-defense project legitimatized by the United Nations Charter. Alleged Iraqi human-rights violations further strengthened the Allied case.

Similarly, the question of peaceful end also depended on whether one interpreted the conflict in a short-term peacekeeping frame or a longer term imperialist one. Senator Robert Dole (R-Kan.) strongly asserted the peaceful end of American policy, "I have implored the President, who also has been there in World War II, that what we are attempting to do in the

Congress of the United States is to strengthen his hand for peace, not to give him a license to see how fast we can become engaged in armed conflict" (ll. 37475–78). Senator Conrad (D-N.D.) challenged this interpretation of Allied motivation. "The sand that Saddam wants, and the oil under it, aren't worth the sacrifice," he said. "And there should be no mistake; the oil is what the war is about" (ll. 27504–07).

Important issues were also raised by the theory of *jus in bello*. Concerns of proportionality and discrimination centered on legitimate war aims, for example, embargo costs to the Iraqi population and the possible occupation of Baghdad. Other questions included uses of inhumane weapons—atomic, biological, chemical; distinctions between civilian and military targets; and protection of the sick and wounded. One example of such concerns was expressed by Senator Timothy Wirth (D-Colo.) "If force must be used," he urged, "we would be well advised to restrict offensive action to air attacks, using armored forces defensively to deter any attempt by Iraq to widen the conflict on the ground. We could, for example, assert the sovereignty of Kuwaiti air space quickly and without great casualty. Then any Iraqi attack on Kuwaiti-sanctioned aircraft in Kuwaiti air space would be dealt with immediately and decisively" (ll. 17548–54).

TALKING THEORY

The Gulf War debate was a war of words that came before the actual war. Realist concerns of power and efficient application of force were as substantial in the debate as they were later on the battlefield, yet post-realist ideas were also important. The debate clearly showed the significance of factors going well beyond the realist model—non-national actors (legislators); nonmilitary actions (rhetoric); and ethics, law, and morality (just war). The constraints of international competition and the discipline of self-control remained important in formulating strategy; at the same time, criticism and interpretation played crucial roles. During the Gulf War debate, political actors engaged in critical thinking as they debated the doctrine of just war. Just war framed, justified, and interpreted the acts involved in fighting the war on the battlefield and in constructing the subsequent peace (see Vaux, 1992).

Just war doctrine is one of the important ways that political and scholarly actors construct contemporary collective meaning. The doctrine provides an ethical, normative frame to structure and limits massive violent actions. Speaking of just war is part of how political actors go about creating both war and justice. Writing about just war and testing its existence in the real world are important scholarly contributions to public policy and political understanding. Our analysis illustrates how political actors use just war doctrine to supplement realism in foreign policy discourse. Actors accentuate or diminish different elements of just-war doctrine to support and oppose the use of coercive force. Just-war doctrine is not only part of the international and domestic struggle for power but also a separate, independent theme in political discourse and culture that helps to shape real-world conflict and cooperation. At the same time, the speakers' use of just-war categories feeds back into just war doctrine itself. Just war rests on a long historical tradition and is usually expounded in general, abstract terms. By grounding it in a specific, contemporary debate, scholars have a much better sense of its relevance and importance in a contemporary context. Just-war analysis is not just an abstruse branch of public international law of war but a dynamic part of collective political life.

Political debate in a democratic forum is part of a process of complex practical reasoning that articulates logics of competition (realism) and cooperation (just war). This process is explicitly normative, thoroughly strategic, and essentially symbolic. Just war is used as a template for integrating interest and justice; for building alliances, domestic and foreign; and for instilling a bias toward the long view into decision making (in part by tending to slow down decision making and in part by implying that just acts are the most strategic in the long term as they produce stability, reduce domestic dissent, and achieve other positive results). The just war schema also operates as a "moving category system," that is, a basic device for sifting, organizing, and evaluating information and perspectives and particularly for doing so when they come from disparate (seemingly contrary, contested, or incommensurable) sources or discourses. Hence, just war theory is not merely a set of principles applied "from above" and fitting poorly into the realist practice of foreign policy decision making. Instead, as postrealism suggests, it is an integral part of the process.

NOTE

1. Textual references are to line numbers in the electronic text of the congressional debate. Thanks to Claudia Dahlerus, Jared Haller, and Nicole Rosmarino for research assistance.

REFERENCES

Beer, F. A. (1981). *Peace against war: The ecology of international violence*. San Francisco: W. H. Freeman.
Beer, F. A. (1987). Just war. In L. Pauling, E. Laszlo, & J. Y. Yoo (Eds.), *World encyclopedia of peace*, I (pp. 508–511). Oxford: Pergamon Press.
Beer, F. A., & Hariman, R. (Eds.) (1996). *Post-realism: The rhetorical turn in international relations*. East Lansing: Michigan State University Press.
Hariman, R. (1989). Before prudence: strategy and the rhetorical tradition. In B. E. Gronbeck (Ed.), *Spheres of argument: Proceedings of the sixth SCA/AFA conference on argumentation* (pp. 108–16). Falls Church, Va.: Speech Communication Association.

Hariman, R. (1995). *Political style: The artistry of power*. Chicago: University of Chicago Press.
Johnson, J. G. (1975). *Ideology, reason and limitation of war: Secular and religious concepts*. Princeton, N.J.: Princeton University Press.
United States of America. (1991). *Congressional Record: Proceedings and Debates of the 102nd Congress, First Session*, vol. 37, nos. 7, 8 (January 11–12). Washington, D.C.: U.S. Government Printing Office.
Vaux, K. L. (1992). *Ethics and the Gulf War: Religion, rhetoric, and righteousness*. Boulder, Colo.: Westview.
Walzer, M. (1977). *Just and unjust wars: A moral argument with historical illustrations*. New York: Basic Books.

Epilogue: Where Do We Stand?

OFER FELDMAN

Previous chapters approach the issue of political language from several empirical, conceptual, and theoretical standpoints. Obviously, other theories and concepts also could be discussed in this volume, and the spectrum of analysis through which political discourse is viewed here clearly could be broader. The editors, however, selected the themes that we consider the most important for better understanding the nature, characteristics, and content of political language in different environments and for examining the functions that language plays in the polity. Though different in subject matter, the chapters of this book complement one another through interlinking the important theme of the power of language as a crucial form of political action. Indeed, several chapters go beyond analysis of the power of political language and its effects and take a clear ideological stance as to what language should do in the public sphere.

Considering again the links between chapters, one can discern a number of underlying bonds: the essence of politics, the power and complexity of language, the role of mass media, and methods of research.

THE ESSENCE OF POLITICS

In emphasizing the centrality of the language in politics, this volume underscores the notion that political society is constituted by language—in other words, the essence of politics is talk. In Western democratic societies, Middle Eastern countries, Russia, and Latin America, discourse dictates what is possible and what is not possible to say at a given time. Words reduce the uncertainties and contradictions, characteristics of abstract concepts and political maneuvers, to the extent that language becomes an important instrument of power, a means for winning political office, a tool for influencing policy, and a weapon for mobilizing the public's support.

The discourse of politicians is constructed, disseminated, and transformed by homing in on a common rhetoric of key words and formulaic phrases used mainly to inform and to interpret the state of polity and the role played by the political elite. To apprise their colleagues and the public about their activities, political issues and the political agenda, politicians and bureaucrats use language to interpret the significance of developing events, to clarify the dynamics of political issues, to reveal their targets, and to control public debate. They go beyond informing others; rather they explain their motives, justify their activities, and endeavor to give meaning to the things that take place in politics.

In Chapter 6, one noticeable example is discussed by Amos Kiewe in his analysis of how the twentieth-century American presidency, in particular, has become labeled the *rhetorical presidency* (Tulis, 1987). This term serves to describe a style of leadership, relying heavily on public discourse, in which rhetoric equals action. In turn, the public has come to consider the rhetorical and the oratorical as primary features of the executive branch of government. Ironically, the public sometimes judges individuals by their words, not by their deeds.

THE POWER OF LANGUAGE

The idea that language is powerful permeates each chapter: language affects political affairs on both domestic and international levels; language influences behaviors and attitudes; and language can shape, change, and reverse opinions. Some chapters explore the kinds of language and symbols that attract political support and votes and shape attitudes toward political institutions and politicians. Maritza Montero and Isabel Rodriguez-Mora (Chapter 8) note that presidential addresses in Argentina, Brazil, and Venezuela between 1990 and 1996 aimed to present and justify certain policies and to convince the public of the appropriateness and potential benefits of those policies. In the usually authoritarian Arab world, Raphael Israeli (Chapter 2) claims that leaders use Arabic, with its strength of expression, its wealth of allusions, and the emotional associations that it evokes, to impress upon the public the supremacy of the Islamic world, and to mobilize support for its leaders.

Carol B. Conaway (Chapter 5) suggests that a particular form of rhetoric within the Jewish tradition—the *midrash*—was a medium used to convey and cultivate the ancient ethnocentric concepts that enabled Jews to retain their collective identity. She argues that this, in turn, affected Jewish political behavior. Indeed, she sees the rabbinic messages about Jewish national identity and claims that Israel is the eternal homeland as more nationalistic than theological. By contrast, in Japan, as Ofer Feldman indicated, leaders of political groups and their aids conduct endless secret political consultations with representatives of other political groups and with government bureaucrats. Quietly, they present to each other their stances on specific issues. They express support for or objections to the views held by other members on these topics and are able to resolve conflicts of opinions by involving all relevant parties in the decision-making process.

The impact of powerful language shifts to the use of slogans. American presidential slogans, as Herbert Barry III suggests in Chapter 13, are targeted toward gaining acceptance of a presidential proposal by associating the proposal with a brief, memorable phrase. By employing words such as "good," "rights," "revolution," "defense," "war," "welfare," and "new," slogans can elicit strong emotional responses. So, too, can metaphors achieve similar results. These emotive diamonds of language inform us about "users" (politicians and the audience) and social and political experiences, argues Christ'l De Landtsheer in Chapter 11. Equally, the rhetoric of just war, as Francis A. Beer and Robert Hariman claim in Chapter 15, is exploited to legitimatize national interests, to shape foreign policy, and to construct the institutions and process of a normative international regime, known simply as the New World Order.

In Chapter 6, Richard D. Anderson, Jr., notes the potent force of linguistic cues in directing the attention of potential political participants and in capturing their political allegiance. He describes this process in particular references to Russia, where adults are acquiring partisan identities for the first time because political parties have not yet established themselves and parents have not yet had sufficient opportunity to supply partisan cues. Peter Suedfeld and his colleagues (Chapter 14) detail how conflicts over environmental issues in Canada reflect relatively low levels of complexity and a focus on power motivation. This pattern is characteristic of mutually hostile, uncompromising positions and, in studies of international crises, has been found to precede the outbreak of war. Thus, the authors suggest that, regardless of the cause, a competitive public communication spiral can undermine the quality and eventual outcome of a debate.

THE COMPLEXITY OF LANGUAGE

This volume also reveals the versatility and diversity of political discourse in regard to the sources of the rhetoric, the content of the message, and the environment in which these messages are produced and disseminated. Often, the sources are those who either already hold political positions—politicians or presidents—or are positioning themselves as candidates for political office. Other individuals and institutions are also directly or indirectly involved in public affairs and likewise employ verbal behavior that influences politics. These include government bureaucrats, representatives of labor unions, members of interest and support groups, and also religious leaders whose messages are of a nationalistic nature. Because so many sources are involved in political discourse, there is a need to identify and differentiate these sources in order to understand the nature and significance of the language produced and used in given social and political milieus.

As some chapters suggest, politicians in Western societies, in addition to maintaining their leadership qualities, negotiation skills, and ability to keep effective working relationships with other politicians and government bureaucrats, must demonstrate a certain rhetorical inclination and skill that allows them to communicate effectively with consequence. Kiewe (Chapter 7) notes that the more successful U.S. presidents in this century, such as Theodore Roosevelt, John F. Kennedy, and Ronald Reagan, have been known for their strong rhetorical abilities. In contrast, those presidents whose terms have been described as less than inspiring are those also considered the least rhetorically gifted. In the case of J. M. Le Pen in France, Simone Bonnafous argues in Chapter 9 that the force of Le Pen's discourse is not only the result of the chosen political themes or style of rhetoric but also a product of his ability to integrate all of these elements into an argumentative structure adapted to a specific context and public.

The content and style of the messages that political communicators produce are also significant variables that need special consideration. In most cases, politicians and other sources decide on the content and timing of their speeches, appeals, and declarations. They tend to focus on issues with which they feel most comfortable, to choose topics that they can handle, or to avoid issues with which they are not familiar or those that can affect their political agendas. Political styles can differ, not only according to nationality but also according to ideology and gender, concludes De Landtsheer in Chapter 11 on European parliamentary rhetoric.

To achieve policy objectives that are difficult to accomplish under normal routines, politicians sometimes resort to a special type of rhetoric, as Kiewe details in his analysis of the preference for crisis rhetoric by American presidents (Chapter 7). In effect, presidents do well when they are in control of defining the crisis. In Latin America, as discussed by Montero and Rodriguez-Mora in Chapter 8, presidents position themselves as heroes and positive protagonists. Their discourse depicts them as experts, as the ultimate team leaders, and as the saviors of their homelands. In other cases, they use political discourse to place themselves above the country's citizens and all other possible political actors. Self-reference here seems to be an important ingredient in presidential discourses and acts to depict presidents as the main actors, working with teams of ministries and consultants, to whom they may manifestly give support and praise.

Leaders of democratic societies have presumably different rhetoric styles than leaders of other types of regimes. In undemocratic societies, Anderson suggests in Chapter 6, rulers and politicians use their public speech to suppress "democratic participation." By restricting their public speech, dictators achieve their objective of discouraging people from taking sides in the political contest. Undemocratic rulers avoid utterances that might draw popular attention to the possibility of a mutually destructive political contest in which the public might try to take sides. Dictators, therefore, prefer to talk about the community as a unified whole, the military threat posed by their foreign rivals, and the threats to the country's unity posed by domestic disorder. Anderson noted that in Russia, for example, utterances by electoral speakers are significantly more likely to draw attention to the reasonableness of the speakers than are utterances by their authoritarian communist predecessors in the Soviet Union. The texts of authoritarian Russians strictly avoid epistemic usage of the frequently occurring, pragmatically ambiguous modals. Speech-act usage of these modals is also quite rare. By contrast, such epistemic usage and speech styles become reasonably frequent in public statements by electoral politicians.

The complexity further lends itself to explicit and implicit uses of language. Arab leaders, Israeli observes in Chapter 2, profusely use Islam in matters of symbolism, historical precedent, and vocabulary in order to survive domestically and further their foreign policy externally. In Japan (Chapter 4), on the other hand, politicians and government officials tend to talk vaguely so as to avoid disclosing their thoughts and honest feeling in public, whereas they reveal their real intentions and opinions only in private, informal, and nonceremonial meetings.

In the case of religious leaders, as detailed by Conaway (Chapter 5), rhetorical analysis can be more elusive than that of secular leaders because the sources of evidence might be the standard fare. The rabbinic concepts of a collective identity linked to the Land of Israel developed in *midrashim* are interpretations that created very positive and enduring concepts of Jewish identity, which could have influenced Jewish political behavior. Because the rabbis were both the spiritual and the political leaders of Jewry during the early centuries of the Common Era and for centuries thereafter, *midrash* was a perfect medium through which to transmit an enduring concept of a land-based Jewish collective identity. The messages within these *midrashim* are a rich vein of Jewish political thought.

In terms of style, discourse of politicians can be explicit, with direct appeals revealing their real thoughts and feelings, or it can use metaphors (typically involving the transferring of a word, a name, and at least some of the meaning that the word ordinarily conveys, to something else) or slogans (a catchword or rallying motto distinctly associated with a political party or other group). Metaphors allow speakers to talk and think about one area of experience in terms of another, and they can influence the way in which large numbers of people conceive of sensitive and controversial aspects of their immediate reality (Jansen & Sabo, 1994: Lackoff, 1991).

Slogans, as discussed by Barry in Chapter 13, can summarize the promises or policies of politicians and their administrations. Metaphors and slogans can be a powerful tools when applied consistently and systematically in a particular social or political context. Political communicators frequently exploit a set of conventional metaphors or slogans to achieve their political objectives of shaping people's attitudes toward politics; creating a certain image of politicians, political institutions, and political parties to the extent that they attract political support and votes; or justifying their activities and policies.

As users of language in everyday social life and because they are capable of decoding messages differently from the way in which they were encoded in texts by the politicians, the public is seen to play an active role in the process by which discourses are both reproduced and transformed. In this context, the audience, "the people in the street," are important players. The audience is tuned to listen to what a particular politician might say on a specific issue or on pending issues in which the public shows interest. This is probably because politics has been so pervasive in their lives that practically all aspects of their routines are governed by politics, not only the regime they live under and the society and environment they live in, but also such matters as health, housing, welfare, standard of living, education, transportation, the food they eat, the goods they consume, and all the rest. Therefore, the audience listens to those who hold the reins of power and the purse of money in order to detect any nuance of policy that could affect any aspect of the people's lives.

As a whole, the chapters in this book indicate directly or indirectly the need to explore political discourse outside formal institutions. Language might be a significant factor in the activities of members of the political elite and other decision makers, but, at the same time, it also constitutes a reciprocal relationship with the audience, "the ordinary citizens." Political discourse not only deals with public affairs that concern and affect a large number of citizens but also with the way in which citizens produce and use political discourse to construct and interpret different messages, ideological arguments, and opinion.

Affecting all of these is the environment in which messages are produced and disseminated. The culture or the context in which messages are transmitted and received can have a great bearing on their meaning. The same message passing in Japan, the United States, Russia, or elsewhere will probably carry different meanings, will result in different interpretations, and will have different implications. Political rhetoric and semantics are influenced by various social and cultural factors that are typical of a specific environment. In Germany, for example, Christa Lang-Pfaff notes in Chapter 3 that political rhetoric was influenced by the country's political system, which has changed radically several times during the twentieth century. As a result, the political language of the present Germany has not only "changed" but "turned around." And in Britain, as Peter Bull suggests in Chapter 12, because of the adversarial political system in which no politician can afford to lose face, a politician's skills in face management in televised interviews are of central importance.

Because readers and listeners of a particular political entity apply to the language an interpretative framework derived from their own culture, different audiences would perceive political speeches and declarations differently. This phenomenon would probably affect each audience, the political agenda, and the reaction of the news media, as well as the general public, in different ways. The chapters in this volume actually talk to each other in this regard.

THE MASS MEDIA

The chapters indicate the growing role and importance of intermediate channels in political discourse. As the primary sources of social and political information, the news media, in particular television and newspapers, are increasingly reporting political issues and events and the activities of politicians (Ansolabeher, Behr, & Iyenagar 1993; Lee & Solomon, 1990). In Britain, for example, Bull (Chapter 12) reveals that, during recent general elections, televised political interviews have played a prominent role and, as such, must continue to be considered one of the most important means of political communication in contemporary British politics.

By selection and exclusion in reporting issues and events of the day, the news media are able to define the news, decide how the news is to be interpreted, and frame particular aspects of perceived reality. The media have affected political attitudes and behavior; influenced the way people construct their images and perceptions of the political world and politicians; and magnified, among other things, the effectiveness of sound bites, brief, memorable statements (Anderson & Opfer, 1992), which, Barry suggests, have become slogans to characterize a presidential administration.

Because of the growing impact of the news media, as detailed in the case of Japan (Chapter 4), politicians try to control the scope and nature of the information disseminated by newspapers and television. Political sources tend to filter the information given to reporters, on the one hand, and to prohibit reporters from publishing other types of information that they consider less than convenient for them, on the other hand. To exploit this contact to their own advantage, media sources tend to develop cozy relationships with media representatives.

In chronicling financial events, Matthew G. Sorley notes in Chapter 10 that the financial media are responsible for identifying, collecting, packaging, and disseminating economic news. The financial press constructs a version not only of economic reality but also of social and political reality. The financial media play a prominent role in facilitating the production and reproduction of such discursive practices and might be implicated as a vehicle of social control. Therefore, the financial press exploits a media narrative to serve social, economic, and political ends.

In the case of land-use debate (Chapter 14), Suedfeld and colleagues detail that newspaper editorials are no more complex than the inherently partisan statements of the source groups; this implies that not much help can be expected from those media in the search for generally acceptable integrative solutions. This is especially true when influential international media focus on dramatic, high-profile components of a particular event and ignore attempts both to defuse the situation and to develop acceptable compromises. Such actions thus encourage continued intractability among the disputants involved.

METHODS OF RESEARCH

Some of the chapters in this volume represent methodological advances suggesting that political discourse can be explored through various approaches and research methods. Discourse analysis, one method employed in several chapters, provides an opportunity to focus on the social text itself and to comprehend better the structure and organization of discourse. The framework allows for a consideration of text function and the possible consequences of the use of particular instantiations of meaning in the text.

Montero and Rodriguez-Mora (Chapter 8) use a qualitative methodological procedure for discourse analysis to examine the discourse of three Latin American presidents to show how they perceive politics and their roles. In Chapter 9, Bonnafous examines the rhetoric of Le Pen to highlight his ideological orientations through an analysis of a televised presentation on one of the most widely viewed programs of political discussion in France. De Landtsheer presents a political semantic analysis of metaphorical discourse within the European Parliament (1981–1993) in Chapter 11. Here, European, national and gender identities among the delegates were tested by means of a quantitative political-style analysis.

Further, a discourse analytic examination of financial press accounts of the 1987 stock market crash is detailed by Sorley (Chapter 10). This chapter focuses on the function and construction of investor categories and the rhetoric of regulation. In Chapter 14, Suedfeld and colleagues examine information campaigns and newspaper coverage concerning the Clayoquot land-use debate for the presence of motivational and cognitive factors that might influence the quality of forest land-use discussions and intergroup relations. They observe the integrative complexity (defined by two cognitive variables, differentiation and integration) of published materials from source groups involved in the debate and from newspapers. In Anderson's analyses (Chapter 6) of the spoken texts of elite members from the authoritarian era in the Soviet Union and texts from the first two years of electoral politics in Russia, he identifies in each corpus of texts, all instances of the three Russian modals capable of expressing pragmatic ambiguity. He then reviews the context of each instance to classify the modality as a content, epistemic, or speech-act usage.

Kiewe (Chapter 7) and Barry (Chapter 13) examine, through several case studies, the nature and function of crisis rhetoric and presidential slogans in the United States. Israeli (Chapter 2) looks at the impact of religion on the content of the discourse of two Arab leaders. In the case of Japan (Chapter 4), I view political discourse through the prism of culture. Conaway produces a text analysis of the rabbinic commentary on the biblical book of Genesis (*Bereshith Rabbah*, or *Genesis Rabbah*) in Chapter 5. Her study focuses on revealing, exposing, and explaining the meanings within the *midrashim* that address the subjects of collective identity and territory. She isolates how the Jews become represented as a unique people and the Land of Israel as the eternal homeland of the people Israel. In contrast, Bull (Chapter 12) reviews research on such aspects as patterns of turn-taking, the frequent occurrence of both interruptions and equivocation, and the central role of self-presentation and face management, so as to consider the degree to which they provide a basis for evaluating the interview performance of both interviewers and politicians.

CONCLUSION

Political reality is constituted by language through the creation of shared meanings, perceptions, and reassurances. Chapter 1 indicates how long many scholars have been aware of the political power of language. Most research in the past emphasized the negative (propaganda) functions of language. This book reveals however, that the rhetoric employed by elected Russian politicians positively affects political participation, European Parliamentary rhetoric creates feelings of European identity and furthers the process of European political integration, European-minded rhetoric by German political leaders finally led to German unification, and Japanese politicians create a political equilibrum in the public sphere through informal political honesty.

More than this, scholarly work that deconstructs propaganda techniques used by political leaders in Latin America, Great Britain, the United States, and France; that discovers crisis patterns in media language in Canada or the Middle East; or that lays bare scientific, religious, or financial bias can be said to contribute to a democratic society.

Democratic society and world peace are ipso facto advanced by political talk, by the worldwide increase of political talk (caused by the globalization of society and the news media), and by the critical study of political talk.

When there is no more political talk, weapons begin to speak. We should therefore take a positive look at political discourse because such discussion might directly affect the quality of the future.

REFERENCES

Anderson, P. A., & Opfer, J. (1992). Explaining the sound bite: A test of a theory of metaphor and assonance. Paper presented at the Western Speech Communication Association Convention, Boise, Idaho.

Ansolabehere, S., Behr R., & Iyenagar, S. (1993). *The media game: American politics in the television age.* New York: Macmillan.

Jansen, S. C., & Sabo, D. (1994). The sport/war metaphor: Hegemonic masculinity, the Persian Gulf and the new order. *Sociology of Sport Journal*, 11, 1–17.

Lackoff, G. (1991). Metaphor and war: The metaphor system used to justify war in the Gulf. *Journal of Urban and Cultural Studies*, 2, 59–72.

Lee, M. A., & Solomon, N. (1990). *Unreliable sources: A guide to detecting bias in news media.* Secaucus, N.J.: Lyle Stuart.

Tulis, J. K. (1987). *The Rhetorical Presidency.* Princeton, N.J.: Princeton University Press.

Index

Adenauer, Konrad, 33, 39, 41
Andreotti, Giulio, 36
Allah (God), 21–23
Arab leaders, 19–20; Arab world, 19, 21
Arafat, Yasir, 7, 20, 25–30
Argentina, 8, 91–105, 196
Aristotle, 6, 16, 31

BBC (British Broadcasting Corporation), 149
Belgium, 137–38, 140
Bonham, Matthew, 13, 130, 143
Brandt, Willy, 39, 41
Brazil, 8, 91–105, 196
Brezhnev, Leonid, 70
Bundestag, 33, 40
Burkhardt, Armin, 9, 13, 34, 41
Bush, George, 79, 80, 83, 84, 161–63, 165, 167–68, 189

Caldera, Rafael, 91–105
Canada, 8, 170, 172, 197
Cardoso, Fernando Henrique, 91–105
Carter, Jimmy, 79, 161–63, 167–68
Chernenko, Konstantin, 70, 71
Chicago Tribune, 173
Chirac, Jacques, 109
Chomsky, Noam, 11

Christian Science Monitor, 173
Clinton, William J., 79, 161–63, 165–68
Cold war, 10, 36, 184
Coolidge, Calvin, 79
Crisis rhetoric, 79–89

Dallas Morning News, 173
De Sola Pool, Isabel, 8, 14, 132–33, 144
Delores, Jacques, 132
Denmark, 137–38, 140
Der Spiegel, 38
Dieckmann, Walther, 6, 14
Diet (Japanese Parliament), 43, 45, 46, 48
Diet members, 43–44, 46–49, 52–54
Dijk, Teun Van, 11
Discourse analysis, 11, 118, 119, 123, 126

Edelman, Murray, 4, 5, 7, 134
Egypt, 20, 23, 29
Europe, 31, 32, 39
European Commission, 10; European Parliament, 129–31, 139, 141; European Union, 36
Extreme Left, 136, 137, 140, 142

Extreme Right, 106, 107, 135–37, 140, 142

Financial press, 117, 118, 201
Ford, Gerald, 79
Foucault, Michel, 12
France, 8, 9, 137–38
Fritzsche, Peter, 9, 13, 33, 41, 130, 134, 144

Gaus, Helmut, 130, 135, 144
German political language studies, 9–10
Germany, 8–10, 31–41, 137–38, 200
Gorbachev, Mikhail, 36, 38
Graber, Doris, 7, 14
Great Britain, 11, 149
Greece, 137–38
Gulf War, 84, 191

Habermas, Juergen, 12
Halifax Chronicle Herald, 173
Hall, Stuart, 11, 14
Holsti, Ole, 129, 144
Honne, 43, 44, 47–49, 53
Hoover, Herbert, 79, 82
Hussein, Saddam, 189–91

Identity: European, 8, 130; Jewish national, 56
Integrative complexity, 171, 174, 181
Iraq, 189–91
Ireland, 137–38
Islam, 20, 21, 23, 26
Israel, 21, 23, 24, 57, 59, 60, 61
Italy, 140

Japan, 43–54
Japanese, 7, 45
Jerusalem, 26–29
Jews, 57, 58, 61, 63
Jihad (Holy War), 25–27, 29
Johnson, Lyndon, B., 80
Journalists, 2, 5
"Just say no," 161
Just war, 184, 188–89, 191

Kennedy, John, F., 79, 85, 86, 198
Koeller, Wilhelm, 134, 144

Kohl, Helmut, 35, 36, 39, 40
Korzybski, A., 11, 15
Kuwait, 189–91

Lasswell, Harold, 2, 3, 7, 8, 134
Latin America, 91, 195
Le Pen, Jean-Marie, 106–15, 198
Los Angeles Times, 173
Luxembourg, 137–38

Magazines, 117
Major, John, 156, 158
Manchester Guardian, 173
Mannheim, Karl, 4, 15
Meadow, Robert, 4, 7
Menem, Carlos Saul, 91–105
Metaphor, 132–34, 199
Midrash (*Midrashim*), 9, 56, 57–63, 196, 199, 203
Mitterrand, François, 37

National Front, 107, 108, 111, 112
Netherlands, 137–38
"New Deal," 82, 161
"New freedom," 161
"New world order," 165, 167, 197
New York Times, 84, 87, 120, 126, 162, 173
Newspapers, 5, 7, 11, 53, 54, 117, 172, 173, 177, 179, 180
Newsweek, 36, 84
Nimmo, Dan D., 30–35, 37
Nixon, Richard, 80, 167

O Estado de Sao Paulo, 93
Orwell, George, 5, 6, 15

Pelster, Theodor, 10, 15
Perelman, Charles, 108, 116
Philosophy of language, 11–12
PLO (Palestinian Liberation Organization), 20, 25–26
Political communication, 7
Political debate, 192
Political discourse, 1–3, 11, 19, 129, 133–35, 200
Political interview, 149–58, 201

Political language, 1–5, 6, 9, 12, 31–33, 35, 41, 43, 195
Political leaders, 5, 7, 56
Political lexicology, 9
Political rhetoric, 1–3, 6, 7, 35, 129, 130, 132
Political semantics, 129
Political slogans, 161–68, 197, 200
Political socialization, 31
Political speech, 1–5
Political style, 1, 198
Political vocabulary, 8–9
Politicians, 2, 5, 7, 10, 64, 66, 68, 134, 151–54, 196, 197, 199, 200
Politische Sprache, 9
Portugal, 137–38, 140
Postmodernism, 12–13
Post-realism, 184–86
Propaganda, 2, 3, 5, 7–8, 112

Radio, 5, 11
Reagan, Ronald, 37, 39, 50, 79, 86–88, 161–65, 167–68, 198
"Reaganomics," 164
Reich, Wilhelm, 5, 16
Rhetoric, 6–7
Rhetorical analysis, 131; rhetorical presidency, 79, 196; rhetorical style, 88
Ricoeur, Paul, 16, 132, 133, 134, 145
Robin, Regine, 9, 16
Roosevelt, Franklin, D., 79, 82, 83, 161–62, 167
Roosevelt, Theodore, 79, 161, 198
Russia, 8, 13, 64–74, 66, 195, 197, 199

Sadat, Anwar, 7, 20–25, 29, 30
San Francisco Chronicle, 173

Sapir, Edward, 12, 16, 145
Schaff, Adam, 4, 6, 16, 145
Schmidt, Helmut, 39
Schmidt, Wilhelm, 10, 16
Semiotics, 1
Shapiro, Michael, 4, 16
Sociolinguistics, 10
Soviet Union, 38, 68, 71, 72, 199
Spain, 137–38
"Star wars" program, 164
"Strategic defense initiative," 164
Symbols, 6

Tatemae, 43, 44, 47, 48, 54
Television, 5, 6, 11, 53, 54, 149, 150
Television program 7/7, 106–8, 110, 111
Thatcher, Margaret, 151, 152, 155
Third Reich, 31, 32
Torah, 56, 57
Toronto Globe and Mail, 173
"Turn-taking," 150, 151, 158

United Kingdom, 149
United States, 13, 65, 79–89, 123, 161, 189–90; president, 79, 80, 189

Vancouver Sun, 173
Veja, 93
Venezuela, 8, 91–105, 196

Wall Street Journal, 118, 120, 126
"War on drugs," 161
Washington Post, 86, 173
Weimar Republic, 31
Wilson, Woodrow, 79, 161
Wittgenstein, Ludwig, 12, 16

Yeltsin, Boris, 72, 73

About the Editors and Contributors

OFER FELDMAN is Associate Professor at Naruto University of Education, Japan. He is the author of numerous journal articles, book chapters, and several books, including *Politics and the News Media in Japan* (1993). His present work centers on political personality and discourse in Japan.

CHRIST'L DE LANDTSHEER is Associate Professor in Communication Studies at the University of Amsterdam (The Netherlands). Among her works are more than 50 publications on political language, including a special issue of *Politics, Groups and the Individual*. She has written on the political role of the press for the Belgian National Broadcasting Company and served as an assistant spokesperson for a member of the Belgian government and as a policy advisor to the Dutch-Belgian Linguistic Union.

RICHARD D. ANDERSON, JR. is Associate Professor of Political Science at the University of California, Los Angeles. He is the author of *Public Politics in an Authoritarian State* (1993), a study of how linguistic behaviors shaped Soviet foreign policy, and of various articles on Soviet foreign policy and on the contribution of discursive change to democratization in Russia. His recent work strives to develop the emerging field of political linguistics by examining the Russian language of politics.

HERBERT BARRY III is Professor of Pharmaceutical Sciences in the School of Pharmacy, with an adjunct appointment as a Professor of Anthropology, at the University of Pittsburgh. Since 1979, he has published reports of his research on psychological influences on personality and performance of the presidents of the United States. The principal variables in these studies are birth order, first name, relationships with parents, and other childhood conditions.

FRANCIS A. BEER has been Professor of Political Science at the University of Colorado, Boulder, since 1975. He has published numerous papers in leading professional journals. His books include *Integration and Disintegration in NATO: Processes of Alliance Cohesion and Prospects for Atlantic Community* (1969) and *Peace Against War: The Ecology of International Violence* (1981) as well as related monographs. He has edited *Alliances: Latent War Communities in the Contemporary World* (1970) and coedited, with Robert Hariman, *Post-Realism: The Rhetorical Turn in International Relations* (1996).

SIMONE BONNAFOUS is Professor of Information and Communication at Paris XII University, France. She has authored works on political and media discourse analysis and published two books, including *L'immigration Prise aux Mots* (1991), and numerous articles about the French extreme right-wing way of speaking and the words related to immigration and immigrated people.

JENNIFER BROUGH is entering the fourth year of the B.Sc. program in biopsychology at the University of British Columbia, Canada. After completing her undergraduate studies, she intends to apply her joint interest in public policy and health care to a graduate program in public administration.

PETER BULL is Senior Lecturer in the Department of Psychology at the University of York (United Kingdom). He has had a series of articles published on political communication, as well as on nonverbal communication. He is the author of *Body Movement and Interpersonal Communication* (1983; paperback version, 1984; Japanese translation, 1986) and *Posture and Gesture* (1987), and is co-editor (with Derek Roger) of *Conversation: An Interdisciplinary Perspective* (1989). His current work focuses on the analysis of political interviews.

CAROL B. CONAWAY is Assistant Professor of Political Science at the College of the Holy Cross, Worcester, Massachusetts. She is the author of several papers on political rhetoric, including "Framing Identity: The Press in Crown Heights" (1996), a study of media discourse used to describe Hasidic Jews and Caribbean-Americans in the Crown Heights conflict. Her present work centers on the discourse of identity, and media and politics.

ROBERT HARIMAN is Professor of Rhetoric and Communication Studies and Endowment Professor of the Humanities at Drake University. He is the author of *Political Style: The Artistry of Power* (1995), editor of *Popular Trials: Rhetoric, Mass Media, and the Law* (1990), and co-editor of *Post-Realism: The Rhetorical Turn in International Relations* (1996).

RAPHAEL ISRAELI is Professor of Chinese, Islamic, and Middle Eastern History at the Hebrew University in Jerusalem. He is the author of fifteen books and more than 80 articles of issues related to China, Islam, and Middle Eastern affairs. His present work focuses on Islamic Fundamentalism, Islam in China, and the French venture into China.

AMOS KIEWE is Associate Professor of Speech Communication at Syracuse University. He is the author of several books and articles, as well as volume editor of *The Modern Presidency and Crisis Rhetoric* (Praeger, 1994). His specialty is political communication and rhetorical criticism.

CHRISTA LANG-PFAFF is a Scientific Assistant at the Free University, Berlin. She has contributed chapters to several books dealing with political language and systems with respect to twentieth-century Germany. Her present work focuses on the political biography and language of Germany.

LORAINE LAVALLEE is a student of social psychology at the University of British Columbia, Canada. Her research focuses on topics in both environmental and health psychology, and she is author of several journal articles in these areas. Currently, she is conducting a province-wide study of human values of forests through the Faculty of Forestry at UBC.

MARITZA MONTERO is Professor at Universidad Central de Venezuela. She has written and edited several books and journal papers in Spanish, English, and French. Her research interests include social identity, alternative modes of political action, and discourse analysis.

ISABEL RODRIGUEZ-MORA is a lecturer in Social Psychology at Universidad de Los Andes, Trujillo, Venezuela, and has published articles in Spanish scientific journals.

MATTHEW G. SORLEY is a master's student at Carleton University, Canada. He is the leader of the Crisis Intervention Team with the Ottawa Distress Centre and is a faculty member of the Crisis Management/Human Psychology program at Algonquin College, Canada. His recent research efforts focus on the discourse and social dynamics of the financial marketplace. Currently, he is conducting research with narratives across a variety of clinical settings.

PETER SUEDFELD is Professor of Psychology at the University of British

Columbia, Canada. His research on adaptation and coping in challenging environments has led to some 200 journal articles and book chapters. He developed the procedure for scoring integrative complexity in archival materials, which has been used to study decision making among national and international leaders, as well as ordinary citizens.